Ferenczi's Turn in Psychoana
■

Ferenczi's Turn in Psychoanalysis

EDITED BY

Peter L. Rudnytsky

Antal Bókay, and

Patrizia Giampieri-Deutsch

New York University Press

NEW YORK AND LONDON

NEW YORK UNIVERSITY PRESS
New York and London

Library of Congress Cataloging-in-Publication Data
Ferenczi's turn in psychoanalysis / edited by Peter I. Rudnytsky,
   Antal Bokay, and Patrizia Giampieri-Deutsch.
       p.   cm.
   Includes bibliographical references and index.
   ISBN 0-8147-7475-X (alk. paper)
       1. Ferenczi, Sandor, 1873–1933.   2. Psychoanalysis—Hungary—
   History.   3. Psychoanalysis—History.   I. Rudnytsky, Peter L.
   II. Bokay, Antal.   III. Giampieri-Deutsch, Patrizia.
   BF109.F47F47   1996
   150.19′52′092—dc20   96-10022
                         CIP

New York University Press books are printed on acid-free paper,
and their binding materials are chosen for strength and durability.

Manufactured in the United States of America

10 9 8 7 6 5 4 3 2 1

■

To

Judith Dupont,

Custodian of Ferenczi's legacy

György Hidas, M.D.,

Founder of the Sándor Ferenczi Society

and

Lívia Nemes, M.D.,

Past President of the Hungarian Psychoanalytic Society

CONTENTS

Part III. Theory and Technique

ACKNOWLEDGMENTS

This project owes its existence to two opportunities afforded me to study and teach in Europe: the first a Fulbright Western European Regional Research Fellowship in 1988–89, during which I met Patrizia Giampieri-Deutsch in Vienna; the second a visiting professorship at Janus Pannonius University in Pécs, Hungary, in 1990–91, which was made possible by Antal Bókay. I wish to thank my coeditors for their friendship and intellectual camaraderie.

In the international culture of psychoanalysis, those who have been touched by the spirit of Sándor Ferenczi and the Hungarian tradition form a unique community, which this book seeks to define and exemplify. I wish to thank all of the contributors for their participation, as well as those who by their scholarship and clinical practice have preserved and enriched Ferenczi's legacy. This book is dedicated to three individuals who nursed the embers of hope during the long eclipse of Hungarian psychoanalysis and Ferenczi's reputation and who have led our celebration of their rebirth.

At New York University Press, this book was conceived with Kitty Moore, gestated under Jason Renker, and born at the hands of Timothy Bartlett. To each of these outstanding editors go our thanks for their patience and expertise.

Antal Bókay would like to thank his wife, Marianna, and son, Csongor; Patrizia Giampieri-Deutsch would like to thank her husband, Johannes, and son, Italo-Léon, as well as the analysts Wolfgang Berner, Wilhelm Burian, Heinrich Donat, Verna Ligeti, and Lívia Nemes.

PETER L. RUDNYTSKY

CONTRIBUTORS

MARTIN S. BERGMANN is a Clinical Professor of Psychology at the New York University Postdoctoral Program and a Training and Supervising Analyst at the New York Freudian Society. He is the author of *The Anatomy of Loving: The Quest of Man to Know What Love Is* (1987) and *In the Shadow of Moloch: The Effect of the Sacrifice of Children on Western Religion* (1992); he is also the coauthor, with Frank Hartmann, of *The Evolution of Psychoanalytic Technique* (1975) and, with Milton Jucovy, of *Generations of the Holocaust* (1982). His eightieth birthday was honored with a *Festschrift, The Spectrum of Psychoanalysis* (1994), edited by Arnold Richards and Arlene Richards.

WOLFGANG BERNER, M.D., is Professor of Psychiatry and Head of the Department for Sex Research at the University of Hamburg. He served as president of the Vienna Psychoanalytic Society from 1984 to 1993. He is the author of articles on criminality, psychotherapy, and the psychoanalysis of perversions.

MICHÈLE BERTRAND, PH.D., is a Professor of Social Sciences at the University of Besançon and a member of the Paris Psychoanalytic Society. Among the books she has written or edited are *Spinoza et l'imaginaire* (1984), *Psychanalyse et sciences sociales* (1989), *La Pensée et le trauma* (1991), and *Pratiques de la prière dans la France contemporaine* (1993).

THIERRY M. BOKANOWSKI, M.D., is a training analyst of the Paris Psychoanalytic Society and a member of the International Association of the History of Psychoanalysis. He is also editor of the *Revue française de psychanalyse*. His previous articles on Ferenczi have appeared in *Études freudiennes, International Review of the History of Psychoanalysis,* and the *Révue française de psychanalyse.*

ANTAL BÓKAY, PH.D., is Associate Professor of Literature at Janus Pannonius University in Pécs, Hungary. He is the author of *Psychoanalysis*

Structuring Poetry: Attila József (1982) and *Trends in Literary Theory* (1992), and of many articles on psychoanalysis, literary theory, and philosophy. He is a founding member of the Sándor Ferenczi Society and coeditor of the quarterly *Thalassa*.

REBECCA CURTIS, PH.D., is Professor of Psychology at the Derner Institute of Advanced Psychological Studies, Adelphi University, and in private practice in New York City. She has edited *Self-Defeating Behaviors* (1989), *The Relational Self* (1991), and *How People Change* (1991).

CHRISTOPHER FORTUNE is a Doctoral Fellow of the Social Sciences and Research Council of Canada in Applied Psychology at the University of Toronto (Ontario Institute for Studies in Education). He is currently researching and writing on Elizabeth Severn's role in the history of psychoanalysis, 1924–33, and preparing an English edition of the Ferenczi-Groddeck correspondence.

JOHN E. GEDO, M.D., retired in 1990 as a Training and Supervising Analyst at the Chicago Institute of Psychoanalysis. Among his many books are *Beyond Interpretation* (1979), *Portraits of the Artist* (1983), *Conceptual Issues in Psychoanalysis* (1986), *The Mind in Disorder* (1988), and *The Biology of Clinical Encounters* (1991). He has also coedited, with George Pollock, *Freud: The Fusion of Science and Humanism* (1976) and, with Mark Gehrie, *Impasse and Innovation in Psychoanalysis* (1993).

PATRIZIA GIAMPIERI-DEUTSCH, PH.D., is a member of the Vienna Psychoanalytic Society and a lecturer in philosophy at the Universities of Vienna and Trieste. She has held visiting professorships in theoretical philosophy and German language and literature at Trieste. The author of numerous articles on contemporary philosophy and the history of psychoanalysis, she is an editor of the Freud-Ferenczi correspondence.

ANDRÉ E. HAYNAL, M.D., is Professor of Psychiatry at the University of Geneva and a former president of the Swiss Psychoanalytic Society. He is academic supervisor of the Freud-Ferenczi correspondence. He is the author of *Depression and Creativity* (1984), *The Technique at Issue: Controversies in Psychoanalytic Method from Freud to Ferenczi to Michael Bálint* (1991), and *Psychoanalysis and the Sciences: Epistemology-History* (1993), and coeditor, with Ernst Falzeder, of *100 Years of Psychoanalysis* (1994).

AXEL HOFFER, M.D., is a Training and Supervising Analyst at the Psychoanalytic Institute of New England, East, and a member of the faculty and a Training Analyst at the Massachusetts Institute of Psychoanalysis. He is an Assistant Clinical Professor of Psychiatry at Harvard Medical School. With his brother, Peter T. Hoffer, he translated Freud's *A Phylogenetic Fantasy* (1987), and he has written the introduction to Volume 2 of the Freud-Ferenczi correspondence. Dr. Hoffer is a member of the editorial board of the *Journal of the American Psychoanalytic Association*.

KATHLEEN KELLEY-LAINÉ is a member of the Paris Psychoanalytic Society and on the editorial board of the *Revue française de psychanalyse*. She is the author of *Peter Pan, ou L'enfant triste* (1992).

MICHELLE MOREAU-RICAUD, PH.D., is a psychoanalyst belonging to the Fourth Group, Psychoanalytic Organization of the French Language, and Maître de Conférences at the Université François Rabelais in Tours. She is also a member of the Bálint Medical Society and a member and editor of the journal of the International Association of the History of Psychoanalysis. She is the editor of *Cure d'ennui: Écrivains hongrois autour de Ferenczi* (1992).

PETER L. RUDNYTSKY, PH.D., is Professor of English at the University of Florida and a Corresponding Member of the Institute of Contemporary Psychoanalysis in Los Angeles. He is the author of *Freud and Oedipus* (1987) and *The Psychoanalytic Vocation: Rank, Winnicott, and the Legacy of Freud* (1991). He is the editor or coeditor of six previous books, including *Transitional Objects and Potential Spaces: Literary Uses of D. W. Winnicott* (1993) and *Freud and Forbidden Knowledge* (1994).

ANN-LOUISE S. SILVER, M.D., is on the medical staff and chair of the Symposium Committee at Chestnut Lodge Hospital, Rockville,

Maryland. She serves on the faculties of the Washington Psychoanalytic Institute, the Washington School of Psychiatry, the Walter Reed Army Medical Center, and the Uniformed Services University of the Health Sciences. She has edited *Psychoanalysis and Psychosis* (1989), *Psychoanalysis and Severe Emotional Illness* (1990), and, with H. J. Silver, *Illness in the Analyst* (1990).

JUDITH E. VIDA, M.D., is a founding member and a Training and Supervising Analyst at the Institute of Contemporary Psychoanalysis in Los Angeles and an Assistant Clinical Professor of Psychiatry at the University of Southern California Medical School. Her essays on Ferenczi have appeared in the *Journal of the American Academy of Psychoanalysis, Psychoanalytic Books,* and the collection *100 Years of Psychoanalysis.*

GYÖRGY VIKÁR, M.D., a pupil of Imre Hermann, was president of the Hungarian Psychoanalytic Association from 1989 to 1992. He is the author of *Cries of Youth* (1980) and *Healing and Self-Healing: Essays on the Elaboration of Psychic Traumata* (1984) and of articles on adolescence, childhood mourning, obsessive-compulsive neurosis, and the psychology of literature.

Introduction: Ferenczi's Turn in Psychoanalysis

■

P E T E R   L .   R U D N Y T S K Y

To those who have come under its spell, the history of psychoanalysis is a subject of inexhaustible fascination. The appeal of psychoanalysis as a guide to living stems ultimately from the way that it enables its adepts to think theoretically about their own experiences. It thus functions, as it were, on a *meta*-level, not removing one from life, but immersing one in it more deeply by adding a dimension of self-conscious reflection to the fluctuating compounds of love and loss, repetition and regeneration, that are the staples of the human lot.[1] In turning to the history of psychoanalysis, then, which inevitably comes down to posterity mainly in the form of written texts, and where we can witness how the personal and professional lives of those who have preceded us are intimately intertwined, we have an opportunity to observe this *meta*-quality of psychoanalysis in a concentrated form.

By any standard, the longest shadow in the history of psychoanalysis continues to be cast by Freud. However much one may disagree with Freud on certain doctrinal points—his views on drives and female sexuality being two notable areas of controversy—and whatever judgments one may make on his character, it cannot be disputed that psychoanalysis originated with Freud and that he is the leading actor in the drama of its development, which traverses the twentieth century and constitutes one of the guiding threads to its intellectual history. On those who knew Freud personally, of course, his impact was overwhelming. Even now, over fifty years after his death, he remains an inescapable presence, not only for those who wish to become psychoanalysts or psychotherapists (or scholars who employ psychoanalytic tools in their research), but for the culture at large, as witnessed by the ongoing skirmishes waged over Freud's reputation and the epistemological status of psychoanalysis. For both individuals and the myriad of interested professional groups, moreover, the ideological, economic, and sheerly narcissistic stakes in these disputes are high; and the self-blinding passion with which they are often conducted is the unfortunate counterpart to the prospective rewards to be derived from a theory that raises experience of all kinds to a higher power of intensity and self-consciousness.

Although Freud stands enduringly at the crossroads, one of the most remarkable features of the history of psychoanalysis since its inception is the exceptional caliber of the men and women whom he attracted as disciples and coworkers. And just as Freud's image is contested within and outside of psychoanalysis, so too have the other gifted individuals—each of whom deserves to be seen as a unique being in his or her own right with a destiny and story to tell—who have left their mark on the movement become objects of positive or negative transference by their contemporaries and successors and pieces in the incessant chess game of writing and rewriting the past.

In singling out any of the stars around Freud's sun for particular attention, one has a natural tendency to want to make the strongest possible case for that figure's eminence. It is because something in the precursor's life and work speaks to our own personal and collective conditions that we initially gravitate to him or her. In championing that thinker's point of view, we are then simultaneously advancing our own ideological agendas. In the best examples of psychoanalytic (as of any other) scholarship, however, a healthy idealization of a given person's achievement is balanced by a recognition of limitations and frailties; and the criticisms that are conversely directed against those who are cast as opponents should be tempered by generous doses of respect and empathy.

This volume seeks to pay tribute to Sándor Ferenczi (1873–1933) and to promote the collective reappraisal of his legacy that is already in progress.[2] Ferenczi, the Hungarian disciple of whom Freud wrote in *On the History of the Psycho-Analytic Movement* that he "outweighs an entire society" (1914,

33) and whom he later lauded in his obituary as one who had "made all analysts into his pupils" (1933, 228), is unquestionably one of the most brilliant orbs in the psychoanalytic firmament. Apart from Freud, he is the first-generation pioneer who addresses most immediately the concerns of contemporary psychoanalysts; and, in some respects, he has come to represent not only a complement but a powerful alternative to Freud as well. By the title of our book, *Ferenczi's Turn in Psychoanalysis,* we mean to evoke both the radical innovations introduced by Ferenczi into psychoanalytic theory and practice and the renewed interest in his work that makes this his time.

Ferenczi's rehabilitation in recent years has much to do with his position in the early history of the psychoanalytic movement. Of the four leading members of the Committee that formed around Freud in 1912 to counter the incipient defection of Jung, there is a fundamental dichotomy between the two conservatives, Karl Abraham in Berlin and Ernest Jones in London, and the two radicals, Otto Rank in Vienna and Ferenczi in Budapest. Insofar as contemporary psychoanalysis is characterized by a shift away from classical drive theory and toward a relational paradigm, Ferenczi and Rank (who in 1923 coauthored a book, *The Development of Psycho-Analysis*) will clearly be more congenial ancestors than Abraham and Jones. Abraham is best remembered for the refinements he introduced into Freud's libido theory. Jones, the only one of the four to outlive Freud, is renowned for his three-volume biography of Freud, completed in 1957, in which he simultaneously settled old scores with his rivals (especially Ferenczi, who had been his analyst, and Rank) and gave definitive shape to the Freud legend. Abraham's intellectual gifts were matched by those of Jones as an administrator, but both remained unswervingly loyal to Freud and thus could not mount a challenge to his authority that might provide a point of departure for subsequent revisionist thinking.

Rank stands at the antipodes from Jones and Abraham, since he broke with Freud after the publication of *The Trauma of Birth* (1924) and, like Jung, became a dissident. As such, however, his influence waned, and his later writings on will therapy and creativity found an audience chiefly among artists, social workers, and cultural critics outside psychoanalysis. By contrast, Ferenczi's decision to remain within the psychoanalytic fold has contributed decisively to his revival, since he is revered by members of the American interpersonal tradition and others who consider themselves psychoanalysts but have been excluded from the International Psychoanalytic Association and who seek to establish their legitimacy by claiming descent from Ferenczi. As I have argued elsewhere (1991), the desire to anoint Ferenczi as the "first object relations psychoanalyst" overlooks Rank's dominant influence on their intellectual partnership and his undeservedly neglected work between 1924 and 1927; but it remains true that Ferenczi is a vital presence for many contemporary psychoanalysts in a way that Rank is not.

Central to Ferenczi's career and legacy is, of course, his relationship to Freud. Our understanding of this relationship has been revolutionized in recent years by newly available documents—above all, the *Clinical Diary*, the private journal Ferenczi kept in 1932, first published in 1985, and the complete Freud-Ferenczi correspondence, publication of which is still in progress as of this writing. The Freud-Ferenczi relationship is extremely complex and will be interpreted in divergent ways by different commentators. Its outcome, in my view, is a tragedy stemming ultimately from the conjunction between Freud's tendency to impose a lethal choice between submission or rebellion on his male heirs and Ferenczi's complementary predisposition to docility and need for approval by authority figures. Throughout most of their long association, Ferenczi sought to find satisfaction in playing the role of Freud's beloved son and resolutely suppressed all murmurs of discontent. Indeed, after Rank's revolt, Ferenczi in 1927 published a scathing review of *Technique of Psychoanalysis*, in which he reaffirmed his loyalty to Freud by castigating Rank for his divagations. But, as I have previously proposed (1991, 54–55), Rank and Ferenczi can be viewed as together comprising the two sides of a single ambivalent filial relationship to Freud, in which neither the former's rebellion nor the latter's obedience led to genuine autonomy. The public opprobrium heaped on Rank finds a counterpart in Ferenczi's private anguish, recorded in the *Clinical Diary* along with the criticisms of Freud that he did not dare to voice openly during his lifetime.

One of the consequences of the release of the *Clinical Diary* and the Freud-Ferenczi correspondence, at least in my judgment, is to show the tendentiousness of Freud's reiterated narratives of their relationship. In the first, a testimonial on the occasion of his fiftieth birthday, for example, Freud affirms that Ferenczi, "who, as a middle child in a large family, had to struggle with a powerful brother complex, had, under the influence of analysis, become an irreproachable elder brother" (1923, 268). This may be true as far as it goes, but an elder brother is conspicuously not a father. Freud, who had been Ferenczi's analyst, omits any reference to his Oedipus complex, which would imply rivalry with himself, and casts him in a favored but still subordinate role. In his obituary, Freud singles out *Thalassa* as Ferenczi's "most brilliant and most fertile achievement" (1933, 228). Ferenczi had begun *Thalassa,* his only book-length monograph, during World War I in close cooperation with Freud, though he delayed its publication until 1924. Freud's enthusiasm is thus understandable. But *Thalassa,* like Freud's *Phylogenetic Fantasy,* which dates from the same period and was first published in 1985 after having been found in London in a trunk of papers that Ferenczi had bequeathed to Michael Bálint, is a flight of evolutionary speculation based on Lamarckian principles and Haeckel's so-called biogenetic law that possesses great antiquarian (and literary) interest. Unfortunately, however, it is scientific rubbish with little or no relevance to the contemporary practice of psychoanalysis.[3]

Indeed, *Thalassa,* among other liabilities, accentuates Freud's phallocentric perspective. Ferenczi contends that, with the loss of an aquatic mode of life and the need to adapt to existence on land, both sexes "developed the male sexual organ, and there came about, perhaps, a tremendous struggle, the outcome of which was to decide upon which sex should fall the pains and duties of motherhood and the passive endurance of genitality" (1924, 103). The culturally determined misogyny that skews this view of sexuality, which holds that there is primordially only one genital organ and defines women exclusively as mothers who submit unwillingly to sexual intercourse, will be apparent to a modern reader; and it was so to Ferenczi as well by the time he wrote the *Clinical Diary.* With hindsight he avowed:

The ease with which Fr[eud] sacrifices the interests of women in favor of male patients is striking. This is consistent with his unilaterally androphile orientation of his theory of sexuality. In this he was followed by nearly all his pupils, myself not excluded. My theory of genitality may have many good points, yet in its mode of presentation and its historical reconstruction it clings too closely to the words of the master; a new edition would mean a complete rewriting. (1985, 187)

Freud, of course, had not seen the *Clinical Diary* when he wrote his obituary of Ferenczi. He did, however, have access to his later papers—including the valedictory "Confusion of Tongues" (1933), which at their final meeting he notoriously urged Ferenczi not to deliver at the 1932 Wiesbaden Congress—in which Ferenczi forged the paradigm shift that has made him so important to contemporary psychoanalysis. It is thus revealing that in the obituary Freud depicts Ferenczi's final period as one of decline after the "summit of achievement" (1933, 229) reached in *Thalassa,* whereas Ferenczi—with complete justification, from a present-day standpoint—had privately distanced himself from *Thalassa* because of its "androphile orientation" and excessive devotion to "the words of the master," and indicted Freud for his demeaning attitude toward women, which Freud vehemently defended to the end of his days.

Although both the 1923 tribute and the 1933 obituary are milestones in Freud's pronouncements on Ferenczi's career, it is above all the unacknowledged but transparent "case history" of Ferenczi in "Analysis Terminable and Interminable" (1937) that shows the defensiveness and unreliability of Freud's version of events.[4] Here Freud takes up Ferenczi's reproach that his analysis with Freud was inadequate because Freud had not analyzed Ferenczi's negative transference. This issue is in turn bound up with the crucial problem of Ferenczi's marriage and Freud's role in it. To summarize briefly, Ferenczi had been involved in a long-standing love affair with a married woman, Gizella Pálos, when in July 1911 he took her daughter Elma into analysis because of her romantic difficulties. Then, after one of Elma's suitors committed suicide on account of her in October, Ferenczi, in December, found himself falling in love with her, at which point Freud advised him to break off the treatment and agreed to take Elma into analysis himself in Vienna. This analysis lasted from January to mid-March 1912; Elma then returned to Budapest and underwent additional analysis with Ferenczi that summer. The situation remained unresolved for over a year, until Ferenczi definitively broke with Elma and she became engaged in December 1913 to an American writer of Swedish extraction named Hervé Laurvik, whom she married and then divorced after a brief period. Ferenczi and Gizella Pálos were finally married on March 1, 1919, only to learn that her ex-husband Géza had died of a heart attack on the same day!

Even this résumé should suffice to delineate the tragic oedipal entanglements of Ferenczi's love life. His intimate dilemmas were bound up with his identity as an analyst, and both were mediated by his relationship to Freud. As the Freud-Ferenczi correspondence shows, Ferenczi continually unburdened himself to Freud, and Freud kept Ferenczi apprised of the details of Elma's analysis.[5] Freud, moreover, made no secret of his strong preference for Gizella over Elma and actively promoted Ferenczi's decision to renounce the daughter in favor of the mother. The upshot was that Ferenczi could never have children, for whom he longed, or even a fulfilling sexual life: Gizella, despite her formidable virtues, was eight years older than he and unable to bear more children, and she was uninspiring to Ferenczi sexually.[6]

Given all this material, now brought to the light of day, it becomes almost unbelievable that Freud could declare in "Analysis Terminable and Interminable" that Ferenczi's analysis with him, which occurred in three abbreviated periods in 1914 and 1916 in the aftermath of the Elma debacle, had a "completely successful" result because he "married the woman he loved and turned into a friend and teacher of his supposed rivals" (1937, 221). This, a variation on the theme of Ferenczi as "irreproachable elder brother," conveniently neglects to mention that Ferenczi's marriage was a source of abiding conflict to him and that he loved not one but *two* women. Freud goes on to assert that his relationship with Ferenczi "remained unclouded" for many years, until for "no assignable external reason, trouble arose." Freud thus places the entire blame for their falling out on Ferenczi's resentment, which he construes as irrational, and refuses to consider that he himself might have been at fault in some way. This stance of self-righteousness and professed objectivity, inimical to the self-criticism and acknowledgment of his own subjectivity that infuses Ferenczi's private and public writings, especially in his later years, constitutes a serious failing on Freud's part. The way these contrasting attitudes are mirrored in Freud's and Ferenczi's views of the analytic process and countertransference, moreover, has led many people today to see the future of psychoanalysis as lying in directions mapped by Ferenczi rather than Freud.

An indispensable window on the Freud-Ferenczi relationship is provided by Ferenczi's correspondence with Georg Groddeck, the maverick director of the Baden-Baden sanatorium and author of the magnificent *Book of the It* (1923), whom he met in 1920 at the psychoanalytic congress in The Hague. Ferenczi and Groddeck soon became fast friends, and Groddeck extended to Ferenczi the wholehearted acceptance that he lacked from Freud. (Groddeck's combination of massage with psychotherapy likewise contrasted sharply with Freud's technique of abstinence.) As Bernard This (1982, 25) has pointed out, moreover, Groddeck's love life fulfilled a fantasy of Ferenczi's, since in 1923 he married Emmy von Voigt, a young woman who had been his patient, as Ferenczi had longed in vain to do with Elma Pálos.

In two key letters to Groddeck, on Christmas-day 1921 and February 27, 1922, Ferenczi vented his accumulated grievances against Freud. In the former, he anatomized the "Palermo incident," which took place during a holiday trip with Freud to Sicily in September 1910 and marked the first moment of crisis in their relationship. As Ferenczi reports, in the only extant account, when he and Freud began on the first evening to work jointly on the Schreber case, Freud sought to dictate to him (as to an amanuensis), and he protested that this was no way to collaborate. Freud then demanded, "Obviously you want the whole thing for yourself?" and thenceforth worked alone every evening, relegating Ferenczi to the role of copyeditor, which knotted his throat with bitterness (Ferenczi and Groddeck 1982, 37). In the same letter, he complained to Groddeck of further somatic symptoms—insomnia, loss of breath, cardiac pains, etc.—and connected these to dissatisfaction with his marriage and suppressed love for his wife's daughter, whom he had been forced to renounce because of Freud's disapproval. This topic recurs in the letter of February 27, where Ferenczi informed Groddeck of a frank conversation he had had with Freud in Vienna, in which Freud "stuck to his earlier opinion, that the main thing in my case was the hate against *him*, who (just as the father had formerly done) blocked my marriage to the younger bride (now step-daughter)." "I must confess," Ferenczi added, "it did me good to be able to speak with the beloved father for once about these feelings of hate" (41). Again, in view of this conversation with Freud in 1922, eight years before Ferenczi first raised in correspondence the issue of Freud's failure to analyze his negative transference, Freud's claim in "Analysis Terminable and Interminable" that their relationship "remained unclouded" for "many years" must be deemed a self-serving distortion.[7]

Ferenczi's relationship with Freud must be set against the backdrop of his early childhood experiences, a deep insight into which is afforded by his letters to both Groddeck and Freud as well as the *Clinical Diary*. The eighth of twelve children, Ferenczi undoubtedly, as Freud suggested in 1923, had to struggle with issues of sibling rivalry. His father, moreover, died in 1888, when Ferenczi was fifteen. But the decisive revelation of the posthumously published sources is that Ferenczi experienced severe emotional and sexual traumas in infancy at the hands of his mother and other female caretakers. Ferenczi writes to Groddeck on Christmas 1921 that he received "too little love and too much severity" from his mother in childhood (Ferenczi and Groddeck 1982, 36). And in a letter of December 26, 1912, to Freud—an extraordinary piece of self-analysis that goes beyond anything in Freud's correspondence with Fliess—Ferenczi tells of having been caught at the age of three (or earlier) in mutual touching with his sister Gisella by a cook, and then threatened with a kitchen knife by his mother. He elaborates: "As a small boy I had a colossal un . . . . rage against my mother, who was too strict with me; the fantasy of murder (which I don't remember with certainty) was immediately turned toward my own person." (The dots after "un" convey Ferenczi's inability to think of the German equivalent of the Hungarian word *tehetetlen,* meaning "inhibited" or "impotent," a parapraxis which enacts the inhibition wrought in Ferenczi by Freud's authority.) Linking past and present, he conjectures: "Now, possibly, I hate Frau G. because she (as earlier the cook and my mother) prevented marriage with Elma (earlier touching my sister). I can also impute to her the threat of cutting off my penis." Completing this train of thought, Ferenczi connects Gizella Pálos and Freud as impediments to his marriage with Elma: "My ucs. placed the responsibility for it in your and Frau G.'s hands" (Brabant et al. 1992, 452–54).[8]

Additional invaluable information about Ferenczi's traumatic experiences in childhood is contained in the *Clinical Diary.* To condense my reading of this material, which I have elaborated elsewhere (1992), Ferenczi was subjected not only to terrifying episodes of abuse by a nursemaid, but also to both extreme harshness and a lack of love from his mother, leaving him, in his words, "emotionally dead" (1985, 85). As excellent papers by Christopher Fortune (1993) and Sue A. Shapiro (1993) have shown, the theme of murder—both of body and soul—figures prominently also in the histories of the two most important patients treated by Ferenczi during his final years, the American women Elizabeth Severn and Clara Thompson, code named in the *Diary* R.N. and Dm, respectively. With regard to Severn's repressed memory of having participated during childhood in the murder of a black man, Ferenczi writes of her "incessant protestations that she is no murderer, although she admits to firing the shots" (1985, 107). Shapiro (1993, 165) quotes Thompson's startling explanation in her college yearbook of a decision to pursue a career in medicine: "To murder people in the most refined manner possible." Since both Thompson and Severn were victims of emotional and sexual abuse by their fathers, as Ferenczi was by his mother and nursemaid, the recurrent motif of murder in their lives is tied to their common fate as incest survivors. The breakthroughs Ferenczi achieved during his final period—including his experiment in mutual analysis with Severn—were made possible by his unique capacity to explore in an atmosphere of trust and shared vulnerability the shattering effects of childhood trauma on himself as well as his patients.[9]

The first volume of the Freud-Ferenczi letters permits me to amplify one point in my reading of the *Clinical Diary*. The complex dialectic whereby Ferenczi enacts a reciprocal soul murder, modeled on his early battles with his mother, with both Freud and his female patients, unfolds throughout his relationship with Freud. Ferenczi's letter of December 26, 1912, in which he speaks of the "fantasy of murder" directed at his mother that he "immediately turned toward my own person," explicitly associates both Gizella and Freud with his mother as agents of castration toward whom he harbors an "*impotent* rage" (Brabant et al. 1992, 452). Freud, to be sure, is also a symbolic father, but this is not a contradiction, since Ferenczi admits the possibility that "my mother's strict treatment (and my father's mildness) had the result in me of a displacement of the Oedipus complex [mother's death, father's love]" (Ferenczi's brackets). Ferenczi's Oedipus complex, that is, took an unusually "complete" form, with ambivalent feelings of love and hate directed toward both parents; but, in addition to the customary rivalry with his father, he sought to obtain from him (and from Freud) the affection of which his mother had deprived him, and with whom he experienced violent conflicts. She was the principal cause of his pathology, which was at bottom not oedipal, but—to borrow Bálint's (1968) salient term—at the preoedipal level of the basic fault. Thus, when his relationship with Freud broke down, Ferenczi reexperienced a dynamic of *maternal* failure, which explains why he should have done his most probing analytic work with female patients.[10]

In this same letter, written at the high tide not only of his romantic crisis but also of Jung's revolt, of which Freud kept him fully abreast, Ferenczi wrestles with the specter of Freud's authority over his disciples that would haunt him to his dying day. Ferenczi here espouses views antithetical to those he would embrace in the *Clinical Diary,* but the anticipation of his later formulations is uncanny:

> *Mutual analysis* is nonsense, also an impossibility. Everyone must be able to tolerate an authority over himself from whom he accepts analytic correction. You are probably the only one who can permit himself to do without an analyst. . . . But what is valid for *you* is not valid for the rest of us. Jung has not achieved the same self-mastery as you. . . . I, too, went through a period of rebellion against your "treatment." Now I have become insightful and find that you were right in everything. (Brabant et al. 1992, 449)

Ferenczi's readiness to sacrifice his own autonomy on the altar of Freud's approval is pathetic. The closest parallel in the history of psychoanalysis is probably Rank's abject letter of apology to Freud and the other members of the Committee on December 20, 1924, in which he confessed that his recent rebellious behavior was due to his unanalyzed "Oedipus and brother complexes" activated by the news of Freud's cancer (Rudnytsky 1991, 35). But just as Rank soon abjured his recantation and completed his painful separation from Freud, so Ferenczi two decades later in his *Diary* not only defended mutual analysis, but also indicted himself for having been "a blindly dependent son" and accused Freud of playing "only the role of the castrating god" and wanting to be "the only one who does not have to be analyzed" (1985, 185, 188).

The preponderantly maternal dimension of Ferenczi's transference to Freud can be seen in two earlier letters. On November 14, 1911, soon after the death of Elma's suitor and as thoughts of marrying her begin to cross his mind, he writes of longing "to commit a terrible act of violence. Dissatisfied with both parents, I wanted to make myself independent!" Responding to Freud's interpretation of his feelings for him as transferential, Ferenczi reiterates his resolve "to make myself independent," adding that "as a parallel process an apparent detachment of libido from Frau G. was playing itself out in me" (Brabant et al. 1992, 311–12). Still earlier, on October 3, 1910, in the wake of the Palermo incident, Ferenczi again draws a poignant analogy between Freud and his future wife: "Just as in my relationship with Frau G. I strive for *absolute* mutual openness, in the same manner—and with even more justification—I believed that this . . . openness, which conceals nothing, could be possible between two ψα.- minded people" (218).

It seems fitting to conclude this argument for why it should now be Ferenczi's turn in psychoanalysis by returning to the Palermo incident and his frustrated desire for a relationship of "absolute mutual openness" with Freud. That the disillusionment at Palermo continued to rankle in Fer- enczi's soul is evident not only from his Christmas 1921 letter to Groddeck but also from the *Clinical Diary,* where Ferenczi asserts that Freud could "tolerate my being a son only until the moment when I contradicted him for the first time (Palermo)" (1985, 185). Ferenczi underwent every vicissitude of emotion toward Freud, including the delusion that Freud was "right in everything"; but his abiding relevance to contemporary readers stems from his courageous willingness to "contradict [Freud] on some essential points" (Brabant et al. 1992, 217), even as he pays unstinting homage to his genius. This last phrase comes from Ferenczi's letter of October 3, 1910, the same one in which he pleads with Freud for complete openness and reviews with him most candidly the Palermo incident of the preceding month.

Every one who embarks on a career in psychoanalysis must come to terms with a transference to Freud. That it is psychoanalytic theory itself that best allows us to contemplate this phenomenon exemplifies the *meta-* quality of psychoanalysis to which I alluded at the outset. Even now, therefore, we are in a situation comparable to that of Freud's original adherents, although our temporal distance means that we can only know

Freud and the other ancestors through their texts, and we likewise have the freedom to choose among many more potential objects of transference. Essentially, however, our options remain the same as those of the first generation. Do we wish to become dissidents, like Jung or Rank? Or disciples, like Abraham or Jones? Or internal critics, like Ferenczi?

In his October 3, 1910, letter, Ferenczi shares with Freud a dream "in which I saw you standing naked before me" (218). Not discounting his homosexual impulses, Ferenczi interprets the dream as expressing his desire for "absolute mutual openness" with Freud. Asking how he could come "to demand still more—indeed everything" from one who had already given him so much, Ferenczi continues with a passage that speaks for all of us who have placed Freud at the center of our lives and work and at times felt daunted when measuring ourselves against his achievement:

But don't forget that for years I have been occupied with nothing but the products of your intellect, and I have also always felt the man behind every sentence of your works and made him my confidant. Whether you want to be or not, you are one of the great master teachers of mankind, and you must allow your readers to approach you, at least intellectually, in a personal relationship as well. My ideal of truth that strikes down all consideration is certainly nothing less than the most self-evident consequence of your teachings. I am convinced that I am not the only one who, in important decisions, in self-criticism, etc., always asks and has asked himself the question: How would *Freud* relate to this? Under "Freud" I understood his teachings and his personality, fused together in a harmonious unity.

So I am and have been much, much more intimately acquainted with you than you could have imagined. . . .

I must come back again and again to the fact that I am aware of the excessiveness of my demands. But I believe that you underestimate much too much the ennobling power of psychoanalysis if you don't believe that it makes people who have completely grasped its meaning absolutely worthy of trust. . . .

Unfortunately—I can't begin, you have to! After all, you are $\Psi\alpha$. in person! (219–20)

The moral of this moving eulogy is not only that it is impossible to separate intellectual from personal concerns in the domain of psychoanalysis, but also that Ferenczi, as Freud's best reader and most gifted pupil, may paradoxically have understood the lessons of this "master teacher of mankind" more profoundly than he did himself. Ferenczi's "ideal of truth" is indeed the ideal of psychoanalysis, and nobody exemplified its "ennobling power" more steadfastly than he. To his credit, he recognized that his greatest discoveries could also be mistakes, that his creativity and healing powers sprang from what, in a postscript to the above letter, he did not scruple to call his "infantile weaknesses and exaggerations." Ferenczi paid his teacher the ultimate tribute of going beyond him and becoming a master in his own right.[11] By doing so, he outgrew Freud's filial epithet— at once honorific yet condescending—of "Paladin and Secret Grand Vizier," and proved himself to be what each of us must become—"$\Psi\alpha$. in person"—and our most trustworthy guide to its future.

Happily, this volume cannot claim to inaugurate the revival of interest in Ferenczi's work, but rather to show the full flowering of his influence on contemporary psychoanalysis. Among the handful of studies of Ferenczi available in English, there is one anthology, expertly edited by Lewis Aron and Adrienne Harris (1993), to which we stand in a sibling relation. But if the controversies around Freud give no signs of simmering down, those around Ferenczi are just beginning to heat up; and the lines of inquiry that have been recently opened will not soon be exhausted.

This collection of essays by fifteen eminent scholars and clinicians from six different countries is the most comprehensive and, I believe, most rigorous examination of Ferenczi's legacy yet attempted. Although the contributors concur in their assessment of Ferenczi's stature, they often disagree in their judgments about his views, which underwent a lifelong evolution, and his place in the history of psychoanalysis. For some, he is a radically iconoclastic figure whose greatest contributions lie in his post-1930 challenge to Freudian orthodoxy; for others, he is ultimately a classical analyst who built on Freud's foundations. Thus, in the spirit of Ferenczi's own tentativeness, the essays in this book constitute a dialogue in which the questions are many and the answers open-ended.

The anthology has been divided into three parts. The essays in Part I, "Contexts and Continuities," set Ferenczi against the backdrop of his political and cultural contexts, assess the history and distinctive features of the Budapest School of psychoanalysis, and trace the ramifications of his influence. Those in Part II, "Disciple and Dissident," address in varying ways the central issue of Ferenczi's relationship to Freud. If, in the end,

Ferenczi was neither a disciple nor a dissident but a psychoanalytic original who defies categorization, it is still between the Scylla and Charybdis of these poles that he had to navigate. Finally, the essays in Part III, "Theory and Technique," take up Ferenczi's innovative contributions to psychoanalytic theory and his controversial ideas about technique. Despite the ease with which the essays fall into these clusters, however, their concerns are overlapping. Thus, Ferenczi's ties to Freud and his views on theory and technique often find their way into Part I; technical and theoretical issues as well as broader concerns of background and influence surface in Part II; and Part III provides a reprise of previously articulated historical and personal themes.

We begin with André E. Haynal's "Freud and His Intellectual Environment: The Case of Sándor Ferenczi." As supervisor of the publication of the Freud-Ferenczi correspondence and author of the influential *The Technique at Issue* (1988) and other books, he is the dean of contemporary Ferenczi studies. Of Hungarian origin, Haynal has used his prestigious positions in both the psychoanalytic and academic worlds, as Ferenczi surely would have wanted him to do, to resist partisanship and bring people together on the common ground of psychoanalysis. In his paper, Haynal, in broad strokes, sketches Ferenczi's intellectual milieu and his ideas with respect to object relations, countertransference, and unconscious communication. By showing how these originated out of the productive tensions in Ferenczi's relationships with Freud and Rank, he makes the point that creativity in psychoanalysis is always a collaborative matter.

The succeeding two essays present complementary perspectives on psychoanalysis in Hungary. Michelle Moreau-Ricaud, a historian of psychoanalysis and practicing analyst in Paris, chronicles "The Founding of the Budapest School." György Vikár, a past president of the Hungarian Psychoanalytic Association and a pupil of Imre Hermann, tells the story from inside in "The Budapest School of Psychoanalysis." Their accounts contain a wealth of information about the sociocultural reasons for the avid reception of psychoanalysis in Hungary, which until World War I was politically united with Austria, and about the members of the Budapest School that formed around Ferenczi.

The final two essays in Part I chart the vicissitudes of Ferenczi's fortunes in America. John E. Gedo is one of this country's most prolific and distinguished analysts, and in "O, Patria Mia" he surveys from his vantage point on Lake Michigan the panorama of those who, like himself, have come from Hungary to enrich American psychoanalysis. His contribution is at once a scintillating piece of intellectual history and a moving personal memoir. Ann-Louise S. Silver's "Ferenczi's Early Impact on Washington, D.C." reflects her geographical and institutional ties to Chestnut Lodge Hospital. Silver highlights Ferenczi's visit to Washington in 1927, his analysis of Clara Thompson, the close associate of Harry Stack Sullivan, and the role played by Frieda Fromm-Reichmann, who worked with Georg Groddeck before becoming director of Chestnut Lodge, as conduits between the old and new worlds. In closing, Silver notes the references to Groddeck in Harold Searles's paper, "The Patient as Therapist to His Analyst" (1972), as an illustration of the ever-widening ripples of Ferenczi's influence on contemporary clinicians.

Axel Hoffer, together with his brother Peter, translated and introduced Freud's rediscovered *Phylogenetic Fantasy* and he has written the introduction to the second volume of the Freud-Ferenczi correspondence. We begin Part II with his "Asymmetry and Mutuality in the Analytic Relationship: Contemporary Lessons from the Freud-Ferenczi Dialogue." In Hoffer's work one can observe a liberal-minded, classically trained analyst coming to grips with Ferenczi's challenge to the Freudian paradigm. Although Hoffer clearly hears Ferenczi's late pleas on behalf of mutuality in the analytic relationship with sympathy, and argues that the analyst must be able to tolerate the tension produced by this inevitable pull within himself, he does not evade the conclusion that while the feelings produced in analysis are indeed real, the relationship is inherently asymmetrical and should remain that way for the good of the patient. Hoffer's critique of Ferenczi is deeply meditated, and his comparison of the partners in mutual analysis to Hansel and Gretel lost in the woods should give pause to even his most ardent admirers.

Thierry Bokanowski, our second French contributor, displays intellectual rigor and flair in "Sándor Ferenczi: Negative Transference and Transference Depression." The nub of Bokanowski's argument is that Ferenczi as a child introjected a primary depression transmitted by his mother, who, it will be recalled, gave birth to twelve children, and that this replayed itself as a transference depression in his relationship with Freud. Bolstering the views I have outlined above, Bokanowski instances the death of Ferenczi's sister Vilma at one year of age, when he himself was five, as a further factor that likely contributed to his mother's depression. Bokanowski does not pathologize Ferenczi, but he does show the origins of many of his concepts in his personal ordeals. A similar stereoscopic focus on the relationship between Freud and Ferenczi and their ideas about theory and technique informs Martin S. Bergmann's "The Tragic Encounter between Freud and Ferenczi and Its Impact on the History of Psychoanalysis." Bergmann, whose lifetime of achievement has recently been honored by a *Festschrift*, *The Scope of Psychoanalysis*, contends that Ferenczi was neither an extender nor a heretic, but the first psychoanalytic modifier, and pleads for a healing of the tragic split between Freud and Ferenczi through an integration of their complementary models of the analytic enterprise.

Kathleen Kelley-Lainé's paper adopts a more critical stance toward Freud. Hungarian by birth, raised in Anglophone Canada, and a member of the Paris Psychoanalytic Society, she brings a polyglot sensibility to bear in "Ferenczi's Mother Tongue." Concentrating on Ferenczi's two major papers on language, "On Obscene Words" (1911) and "Confusion of Tongues between Adults and the Child," Kelley-Lainé proposes that he experienced a "bilingual splitting" between Hungarian, his mother tongue, and German, metaphorically the paternal language of Freud. As long as Ferenczi confined himself to Freud's theoretical discourse, all was well, but once he attempted to speak in his own idiom, Freud became frightened and turned away. Part II concludes with Christopher Fortune's "Mutual Analysis: A Logical Outcome of Sándor Ferenczi's Experiments in Psycho-analysis." Fortune here pursues his already widely cited research on Eliza-beth Severn, the patient known in the *Clinical Diary* as "R.N." with whom Ferenczi took the leap of mutual analysis. Carefully weighing the factors that led Ferenczi to resort to this extreme measure, Fortune sees it as having been at once "a hero's and a fool's journey," an immensely productive and illuminating but also dangerous and ultimately impossible experiment.

The essays in Part III exhibit no less diversity than those of the foregoing sections. In "Hermann's Concept of Clinging in Light of Modern Drive

Theory," Wolfgang Berner, a former president of the Vienna Psychoanalytic Society, argues that Imre Hermann's early understanding of attachment remains more sophisticated than that of his renowned British scion, John Bowlby. Berner bolsters his contention with case materials drawn from his work with pedophilic patients, and his effort to reconcile attachment with drive theory exemplifies the belief of a classical analyst in the underlying compatibility between the heritages of Ferenczi and Freud.

Because shame is linked to body image, it can reflect anxieties of castration or mutilation. In "Castration and Narcissism in Ferenczi," Michèle Bertrand, a philosopher and psychoanalyst in Paris, investigates Ferenczi's understanding of the connections between these two pivotal psychoanalytic concepts. Although in his earlier writings Ferenczi adhered to Freud's definition of the castration complex as pertaining specifically to the threatened loss of the penis, he came increasingly to emphasize broader concerns of trauma, psychic pain, and narcissistic injury. Examining many of Ferenczi's papers, including those on war neuroses, tics, and Gulliver fantasies, as well as *Thalassa,* Bertrand deftly balances his perspective and Freud's, concluding that castration must be defined more broadly to include all of its avatars.

As befits Ferenczi's own commitment to psychoanalysis as a means of therapy, even for the most disturbed patients, the last three essays in this volume directly address issues of technique. Like Bertrand, Patrizia Giampieri-Deutsch is both a philosopher and a practicing analyst. She is, moreover, one of the coeditors of the Freud-Ferenczi correspondence. Contrary to the widespread tendency to oversimplify Ferenczi by focusing on only one phase of his work, Giampieri-Deutsch's "The Influence of Ferenczi's Ideas on Contemporary Standard Technique" attends to each of his major technical experiments—activity, relaxation, and mutual analysis—and stresses the need for historical contextualization. While giving due weight to the originality of Ferenczi's ideas on transference, countertransference, repetition, and empathy, Giampieri-Deutsch resists any attempt to cast Freud and Ferenczi as polar opposites. The classical temperament of Giampieri-Deutsch, a member of the Vienna Psychoanalytic Society, recalls that of Wolfgang Berner.

By contrast, Rebecca Curtis, a psychoanalyst trained in the interpersonal tradition, proffers "A New World Symphony: Ferenczi and the Integration of Nonpsychoanalytic Techniques into Psychoanalytic Practice." With the aid of several clinical vignettes, Curtis defends the blending of psychoanalytic and other therapeutic methods derived from cognitive, encounter, experiential, and gestalt traditions. Agreeing with Giampieri-Deutsch about the dangers of schematization, Curtis invokes Ferenczi to admonish analysts about their own resistances to change.

Our final essay is Judith E. Vida's "The 'Wise Baby' Grows Up: The Contemporary Relevance of Sándor Ferenczi." A psychiatrist with impeccable analytic credentials, Vida is a founding member of the freestanding Institute of Contemporary Psychoanalysis in Los Angeles. She expounds Ferenczi's memorable concept of the "wise baby," heretofore used principally as a pejorative tag for Ferenczi himself, as a metaphor for the premature ego development that results from childhood trauma. After reviewing Ferenczi's allusions to the wise baby, Vida presents the case history of a patient who both exemplifies Ferenczi's notion and highlights its possible limitations. If, in the end, Vida accepts the traditional diagnosis of Ferenczi as a wise baby, it is because, like her patient, he has something to teach us that disturbs our complacency and we may still be not quite ready to hear.

NOTES

1. As Louis A. Sass has remarked, the paradoxical concept of human subjectivity as "both a knowing subject and a primary object of knowing" was decisively introduced by Kant, whose self-reflexive focus "had the effect of turning subjectivity into a prime object of study, an empirical entity that would itself be investigated by newly developing human sciences that aspired to specify the nature or explain the sources of these very categories or cultural forms" (1994, 80–81). If, as Sass's account implies, psychoanalysis has its philosophical roots in the Kantian tradition, it must likewise acknowledge its kinship to schizophrenia, which represents this modern condition of hyper-consciousness in its diseased form. (Freud's 1910 monograph on Schreber, which forms the backdrop to the "Palermo incident" with Ferenczi—to be discussed later—and harks back to the themes of paranoia and homosexuality in his relationship with Fliess, provides the textual conjunction between psychoanalysis and schizophrenia.) But although self-consciousness has a potentially paralyzing effect, it can, I believe, also lead to health, much in the manner of Wittgenstein's philosophy, which, as Sass shows, seeks to tread the tightrope of thought in order to restore human beings to the ground of ordinary

experience. The continuity between the philosophies of Kant and Wittgenstein is thus ultimately a variation on the Romantic topos of an "odyssey of consciousness," which, as I have argued in *Freud and Oedipus* (1987), underlies the psychoanalytic enterprise.

2. In English, see above all Haynal (1988), Stanton (1991), and Aron and Harris (1993). Among the works in other languages are Sabourin (1985), Harmat (1988), and Bertrand et al. (1994).

3. The titles by which both these texts are known in English are embellishments of their sober German originals. *Thalassa* is actually *Versuch einer Genitaltheorie;* and *A Phylogenetic Fantasy,* one of Freud's seven lost metapsychological papers, *Übersicht der Übertragungsneurosen.* But given their unscientific nature, the desire of their English translators to cast them as imaginative works is readily comprehensible.

4. A similar score-settling vis-à-vis Rank occurs in *Moses and Monotheism* (1939, 125). In this powerful deployment of public narratives to promote his own view of personal and ideological conflicts, which goes back to the *History of the Psycho-Analytic Movement* (1914), Freud sets a precedent for Jones in his biography.

5. Ferenczi's infatuation with Elma Pálos followed, from Freud's perspective, hard on the heels of Jung's imbroglio with his patient Sabina Spielrein and ran concurrently with Jones's affair with the morphine-addicted Loe Kann, whom he brought to Vienna for analysis with Freud in October 1912. It is not difficult to sympathize with Freud's exasperation at the sexual exploits of his lieutenants. See also Ernst Falzeder's (1994) discussion of Freud's own countertransferential struggles during this period with his "grand-patient," Elfriede Hirschfeld, and her role in his quarrels with Jung and Oskar Pfister in Zurich.

6. In an undated letter to Freud probably from the summer of 1912, Ferenczi states that he has "constantly sought to come to grips with painful insights that have to do with Frau G.'s age and the sexual intercourse with her that is not entirely satisfying physically" (Brabant et al. 1992, 383). There is no reason to think that Ferenczi and Elma ever consummated their relationship. Ferenczi's grief over his childlessness gives an ironic twist to Freud's praise of *Thalassa* as his "most fertile" achievement. Although this appears to be inadvertent, there is deliberate cruelty in Freud's exhortation, in a letter of May 12, 1932, that Ferenczi "leave that island of dreams which you inhabit with your fantasy-children and once again join in mankind's struggles" (Dupont 1985, xvi; see Stanton 1991, 49).

7. This letter to Groddeck also appears to call into question Ferenczi's assertion that Freud had overlooked his negative transference. But although it confirms that his hostility toward Freud came up in conversation between them, and indeed that Freud had evidently alluded to it on at least one prior occasion, it does not contradict Ferenczi's allegation that it had not figured during his three periods of *analysis* by Freud, and that he had rather arrived at this insight independently through self-analysis. Ferenczi's crucial letter of January 17, 1930, and other relevant documents, is quoted by Judith Dupont in her introduction to the *Clinical Diary* (1985, xiii).

8. I have cited only the most salient details of this letter, which consists of an extended exegesis of a dream. Among much else, Ferenczi alludes to an experience

of having been forced to perform fellatio at the age of five by an older playmate and rehearses the same symptoms of breathlessness, insomnia, and chills detailed in the Christmas 1921 letter to Groddeck. Of particular note to Freud scholars, Ferenczi interprets his dream as an attempt to ward off the threat of castration incurred by his illicit sexual desires for Elma by comparing them not only to his father's relations with his mother but also to Freud's *voyage de lit-à lit* in Italy with his sister-in-law Minna Bernays. Although Ferenczi dismisses this as "only an infantile thought," it provides an important piece of corroboration for the theory, espoused preeminently by Peter Swales, that Freud engaged in an affair with Minna Bernays.

9. In the *Clinical Diary,* Ferenczi describes the partners in mutual analysis as "two equally terrified children who compare their experiences, and because of their common fate understand each other completely and instinctively" (Ferenczi 1985, 56). For a critique of this model of analysis, see Axel Hoffer's contribution to this volume.

10. A striking analogue to the multiple levels of Ferenczi's emotional life, in which the mother rather than the father is the chief instigator of trauma, with corresponding (and explicitly formulated) consequences for the theory of the Oedipus complex, is found in the case of Harry Guntrip (Rudnytsky 1991, 115–48).

11. On the eve of his rupture with Freud, Jung, in a letter of March 3, 1912, quoted to Freud an extended passage from Nietzsche's *Thus Spoke Zarathustra,* which begins: "One repays a teacher badly if one always remains nothing but a pupil." As I have previously argued (1987, 221–23), had Freud been a better Nietzschean and a more magnanimous soul, he would have issued this warning himself, instead of having it flung at him as a reproach by his heir apparent. The passage likewise glosses Ferenczi's relationship to Freud, and it is ultimately he (and, in a different way, Rank) who best embodies the Nietzschean spirit in psychoanalysis.

REFERENCES

Aron, L., and A. Harris, eds. 1993. *The Legacy of Sándor Ferenczi.* Hillsdale, N.J.: Analytic Press.

Bálint, M. 1968. *The Basic Fault: Therapeutic Aspects of Regression.* New York: Brunner/Mazel, 1979.

Bertrand, M., T. Bokanowski, M. Dechaud-Ferbus, A. Driant, M. Ferminne, and N. Khouri. 1994. *Ferenczi, patient et psychanalyste.* Paris: Harmattan.

Brabant, E., E. Falzeder, and P. Giampieri-Deutsch, eds. 1992. *The Correspondence of Sigmund Freud and Sándor Ferenczi. Volume 1, 1908–1914.* Supervised by A. Haynal. Trans. P. T. Hoffer. Cambridge, Mass.: Harvard University Press, 1993.

Dupont, J. 1985. Introduction to Ferenczi 1985, pp. xi–xxvii.

Falzeder, E. 1994. My Grand-Patient, My Chief Tormentor: A Hitherto Unnoticed Case of Freud's and the Consequences. *Psychoanal. Q.,* 53:297–331.

Ferenczi, S. 1924. *Thalassa: A Theory of Genitality.* Trans. H. A. Bunker. New York: Norton, 1968.

———. 1985. *The Clinical Diary of Sándor Ferenczi.* Ed. J. Dupont. Trans. M. Bálint and N. Z. Jackson. Cambridge, Mass.: Harvard University Press, 1988.

Ferenczi, S., and G. Groddeck. 1982. *Briefwechsel 1921–1933.* Ed. J. Dupont. Frankfurt am Main: Fischer, 1986.

Fortune, C. 1993. The Case of "RN." Sándor Ferenczi's Radical Experiment in Psychoanalysis. In Aron and Harris 1993, pp. 101–20.

Freud, S. 1914. *On the History of the Psycho-Analytic Movement.* In *The Standard Edition of the Complete Psychological Works.* Ed. and trans. J. Strachey et al. 24 vols. 14:7–66. London: Hogarth Press, 1953–74.

———. 1923. Dr. Sándor Ferenczi (On His Fiftieth Birthday). *S.E.*, 19:267–69.

———. 1933. Sándor Ferenczi. *S.E.*, 22:227–29.

———. 1937. Analysis Terminable and Interminable. *S.E.*, 23:216–53.

———. 1939. *Moses and Monotheism. S.E.*, 23:7–137.

Harmat, P. 1988. *Freud, Ferenczi und die ungarische Psychoanalyse.* Tübingen: Diskord.

Haynal, A. 1988. *The Technique at Issue: Controversies in Psychoanalytic Method from Freud and Ferenczi to Michael Bálint.* Trans. E. Holder. London: Karnac, 1989.

Rudnytsky, P. L. 1987. *Freud and Oedipus.* New York: Columbia University Press.

———. 1991. *The Psychoanalytic Vocation: Rank, Winnicott, and the Legacy of Freud.* New Haven: Yale University Press.

———. 1992. Le meurtre du patient par l'analyste. *Le Coq-Héron,* 125:19–23.

Sabourin, P. 1985. *Ferenczi, paladin et grand vizir secret.* Paris: Éditions Universitaires.

Sass, L. A. 1994. *The Paradoxes of Delusion: Wittgenstein, Schreber, and the Schizophrenic Mind.* Ithaca, N.Y.: Cornell University Press.

Shapiro, S. A. 1993. Clara Thompson: Ferenczi's Messenger with Half a Message. In Aron and Harris 1993, pp. 159–74.

Stanton, M. 1991. *Sándor Ferenczi: Reconsidering Active Intervention.* New York: Aronson.

This, B. 1982. "Schrei nach dem Kinde": Le cri de Ferenczi. *Le Coq-Héron,* 85:23–30.

PART I

Contexts and Continuities

One

Freud and His Intellectual Environment: The Case of Sándor Ferenczi

■

A N D R É E . H A Y N A L

Freud has changed our view of human relationships: our present conception of human communication—whether in larger or smaller groups, whether verbal or nonverbal—is inconceivable without the pioneering work of Freud and his circle. In opposition to the widespread image, Freud did not elaborate his thoughts on these problems alone, but beginning with the first flowering of his theory, the *Project for a Scientific Psychology* (1895), which emerged in correspondence with Wilhelm Fliess, he developed them in close contact with his circle and the friends who surrounded him. His study of human relationships, starting from his observations and his difficulties in therapeutic practice, was conducted above all with the aid of two of his collaborators, Sándor Ferenczi and Otto Rank.

The closeness of Freud's relationship with Rank cannot be overstated. Few people today realize that the term *Verleugnung* (disavowal) derives from Rank (1927–28, 12), that Rank (1911) wrote an early article on narcissism, which was quoted by Freud on the first page of his "On Narcissism: An Introduction" (1914a, 73), and that he became for a time the author of sections in Freud's *Interpretation of Dreams*. The thrust to clarify the problems of human relationships, which led to a remarkable advance in our under-

An earlier version of this chapter appears in Lewis Aron and Adrienne Harris, eds., *The Legacy of Sándor Ferenczi* (Hillsdale, N.J.: Analytic Press, 1993), pp. 53–74. Copyright © by The Analytic Press, Inc. It has been presented at "Psychoanalysis and Culture: The Contributions of Sigmund Freud," Stanford University, January 1991, and at the Fourth International Conference of the Sándor Ferenczi Society in Budapest, July 1993.

standing, was itself the result of an intense and intimate dialogue between Freud and his intellectual environment.

A useful point of departure for assessing the collaborative nature of Freud's achievement is provided by a letter written by Michael Bálint on May 31, 1957, to Ernest Jones:

It is true that whenever a crisis broke out Freud invariably showed himself what he really was, a truly great man, who was always accessible and tolerant to new ideas, who was always willing to stop, think anew, even if it meant reexamining even his most basic concepts, in order to find a possibility for understanding what might be valuable in any new idea. It has never been asked whether something in Freud has or has not contributed to a critical increase of tension during the period preceding a crisis. Still less has any analyst bothered to find out what happened in the minds of those who came into conflict with Freud and what in their relationship to him and to psychoanalysis led to the exacerbation. We have been content to describe them as the villains of the piece. . . . Maybe Rank's case is less suitable for this examination, but I am quite certain in Ferenczi's case one could follow the development, which, prompted by the characters of the two protagonists, led to the tragic conflict.[1]

It is generally agreed that Fliess had a significant influence on Freud's early discoveries, although opinions differ as to its nature: for some scholars he merely played the role of a screen upon which Freud could project his ideas, whereas others see him as an intellectual partner who enabled Freud to connect the biology of his time to his literary and philosophical heritage of German Romanticism. Whatever the exact truth of the matter in the case of Fliess, the idea of Freud the Master in the company of eager students is clearly too simple.

Just how wide of the mark this image is becomes clear when we realize that Ferenczi, at the time he and Freud first met in 1909, was already a mature and well-established figure. At thirty-five years of age, his student days in Vienna were far behind him. The son of a cultivated family, he was the author of some sixty scientific works, a neuropsychiatrist who gave expert legal testimony, and a poet in his spare time—in short, a typical member of the Budapest intelligentsia. This community, as distant from provincial Hungary as New York is from the American Midwest, was composed of émigrés of the various territories belonging to the monarchy: German speakers (commonly referred to as *Schwaben* or, more precisely, *Donauschwaben*), Hungarians originating from the distant provinces (such as the multiethnic principality of Transylvania, which had remained independent for centuries), and Jews from western Poland (territory belonging to the Double Monarchy since the time of Maria Theresa). This Judeo-Hungarian intelligentsia, to which Ferenczi belonged, played an immensely important role in the transformation of the cultural life of Budapest, putting it in the same league as Vienna and Prague.

Freud's first meeting with Ferenczi resulted in a mutual enthusiasm and a friendship that Freud was later to describe as "a community of life, thought, and interests" (January 11, 1933).[2] They worked side by side, their dialogue resulting in an intense exchange of ideas, in intimacy, and also in controversy. In the scientific domain, they constantly shared their thoughts and projects. Many of Ferenczi's conceptions reappear in the works of Freud, often after a prolonged period of gestation, blended with his own ideas. Freud evidently needed such stimulating company—Fliess, Rank, Ferenczi, and for a time even Groddeck were to be situated in this context.

To these scientific links must be added personal ones, which were more complex and more profound: Freud's hopes that his daughter Mathilde might marry Ferenczi, their voyage to America with Jung during which they analyzed each other's dreams in a sort of "mutual analysis," and numerous holidays together, with their attendant pleasures and difficulties. These holidays were preceded by several months of preparation, studying the Baedeker, timetables, and so on. Nor can we forget the three periods of Ferenczi's more formal analysis with Freud in 1914 and 1916, where Ferenczi's relationships with his future wife, Gizella, and her daughter, Elma, became important issues. Ferenczi was not satisfied and wished for a deeper understanding by Freud: this dissatisfaction is a recurrent motif in their relationship. The interactions of Ferenczi and Freud with other analysts—Jung, Rank, Jones, Groddeck, Abraham, Eitingon, Reich, etc.—also have their role to play in this contentious history of psychoanalysis.

It is worth remembering that Freud treated his patient Ida Bauer ("Dora") from October to December 1900 and seems to have written her case history in a single burst of impassioned enthusiasm, between January 10 and 25, 1901, breaking off work on *The Psychopathology of Everyday Life* (1901), which he was then writing. As we know, the publication of the Dora case gave Freud a great deal of difficulty and dragged on for five years until 1905 (Marcus 1976). In Freud's social and professional situation it required a great deal of courage and integrity to publish what actually was the chronicle of a failure, not to mention the problems of medical discretion and professional secrecy.

Even at this early date Freud was aware of dangers inherent in the analyst's involvement in the therapeutic process, but he nonetheless recurrently found himself becoming aroused by his own affective responses. In the correspondence with Fliess, for example, he writes on December 21, 1899, of his patient, Mr. E.: "He demonstrated the reality of my theory in my own case, providing me in a surprising reversal with the solution, which I had overlooked, to my former railroad phobia. For this piece of work I even made him the present of a picture of Oedipus and the Sphinx" (Freud and Fliess 1985, 392).

By the time of the Dora case, Freud's experience of the forces present in analytic treatment was already considerable and his ideas on the subject were well developed. As early as 1895 he wrote of the phenomenon of transference that "this happens when the patient's relation to the physician is disturbed, and it is the *worst [ärgste]* obstacle that we can come across," but added that even so it is "the special solicitude inherent to the treatment" and we can "reckon on meeting it in every comparatively serious analysis" (Freud and Breuer 1895, 301–2; italics added), since "these drawbacks . . . are inseparable from our procedure" (266). After a great deal of internal struggle, he admitted to Oskar Pfister in a letter of June 5, 1910, that "transference is indeed a cross" (Freud and Pfister 1963, 39). Following the triangle formed by Breuer, Anna O., and himself, Freud was to find himself, on at least two occasions, involved in analogous situations that were even more delicate: with Sabina Spielrein and Jung (1908–9), and a few years later with Elma Pálos and Ferenczi (1911–12). The recognition of these phenomena therefore occurs not only in his clinical practice but also, it seems, in extra-analytic experiences involving other people. The correspondence between Freud and Jung (1974) and the material published concerning Sabina Spielrein (Carotenuto 1980) bear witness to this.

Gradually Freud came to place increasing emphasis on affective experiences and their repetitive character (affectionate, erotic, hostile, etc.) in the transference. To Jung he wrote on December 6, 1906, that "the cure is effected by love" (Freud and Jung 1974, 13). One month later, on January 30, 1907, in the *Minutes of the Vienna Psychoanalytic Society,* we find him making a similar statement: "Our cures are cures of love" (Nunberg and Federn 1962, 101). On January 19, 1908, he wrote to Karl Abraham: "Back to technique. You are right, that was the most taxing of all to acquire, and that is why I want to spare those who follow in my footsteps part of the grind—and part of the cost" (Freud and Abraham, 1965, 24). At the psychoanalytic congress in Salzburg over Easter in 1908, Freud presented the analysis of the Rat Man (1909), speaking for almost five hours without a break, driven by the need to express himself on a subject that obviously preoccupied him. He acknowledged this need to Abraham in July 1912: "I have to recuperate from psychoanalysis by working, otherwise I should not be able to stand it" (Freud and Abraham 1965, 120); and also to Ferenczi: "I was depressed the whole time and anaesthetized myself with writing—writing—writing" (Freud and Ferenczi 1992, 325).

This suffering stems from Freud's affective involvement in his analytic work. As he wrote to Jung on March 9, 1909: "To be slandered and scorched by the love with which we operate—such are the perils of our trade, which we are certainly not going to abandon on their account. *Navigare necesse est, vivere non necesse* [it is necessary to sail, not to live]." Moreover, " 'In league with the devil and yet you fear fire?' " (Freud and Jung 1974, 210–11). Thus he came to write, on June 7, 1909, again to Jung, about the latter's involvement with Sabina Spielrein:

Such experiences, though painful, are necessary and hard to avoid. Without them, we cannot really know life and what we are dealing with. I myself have never been taken so badly, but I have come very close to it a number of times and had *a narrow escape.* I believe that only grim necessities weighing on my work, and the fact that I was ten years older than yourself when I came to psychoanalysis, have saved me from similar experiences. But no lasting harm is done. They help us to develop the thick skin we need and to dominate "counter-transference," which is after all a permanent problem for us; they teach us to displace our own affects to best advantage. They are a *"blessing in disguise."* (230–31; italicized phrases in English in original)

This 1909 letter contains Freud's first recorded use of the term "counter-transference." It first appears in a published work a year later in "The Future Prospects of Psycho-Analytic Therapy" (1910). The importance of the sentiments of the analyst became increasingly clear to him. On April 7, 1909, he wrote to Abraham that it was precisely those cases in which he had the greatest personal interest that had failed, "perhaps just because of the intensity of feeling" (Freud and Abraham 1965, 63).

Some months later, in August 1909, Freud, Ferenczi, and Jung embarked on their voyage to America, where Freud gave his famous lectures on the occasion of the twentieth anniversary of the founding of Clark University in Worcester, Massachusetts. (Incidentally, it is from Freud himself that we know of the astonishing way in which his five Clark lectures were composed; during their regular walks, Ferenczi would sketch out a lecture, which Freud would deliver half an hour later; Freud 1933, 227.) Clearly, he was preoccupied at this time with problems that he had been seeking to clarify for years, and which now became the subject of intense discussion during the voyage.

However, the working through of these problems required a sense of perspective. Thanks to his position, simultaneously engaged in and yet distant from these theoretical difficulties, the possibility of *understanding* emerged in Freud and led him to the idea of the countertransference and, more generally, to consider the emotional involvement of the psychoanalyst in the treatment. He later noted that many important communications between analyst and patient take place "without passing through the *Cs.*," because "the *Ucs.* of one human being can react upon that of another" (1915b, 194).

Freud's interest in nonverbal means of communication during analysis likewise prompted him and Ferenczi to reexamine the mysterious regions of parapsychology and the occult. The influence of Ferenczi may have helped to revive not only Freud's but also Jung's interest in the occult (Jung wrote his doctoral thesis on the subject). Significantly, their trip to America ended with a detour to Berlin, where Ferenczi met with the clairvoyant Frau Seidler in order to deepen his understanding of *Gedankenübertragung,* a German word that can be translated as "thought transference" or "thought transmission." Ferenczi was later to engage in further exploratory sessions with a certain Mrs. Jelinek in Budapest (November 20, 1909), with Professor Alexander Roth (November 23, 1913), and with one Professor Staudenmeier (July 3, 1912); later he asked his brother to go and see Frau Seidler

(October 14, 1909; November 8, 1909). Freud, meanwhile, gave advice on the way in which these experiments should be conceived (October 11, 1909; October 22, 1909; November 10, 1909). Ferenczi also conducted experiments with his patients (August 17, 1910; November 16, 1910), with his friend and later wife Gizella Pálos (November 22, 1910), and with himself as medium (December 19, 1910). These served, as Freud wrote on August 20, 1910, "to shatter the doubts about the existence of thought transference" (Freud and Ferenczi 1992, 211). It was, of course, difficult for Freud and his colleagues to discuss these embarrassing and forbidden topics. Freud wrote to Jung on December 31, 1911, that a paper on countertransference was "sorely needed," but added, "of course we could not publish it, we should have to circulate copies among ourselves" (Freud and Jung 1974, 476). The previous year he had remarked to Ferenczi, who was heading in the same direction concerning the occult: "I would like to request that you continue to research in secrecy for two full years and don't come out until 1913; then, certainly, in the *Jahrbuch,* openly and aboveboard" (Freud and Ferenczi 1992, 240).

These reflections were to lead, from the end of 1911 through the two years and half which followed, to Freud's publication of six papers on technique (1911, 1912a, 1912b, 1913, 1914b, 1915a), which he had considered making part of a series (in 1918 they were reprinted under the title *On the Technique of Psycho-Analysis*). However, Freud never completed a systematic treatise on technique—an *Allgemeine Methodik der Psychoanalyse (General Methodology of Psycho-Analysis)*—perhaps a sign that he saw this as an unfinished chapter in his work.[3]

In his technical essays, moreover, Freud limited himself to the most cautious formulations and "essentially negative advice." As he later wrote to Ferenczi: "I thought that the most important thing was to underline what should not be done and to highlight the temptations that might put the analysis in jeopardy" (January 4, 1928). Freud addressed these papers mainly to beginners, but the broader theoretical questions were not yet resolved.

At this stage Freud and Ferenczi collaborated more than is sometimes realized. Only later, in the mid-1920s, did their views diverge in ways that were important for the evolution of psychoanalysis. Ferenczi was already proving himself to be a very fine clinician, sensitive to even the most subtle interactions that occur during treatment. His "On Transitory Symptom-Constructions during the Analysis" (1912) is noteworthy in this respect, as are his short clinical notes, "To Whom Does One Relate One's Dreams?" (1913), "A Little Chanticleer" (1913), "Falling Asleep during the Analysis" (1914), and "The 'Forgetting' of a Symptom and Its Explanation in a Dream" (1914). All these papers are of inestimable value and foreshadow his later theoretical work, with its profound understanding of the forces of transference and countertransference and its attention to the dynamics of empathy and regression. Ferenczi's relational and interactional clinical method, which remains his most lasting contribution, has been taken up in various forms by virtually the entire psychoanalytic community (e.g., object relations, interpersonal, and self psychological schools), though he is seldom given credit for the development of this technique, which relies on direct experience and intersubjectivity.

When, in 1913, Freud published *Totem and Taboo,* Ferenczi immediately noted in a letter that it contained a passage espousing "the idea of transmission by unconscious understanding" (Freud and Ferenczi 1992, 494). Freud in his work had written: "For psycho-analysis has shown us that everyone possesses in his unconscious mental activity an apparatus which enables him to interpret other people's reactions, that is, to undo the distortions which in other people have imposed on the expression of their feelings" (1912–13, 159). After the Budapest Congress in 1918, Freud abandoned this question and seems to have preferred to leave it to others in his intellectual circle, notably Ferenczi and Rank, offering them encouragement in the form of a prize for the best study on the correlation of theory and technique (Freud 1922). Apparently, his hopes were high.

Originally, Ferenczi and Rank had intended to submit their joint work, *The Development of Psycho-Analysis* (1923), for this prize, but later they decided against doing so. In this work they put a special stress on reexperiencing *(Wiedererleben)* during treatment, thus advancing the debate over technique a stage further. In this way the question of the emotions *(Gefühle)* came up again, though in a more developed and better conceived form, under the keyword of "experience" *(Erlebnis).* At first, Freud accepted this point of view, writing to the Committee in January 1924: "I think that the joint work [of Rank and Ferenczi] is a corrective to my conception of the role of repetition or of acting out *(agieren)* during analysis" (Jones 1957, 351). He likewise characterized it one month later to the Committee as a "refreshing intervention that may possibly precipitate changes in our present analytic habits" (Freud and Abraham 1965, 345–46). However, in this latter letter, Freud added: "For my part, I shall continue to practice a 'classical' form of analysis."

After the controversies surrounding *The Development of Psycho-Analysis* and Rank's *Trauma of Birth* (1924), two lines of thought become more distinct. On the one hand, we find the Berlin school and Jones; on the other, the Budapest group and Rank. Supported by Sachs, Abraham in two February 1924 letters to Freud criticized the technique of Rank and Ferenczi as an "ominous development" and a "manifestation of regression in the scientific field" (Freud and Abraham 1965, 349–50). The path taken by Ferenczi and Rank seemed to the Berliners, as Abraham insisted to Freud on March 8, 1924, to "lead away from psychoanalysis" (330; see also the March 10, 1924, letter from Sachs to Freud in Jones 1957, 71). Freud underlined the difference between the two methods—the one aiming at experience, the other at insight and enlarging consciousness (see his February 15, 1924, letter to the Committee in Freud and Abraham 1965, 344–48)—though he seems at first not to have taken this difference too seriously. As he wrote to Abraham on March 4, 1924, "It would become plain whether one side had exaggerated a useful finding or the other had underrated it" (Freud and Abraham 1965, 353).

By this time Freud had become displeased with Jones, due in large part to his disputes with Rank concerning their respective competence in psychoanalytic publishing. On January 7, 1922, Freud criticized Jones severely: "I had to find out that you had less control of your moods and passions, were less consistent, sincere, and reliable than I had a right to expect of you and than was required by your conspicuous position." Freud went on to take Jones to task for his "unjust susceptibilities," especially with respect to Rank (Jones 1957, 54). Jones attempted to justify himself, replying on April 10, 1922, that "unfortunately Rank and I have not found it easy to be business collaborators. . . . Rank has also exercised [arrogance] freely towards me. . . . But may I not claim also a little of the same right?" (Brome 1982, 143). Freud apologized to Jones, though without changing his underlying attitude, as he confided to Rank on July 8, 1922: "In fact these reactions are aimed at me but displaced onto you."[4] He reiterated twelve days later: "Jones' reaction is understandable, Abraham's greediness is probably the result of jealousy." Freud seems to have hoped that Ferenczi could serve as a mediator, as he indicates in the letter of July 20: "Because of his open friendliness [Ferenczi] is perfectly suited to the role of reconciliation. What is more, he has a greater influence on Jones thanks to analysis."[5] Freud was fully on the side of Rank and even assured him on June 4, 1922, that he would prefer him to anyone else as future leader of the psychoanalytic movement.

Freud thought it very important that Ferenczi and Rank should get to know each other and collaborate. As he wrote to Ferenczi on August 24, 1922: "I am very pleased by your greater intimacy with Rank, it augurs well for the future." And the same day he wrote to Rank: "Your agreement with Ferenczi pleased me enormously." He continued in the same vein on September 9: "Your association with Ferenczi has my entire support, as you know." Consequently, the axes Rank-Ferenczi and Abraham-Jones diverged to an ever greater extent. It is not difficult to see on which side Freud's sympathies lay. Little by little, Freud added, Max Eitingon was "also implicated in the difficulty with Jones, of which he hardly knew anything." On March 26, 1924, Freud wrote to Ferenczi: "And now to personal matters. All the preceding should do no more than add a little spice to our work and keep us occupied in friendly dispute. Personal affairs are unpleasant. I fear that we cannot separate them from objective matters, except as far as you and I are concerned. In this I am much closer to your way of thinking."

Technique thus comes into question and becomes the center of the discussion. In fact, Freud's technical modification in the Wolf Man case (1918) of setting a termination date for the treatment underlay Rank's ideas concerning the trauma of birth, as Ferenczi attested to Freud on February 14, 1924: "The mere fact of always fixing a limit gave Rank the opportunity to discover the repetition, during analysis, of the reactions of his patients." This demonstrates (if proof were necessary) the interdependence of technique and theory, and marks the limits of the possible reconstructions in analytic treatment. Although Freud had originally been of the opinion that "activity of such a kind on the part of the analyzing physician is unobjectionable and entirely justified" (1919, 162), in a January 1924 letter to the Committee he expressed reservations that might be described as pedagogical in nature: "Ferenczi's active therapy is a dangerous temptation for ambitious beginners" (Jones 1957, 351).

Although in a letter to Freud on April 21, 1909, Ferenczi had compared the processes that take place during analysis to chemical reactions "like in a test-tube" (Freud and Ferenczi 1992, 53), and as late as "The Elasticity of Psycho-Analytic Technique" (1928) he was of the opinion that, regardless of the patient, each completely analyzed analyst "will inevitably come to the same objective conclusions in the observation and treatment of the same psychological raw material, and will consequently adopt the same tactical and technical methods" (89), because of his double experience in the roles of analyst and analysand Ferenczi came to the painful realization that analysis is not an instrument that functioned independently of the person who uses it.[6] His experiences caused him increasingly to see the attitude of the analyst as a variable in the therapeutic equation and therefore this became the center of his interest. The frustration resulting from his inability to distinguish, in the network of analytic relations, between "transferential" and "real" emotions brought him closer to Freud, who had categorically declared that transferential love is a "true" love (1915a) and that affective exchange provides a particularly important form of leverage in analytic treatment, since "it is impossible to destroy anyone *in absentia* or *in effigie*" (1912a, 108). Ferenczi, however, never lost sight of the extent to which analysands suffer from the "hypocrisy" (1933, 159) of self-imposed abstinence on the part of the analyst.

Ferenczi's experiences led him to a radicalization of the concept of transference. By 1926 he considered "*every* dream, *every* gesture, *every* parapraxis, *every* aggravation or improvement in the condition of the patient as above all an expression of transference and resistance" (1926, 225).[7] In this, he is the predecessor of the positions generally held, at least officially, today. The path followed by Ferenczi likewise resulted, as far as the contribution of the analyst to the analytic encounter is concerned, in his technical experiments with active therapy and methods of relaxation and, finally, with mutual analysis, and emboldened him to speak openly and without taboo—as in "Confusion of Tongues between Adults and the Child"

(1933)—about the role played by adults, and the atmosphere they create, in the child's development and, in extreme cases, in infantile traumas.

Diverging increasingly from Freud, Ferenczi came close to a new conception, a sort of field theory that anticipates later developments in psychoanalysis, at a time when the basis of field theory, as well as of Gestalt therapy and existentialism, had not yet been laid. Rank followed with his new ideas. These were also formulated in close contact with Freud. On March 20, 1924, Freud could still write to Ferenczi: "My confidence in you and Rank is unconditional." It would seem that Freud's renewed interest in the problem of separation anxiety, in *Inhibition, Symptoms and Anxiety* (1926, 94, 150–52), can best be understood in the context of his dialogue with Rank. Rank replied with a work that is little known today, *Fundamentals of a Genetic Psychology* (1927–28). Starting from the "psychoanalytic situation," he develops an interpretation of object loss as being a loss of the milieu *(Milieuverlust)* (1:28), explores the relation with the mother, and examines the "tendency to go backwards," that is, regression: "I consider all the child's affective relations, both positive and negative, as normally being directed towards the mother and I suppose that, later, they are merely transferred to brothers, sisters, and the father (as well as to other people)" (37). Rank treats the entire psychoanalytic situation as a "transferential phenomenon" and declares that "whole chapters of psychoanalytic theory are no more than projections in to the past (and perhaps even into prehistory) of the analytic situation" (38).

In my view, it is here that modern post-Freudian psychoanalysis begins to emerge. The dialogue with Freud gave Ferenczi and Rank the impetus to explore the themes of regression and early relationships with the mother centered on the interaction that takes place in the psychoanalytic situation, and resulted in their wondering how a psychoanalytic theory could be developed on the basis of this communication. Even though Freud did not really continue to collaborate in this evolution, and Rank as well as Ferenczi began to assume a certain distance from him, it is undeniable that these are new flowers on the Freudian tree. Despite his preoccupation with issues concerning the father, Freud nevertheless participated in the dialogue with great interest, at least until 1926, that is, until his seventieth year.

It was Jones who disseminated the legend that both Ferenczi and Rank were, at the end, mentally ill. I believe the opinion of Bálint is more judicious, according to whom "the historic event of the disagreement between Freud and Ferenczi acted as a trauma on the psychoanalytic world" (1968, 152). The fact that even so intimate a friendship as that between Freud and Ferenczi could be disturbed by these problems rendered analysts extremely circumspect in their discussions of "technique." Regression and, above all, countertransference temporarily disappeared from debate in the 1930s. Thanks to his emigration, Michael Bálint, the student of Ferenczi and admirer of Freud, brought awareness of these problems to Great Britain, where similar ideas were being discussed (by Margaret Little among others), and where Donald Winnicott (1949), Paula Heimann (1950), and many others later took up the subject of countertransference.

The interest, sparked by Ferenczi and Rank, in the first years of life and the relation with the mother came into bloom in England after World War II, a delayed flowering that took place for the most part without its intellectual roots being recognized. Important contributions on these subjects were made by authors as diverse as Melanie Klein (an analysand of Ferenczi's), John Bowlby (who refers to Imre Hermann), Margaret Mahler, and René Spitz—the two latter being Hungarian and influenced by that country's psychoanalytic traditions.

This extension of Ferenczian creativity with respect to object relations, countertransference, and psychoanalytic communication, and the fundamental perspectives opened up by Freud, were to lead to a new paradigm, and despite the lively debate, the two protagonists remained faithful to each other. The controversy resulted neither in enmity nor in defection, even though it could no longer be resolved. On April 2, 1933, Freud wrote: "The differences between us . . . can wait . . . it is more important to me that you should recover your health." A few weeks later, Ferenczi died— not without having given Freud a last piece of advice, which expresses all his concern for him: "I advise you to take advantage of what time remains, since the situation is not imminently threatening, to leave for a more stable country, England, for example. Take some patients with you and your daughter Anna" (March 29, 1933). These touching words and the surprising foresight of a dying man bear witness to a relationship more solid than any differences of opinion.

Ludwig Wittgenstein declares: "I believe that my originality (if that is the right word) is an originality belonging to the soil rather than to the seed. (Perhaps I have no seed of my own.) Sow a seed in my soil and it will grow differently than it would in any other soil. Freud's originality too was like this, I think" (1977, 36).

Clearly, the ideas of Ferenczi developed in the context of an intimate relationship of intellectual exchange with Freud—in his soil, one might say. According to Bálint, Freud was much impressed by the unpublished works of Ferenczi when they were presented to him after his death,[8] and he wrote that it would be virtually impossible to disentangle the precise origins of their various ideas.[9] Fortunately, this task is not ours since we are, in our efforts and processes of psychoanalytic thought, the inheritors both of Freud's genius and of those equally exceptional individuals whom he succeeded in drawing around him—men such as Sándor Ferenczi, who remains a model for the creative development of Freudian ideas, a testament to the durability of the foundation created by Sigmund Freud.

NOTES

1. Unpublished manuscript, Bálint Archives, Geneva.

2. Still unpublished letters between Freud and Ferenczi will be cited in the text by their dates and are translated by the author.

3. See James Strachey's Introduction to the technical writings from 1911 to 1915 in *S.E.*, 12:85–88.

4. Unpublished letter, Bálint Archives, Geneva.

5. In 1913, Jones had undertaken two months of analysis with Ferenczi in Budapest.

6. The metaphor "psycho*analysis*" probably stems from chemical analysis. In his 1885 *curriculum vitae* Freud stressed that he had studied chemistry for three semesters with Professor E. Ludwig, who specialized in the analysis of gases. (See Haynal 1991, 123, and Freud 1919, 159.)

7. Freud never felt completely comfortable with this radicalization. In an implicit reply to Ferenczi, he wrote: "Not every good relation between an analyst and his subject during and after analysis was to be regarded as a transference" (1937, 222).

8. "He expressed his admiration for Ferenczi's ideas, until then unknown to him" (Bálint, in Ferenczi 1985, 219).

9. "A number of papers that appeared later in the literature under his or my name took their first shape in our talks" (1933, 227–28).

REFERENCES

Bálint, M. 1968. *The Basic Fault: Therapeutic Aspects of Regression*. London: Tavistock Publications.

Brome, V. 1982. *Ernest Jones: Freud's Alter Ego*. London: Caliban Books.

Carotenuto, A. 1980. *A Secret Symmetry: Sabina Spielrein between Freud and Jung*. Trans. A. Pomerans et al. New York: Pantheon, 1982.

Ferenczi, S. 1926. Contra-indications to the "Active" Psycho-Analytical Technique. In *Further Contributions to the Theory and Technique of Psycho-Analysis*. Ed. J. Rickman. Trans. J. Suttie et al., pp. 217–30. London: Maresfield Reprints, 1980.

———. 1928. The Elasticity of Psycho-Analytic Technique. In Ferenczi 1955, pp. 87–101.

———. 1933. Confusion of Tongues between Adults and the Child. In Ferenczi 1955, pp. 156–67.

———. 1955. *Final Contributions to the Problems and Methods of Psycho-Analysis*. Ed. M. Bálint. Trans. E. Mosbacher et al. London: Maresfield Reprints, 1980.

———. 1985. *The Clinical Diary of Sándor Ferenczi*. Ed. J. Dupont. Trans. M. Bálint and N. Z. Jackson. Cambridge, Mass.: Harvard University Press, 1988.

Freud, S. 1911. The Handling of Dream-Interpretation in Psycho-Analysis. *S.E.*, 12:91–96.

———. 1912a. The Dynamics of Transference. *S.E.*, 12:99–108.

———. 1912b. Recommendations to Physicians Practicing Psycho-Analysis. *S.E.*, 111–20.

———. 1912–13. *Totem and Taboo*. *S.E.*, 13:1–161.

———. 1913. On Beginning the Treatment. *S.E.*, 12:123–44.

———. 1914a. On Narcissism: An Introduction. *S.E.*, 14:73–102.

———. 1914b. Remembering, Repeating, and Working Through. *S.E.*, 12:147–56.

———. 1915a. Observations on Transference-Love. *S.E.*, 12:159–71.

———. 1915b. The Unconscious. *S.E.*, 14:166–204.

———. 1918. From the History of an Infantile Neurosis. *S.E.*, 17:7–122.

———. 1919. Lines of Advance in Psychoanalytic Therapy. *S.E.*, 17:159–68.

———. 1922. Prize Offer. *S.E.*, 17:270.

———. 1926. *Inhibition, Symptom, and Anxiety*. *S.E.*, 20:87–172.

———. 1933. Sándor Ferenczi. *S.E.*, 22:227–29.

———. 1937. Analysis Terminable and Interminable. *S.E.*, 23:216–53.

Freud, S., and K. Abraham. 1965. *A Psychoanalytic Dialogue: The Letters of Sigmund Freud and Karl Abraham*. Ed. H. C. Abraham and E. L. Freud. New York: Basic Books.

Freud, S., and J. Breuer. 1895. *Studies on Hysteria*. *S.E.*, 2.

Freud, S., and S. Ferenczi. 1992. *The Correspondence of Sigmund Freud and Sándor Ferenczi. Volume 1, 1908–1914*. Supervised by A. Haynal. Trans. P. T. Hoffer. Ed. E. Brabant, E. Falzeder, and P. Giampieri-Deutsch. Cambridge, Mass.: Harvard University Press, 1993.

Freud, S., and W. Fliess. 1985. *The Complete Letters of Sigmund Freud to Wilhelm Fliess, 1887–1904*. Trans. and ed. J. M. Masson. Cambridge, Mass.: Harvard University Press.

Freud, S., and C. G. Jung. 1974. *The Freud/Jung Letters*. Ed. W. McGuire. Trans. R. Manheim and R. F. C. Hull. London: Hogarth Press.

Freud, S., and O. Pfister. 1963. *Psychoanalysis and Faith: Dialogues with Oskar Pfister*. Ed. H. Meng and E. L. Freud. New York: Basic Books.

Haynal, A. 1991. *Psychoanalysis and the Sciences: Epistemology—History*. Berkeley: University of California Press, 1993.

Heimann, P. 1950. On Counter-transference. *Int. J. Psycho-Anal.*, 31:81–84.

Jones, E. 1957. *The Life and Work of Sigmund Freud: The Last Phase, 1919–1939*. Vol. 3. London: Hogarth Press, 1980.

Jung, C. G. 1961. *Memories, Dreams, Reflections*. Ed. A. Jaffé. Trans. R. and C. Winston. New York: Vintage, 1963.

Marcus, S. 1976. Freud and Dora: Story, History, Case History. In T. Shapiro, ed., *Psychoanalysis and Contemporary Science: An Annual of Integrative and Interdisciplinary Studies*. Vol. 5. New York: International Universities Press.

Nunberg, H. and E. Federn, eds. 1962. *Minutes of the Vienna Psychoanalytic Society, 1906–1908*. Trans. M. Nunberg. Vol. 1. New York: International Universities Press.

Rank, O. 1911. Ein Beitrag zum Narzissismus [A Contribution to narcissism]. *Jahrbuch für psychoanal. und psychopath. Forschungen*, 3:401–26.

———. 1927–28. *Grundzüge einer genetischen Psychologie auf Grund der Psychoanalyse der Ich-Struktur* [Fundamentals of a genetic psychology based on a psychoanalysis of ego structure]. 2 vols. Leipzig: Deuticke.

Winnicott, D. W. 1949. Hate in the Counter-transference. *Int. J. Psycho-Anal.*, 30:69–74.

Wittgenstein, L. 1977. *Culture and Value*. Ed. G. H. von Wright. Trans. P. Winch. Chicago: University of Chicago Press.

Two

The Founding of the Budapest School

∎

MICHELLE MOREAU-RICAUD
(Translated by Paul V. Taylor)

In 1914, Freud wrote that "Hungary, so near geographically to Austria, and so far from it scientifically, has produced only one collaborator, S. Ferenczi, but one that indeed outweighs a whole society" (33). In 1923 he added a footnote: "In Hungary a brilliant analytic school is flourishing under the leadership of Ferenczi" (34). When Freud wrote *On the History of the Psycho-Analytic Movement,* becoming the first historian of this new field of research, the Hungarian Psycho-Analytic Association had been in existence for only one year and had not yet produced the famous analysts who were later known as the Budapest School. Drawing on the correspondence between Freud and Ferenczi, I will recount the arduous process by which Ferenczi introduced psychoanalysis into his country and founded his school.

Historical and Cultural Background

I shall begin by sketching the cultural and historical context in which the Budapest School came into being, then chronicle the key events in the life of the Hungarian Psychoanalytic Association. Let us quickly recall some-

An earlier French version of this chapter was given in Paris in October 1988 to a conference on the Freud-Ferenczi correspondence organized by the International Association for the History of Psychoanalysis and published in the *Int. Rev. Hist. Psychoanal.* (Paris: Presses Universitaires de France, 1990), pp. 419–37. The author wishes to thank Drs. Judith Dupont and André Haynal for permission to consult as yet unpublished letters from the Freud-Ferenczi correspondence, which will be cited simply by their dates.

thing of Hungary's history as a background to its cultural reception of psychoanalysis.[1]

In February 1908, when Freud and Ferenczi began their exchange of letters, Austria and Hungary were still politically united. In 1526, Hungary had allied itself with the House of Habsburg in order to free itself from the Turkish invaders. That marriage of convenience, however, was never really accepted by the Hungarian people, and in the eighteenth and nineteenth centuries two nationwide armed insurrections tried vainly to liberate the country from absolute imperialism. During the second of these, in 1848, the poets Sándor Petőfi and Mihály Tompa exhorted their compatriots to fight to liberate themselves; and Sándor Ferenczi's father, Bernát Fränkel, a Jewish immigrant from Kraków, enlisted in the Hungarian army at the age of eighteen and conducted himself in exemplary fashion. Later, in 1879, when he came to make his name sound more Hungarian by changing it to "Ferenczi," he could have created the appearance of nobility by writing it with a "y," but, convinced democrat that he was, he refused. He took up residence at Miskolc and became a bookseller and printer, and set about publishing the revolutionary poems of Tompa.

With the failure of the 1848 uprising, Hungary experienced a period of ferocious oppression. Then, with the compromise of 1867, the establishment of the twin monarchy transformed the status of Hungary from a colony to a political and cultural state with relative autonomy. Nonetheless, the shadow of past uprisings lingered in the national memory. We can see their influence on the politics, arts, literature, and community life of Budapest in 1900.

Prior to the outbreak of World War I, the country was on the way to modernization, although its economy was retarded by the feudal structure of the agricultural sector. The politics of latifundia were as unproductive as ever. Aristocratic families—such as the Esterházy—and the Catholic church owned most of the land. The gap between the capital and the countryside widened. Budapest became a grand metropolis, an industrial and cultural center. In particular, Jewish intellectuals gathered there and were integral to this period of intense expansion. Modern means of communications were developed; a railway network linked Budapest to the rest of the country as well as to Vienna. This was significant for the development of psychoanalysis, since Ferenczi often traveled to Vienna, a distance of some 200 kilometers.

This period of expansion was a greatly troubled one. On the one hand, there were the problems of the different nationalities (Hungary being a mosaic of people, languages, and religions); on the other, there were political conflicts, both internal and with Vienna, as well as social problems, unemployment, and poverty. The correspondence between Freud and Ferenczi contains echoes of these problems and, later, of World War I and the Bolshevik revolution.

In 1914, the Austro-Hungarian Empire entered World War I on the side of the Germans. Although Hungary had little alternative, at the end of the war it was penalized by being deprived of two-thirds of its territory and more than one-half of its population. The humiliation of the treaty of Trianon (1920) was an enduring one. Hungary then had to face a grave economic and political crisis, which ultimately provoked two revolutions. The first, known as the "Chrysanthemum" or "Aster" revolution, brought about a liberal republic on November 16, 1918, which was headed from January 1919 by the "red" Count Mihály Károlyi. The second, in March 1919, was a Bolshevik revolution, which set up the Republic of Councils led by Béla Kun. This commune lasted only 133 days, but it introduced a number of social changes, and during this time, psychoanalysis experienced a brief moment of triumph.

The counterrevolution that followed, led by Admiral Miklós Horthy, introduced a reign of terror and established a regime not unlike that of Pétain in France or Franco in Spain. It is unlikely that Horthy's regime could have survived without the split between the backward, conservative countryside, and the progressive capital. With its organizational base in the provincial city of Szeged, and in stark opposition to the direction taken by Budapest, Horthyism stressed traditional and feudal values. The capital welcomed psychoanalysis in a spirit of renewal, but, like other progressive institutions, the Hungarian Association was to suffer because of its links with the Bolsheviks. Nevertheless, even under Horthy, it continued to develop and to attract a wider following. The urban cultural context in which psychoanalysis established itself merits closer attention.

In Budapest, more than in Vienna, the relationship between psychoanalysis and literature was like that of two "communicating vessels," to use an image dear to the surrealists. This symbiotic relationship was typified by Ferenczi. Warm and open to new ideas in every field, he was not afraid to mix with the avant-garde literati. He attended their meetings and passed his reluctantly bachelor evenings with writers gathered around specially re-served café tables. As he lived in the Royal Hotel (where he had a room on the third floor), he was easily able to join his friends from the review *Nyugat (Occident)* at the Café Royal or elsewhere.[2] Here Ferenczi rediscovered the carefree life of a student, such as he had known and enjoyed at Vienna, and avoided the risk of becoming like one of those bespectacled people who read late into the night or "find things to eat more often at the pharmacist than in the kitchen." We run this risk, Ferenczi warns in "Reading and Health" (1901), published in *Gyógyászat (Therapeutics),* if we do not know how "to moderate our intellectual work, notwithstanding our thirst for knowledge, our ambitions, or the vanity that spurs us on" (176). As for Ferenczi at this time, he seems to have been able to put into practice his own healthy advice.

In all likelihood, his gregarious nature and his curiosity fostered his integration into the avant-garde movements and support of the literary revolution. The degree of Ferenczi's immersion in literary culture is amus-ingly revealed in his slip of the tongue, which Freud added in 1910 to *The Psychopathology of Everyday Life:*

> When I was in the first form at the *Gymnasium* I had, for the first time in my life, to recite a poem in public (i.e., in front of the whole class). I was well prepared and was dismayed at being interrupted at the very start by a burst of laughter. The teacher subsequently told me why I had met with this strange reception. I gave the title of the poem "Aus der Ferne" ("From Afar") quite correctly, but instead of attributing it to its real author I gave my own name. The poet's name is Alexander (Sándor [in Hungarian]) Petőfi. The exchange of names was helped by our having the same first name; but the real cause was undoubtedly that at that time I identified myself in my secret wishes with the celebrated hero-poet. Even consciously my love and admiration for him bordered on idolatry. The whole wretched ambition-complex is of course to be found as well behind this parapraxis. (Freud 1901, 85)

The theme of Ferenczi's "wretched ambition," present in both the passage from "Reading and Health" and this anecdote from his schooldays, is a key to his relationship with Freud.

Later, after his meeting with Freud and his conversion to the cause of analysis, he became a mediator between the two camps of literature and psychoanalysis. Under his influence, many poets underwent a therapeutic analysis. One of them, Géza Szilágyi, became an analyst and practiced until 1941. The supremely gifted Attila József sought treatment successively with Samu Rapaport, Edit Ludowyk-Gyömrői, and Robert Bak. Psychoanalysis was a source of inspiration for his work. A poem dedicated to Bak, "You Have Made Me a Child Again," refers to psychoanalysis, which, however, did not prevent his suicide in 1937.

Frigyes Karinthy was another writer who, after the death of his wife in the influenza epidemic of 1918, sought analysis from Ferenczi; but then, in a series of articles, he rather poked fun at analytic discoveries. Fearing that he might join the ranks of those attacking psychoanalysis, Ferenczi wrote him a letter that was published in *Nyugat* under the title "Science that Lulls and Science that Awakens" (1924).

Géza Csáth (also called Joseph Brenner), a neurologist and writer who had become an opium addict, also consulted Ferenczi. Known primarily to pharmacologists and literary scholars, he was the author of the *Diary of a Madwoman* (1911), inspired by his reading of *Studies on Hysteria* (1895). He had much in common with Dezső Kosztolányi, a poet and author of the stories *Silent Film with Heartbeats* (c. 1926–30) and *The Kleptomaniac Translator* (1935).[3] Kosztolányi was also a journalist, and in April 1918 he interviewed Ferenczi about the problems of the war and the prospects for peace for the literary review *Esztendő (The Year)*. His wife, Ilona, had been treated by Ferenczi; and we know from Ferenczi's letter to Freud of May 31, 1927, that it was this patient who told him the story of Arpad, the boy who imagined himself "a little chanticleer" and influenced Freud's theories of castration. Finally, but of particular note, there was Endre Ady, the "poet laureate of the people" and the most popular poet at the beginning of this century. His revolutionary poems, such as "The Marriage of Hawks," inspired by the French modernists Baudelaire and Verlaine, frankly speak of lust and desire and exemplify the intertwining of literature and psychoanalysis.

Thus, Budapest at the turn of the twentieth century was a place of cultural ferment. The intellectuals, conscious of the backwardness of their country and of the rift between the provinces and the capital, sought to foster social and economic change. They were extremely active and played an important role in transforming attitudes by means of educational circles and especially by founding journals where modern ideas could be disseminated.

Among the forty or so thriving journals in Budapest, three warrant special mention. At the end of the nineteenth century, *Gyógyászat* was set up in opposition to the established medical journal, *Orvosi Hetilap (Medical Weekly)*. It was essentially the work of one man, Miksa Schächter, a doctor turned publisher whose aim was, as Ferenczi wrote in a 1917 tribute, to defend truth and medical ethics against all attacks. Ferenczi was influenced to such a degree by Schächter that he was nicknamed "little Schächter." He had originally decided to be one of the journal's collaborators, following an experience he had of automatic writing. The two doctors joined forces to bring about "a moral purging," and *Gyógyászat* published much of Ferenczi's preanalytic work.

In one of these articles, "On the Intermediate Sex" (1906), Ferenczi fought to protect homosexual patients from oppression before the Humanitarian Scientific Committee in Berlin. Still earlier, he published "On the Organization of the Work of Assistant Physicians in the Hospitals" (1903). Given as a paper to the Medical Society, it defends the status of the assistants, "the Faculty's Cinderellas," who were exploited and then dismissed. On their behalf, he pressed for higher salaries, better working conditions, and proper training. Ferenczi's political commitment at this time was tenacious. Later edited by Lajos Lévy—first Ferenczi's pupil, then his personal physician—*Gyógyászat* continued to give considerable space to analytic publications.

Huszadik Század (The Twentieth Century), the second of the three journals, was nonmedical and started by the intellectual democrats, among whom was the sociologist Oszkár Jászi, who in 1914 became the founder of the Radical Party. It appeared bimonthly from 1900 and sought to combat the conservatism of Hungarian society. *Huszadik Század* launched the Society of Social Sciences in 1901. The journal focused on social questions, and political scientists and jurists sparked debate in its columns. It was receptive to foreign literatures, especially those of England and

France, and always on the lookout for new ideas. Ferenczi became responsible for the section on psychoanalysis. We now know that it was for this journal rather than for Schächter's that—as Freud recalled in his tribute to Ferenczi on his fiftieth birthday (1923, 267)—he refused to review *The Interpretation of Dreams* at the time of its publication, having judged it to be of no interest.

Finally, *Nyugat,* an even more prestigious review, appeared in 1908. It was an avant-garde journal associated with the liberal, progressive left. Its editor, Ignotus (Hugo Veigelsberg, 1869–1949), a critic and essayist, was also the first to translate Freud into Hungarian and the first nonclinical member to join the group that grew into the Budapest School. Ferenczi respected the "moral courage" with which he defended analysis. He paid him tribute in a 1924 article, "Ignotus the Understanding," where he described Ignotus as his "forum," the "sensitive litmus paper" on whom he could test out the validity of his ideas. *Nyugat* championed the cause of analysis. Freud's lecture to the 1918 Budapest Congress, "Lines of Advance in Psycho-Analytic Therapy," was originally published in Hungarian in this journal.

Many writers took an active part in *Nyugat*. Its principal collaborators were literary figures of the highest order—Szilágyi, Kosztolányi, and Ady, as well as Mihály Babits. The central person was Ady, who took his poetic vocation seriously and used *Nyugat* to foster a literary revival and the opening of Hungary toward Western Europe.

In addition to publishing journals, the intellectuals congregated in literary, artistic, and political societies, the best known of which were the Galileo Circle and the Sunday Circle. Founded in 1908 by Karl Polányi, editor of *Szabad Gondolat (The Free Thought),* the Galileo Circle was a socialist forum comprised of freethinkers, especially students, who later supported Ferenczi's nomination to a chair of psychoanalysis at the University of Budapest. The sights of the Galileo Circle were set on the struggle against clericalism, the army, and the bureaucracy.

We know from Paul Ignotus, Hugo's son, that Ferenczi was a member of the Galileo circle; he gave a large number of lectures and published material in *Szabad Gondolat*. Many of those who later became analysts— for example, Imre Hermann and Jenő Hárnik—were regular attenders.

The Sunday Circle, chiefly devoted to fine arts, was founded in 1915 by the sociologist Karl Mannheim and the literary critic György Lukács. It provided a meeting place for philosophers, writers, artists, and musicians, including Béla Bartók, and counted among its members such future analysts as René Spitz, Edit Ludowyk-Gyömrői, and Júlia Láng, Mannheim's wife.

One can gather from the foregoing how Hungarian analysts were actively engaged in the political and social conflicts that shaped their country. They did not live in an ethereal world, but took part in debates and experimented with new ideas. Their intellectual milieu was based firmly in these centers of reflection and struggle for progress and renewal. In short, one cannot imagine a more auspicious setting than Budapest to welcome the infant science of psychoanalysis, one of many catalysts in the social development of Hungary, a country that would, in its turn, foster the growth of Freud's ideas.

The Founding of the Psychoanalytic Association

The early history of the Hungarian Psychoanalytic Association can be divided into four periods: (1) 1908–1913: the years of preparation and foundation; (2) 1913–1918: the years of turmoil; (3) 1918–1919: the years of triumph; and (4) 1919–1939: the years of reorganization and defeat.

The first meeting between Freud and Ferenczi, which resulted in the spread of the analytic movement to Hungary, took place at Freud's home on February 2, 1908. The idea for the meeting had emanated from Fülöp Stein, a doctor who founded the temperance movement in Hungary and was a friend of Ferenczi's. Stein had previously met Jung and asked him for more than a year to make the necessary introductions.[4]

Prior to their meeting, on January 18, Ferenczi wrote his first letter to Freud, which clearly reveals his keen anticipation. For a year Ferenczi had been attracted to Freud's research, and he asked for his help with a lecture. He wanted to present Freud's discoveries to a medical audience ignorant of psychoanalysis. As his refusal to review *The Interpretation of Dreams* shows, Ferenczi at first rejected Freud's theories, but he soon came to accept them unreservedly.

At the time of their meeting, Freud was fifty-two and Ferenczi thirty-five. The two researchers experienced a *coup de foudre,* which led to twenty-five years of exchanges and contacts. Freud invited his "dear son" on trips, congresses, and even on holidays. Meeting followed meeting; they exchanged patients, but most of all they exchanged letters—1,350 in all—which were, as Freud wrote on November 21, 1909, "the best way of exchanging ideas about scientific matters" (Brabant et al. 1992, 107).

Ferenczi was invited to become a member of the Vienna Society and its Budapest correspondent, and he launched the movement that resulted in the creation of the Budapest School. Having embraced the cause of analysis, he employed a strategy of infiltrating the medical network. He tried to initiate his confrères into this new science by giving lectures to the Royal Society of Medicine. The first, "Actual- and Psycho-neuroses in the Light of Freud's Investigations and Psychoanalysis" (1908), shows his pedagogical talent. Ferenczi empathized with members of the audience who were hostile to the new theory, confessing his ancient resistance and even his "aversion" to it, and justified his change of heart on scientific grounds.

Despite his best efforts, he still clashed with the medical profession. Opposed by a "clinicians' conspiracy" (Brabant et al., 1992, 153), as he bitterly termed it in a letter to Freud of March 22, 1910, he found allies among writers, artists, and intellectuals in the Society of Social Sciences who included him in their debates, and among the patients who consulted him.

Notwithstanding Freud's moderating influence, Ferenczi's impatience to form a psychoanalytic society led him to increase the number of lectures so that he could "sift out" the best potential candidates. In May and June of 1910, he offered another cycle of twelve lectures (three per week), scheduled from 9:00 to 11:00 pm. Only a handful of those who attended, however, were medical doctors; most were musicologists, jurists, philosophers, and students. In the autumn of 1910, he first tried to found the psychoanalytic society, but there were still too few doctors among those wanting to be members. Not only that, but the two doctors who had been approached, Imre Décsi (our "little local Freud") and Stein, did not reply. The future of psychoanalysis lay elsewhere.

First of all, there was the movement as a whole. At the 1910 Nuremburg Congress, Ferenczi proposed the founding of an International Psychoanalytic Association (of which he would become the president for a few weeks in 1918). Then, at the local level, there were the Free School of Sociology, the attention paid to Freud in the press, and the Galileo Circle, which was clamoring after him. So, as Ferenczi wrote to Freud on March 8, 1912, the "analytic fever" hit Budapest: "Lay circles are talking—and physicians are cursing about nothing else" (Brabant et al. 1992, 354).

In 1913, for tactical reasons that related to the incipient dissidence of Jung in Zurich, Ferenczi decided to establish the Budapest group before the Munich Congress. Its first committee came into existence on May 19, 1913, and consisted of Ferenczi as president, István Hollós as vice-president, Sándor Radó as secretary, Lévy as treasurer, plus Ignotus, who represented "the public." It was Ignotus, as Ferenczi told Freud on May 28, 1913, who immediately suggested translating Freud's article, "The Claims of Psycho-Analysis to Scientific Interest" (1913), for *Nyugat*. Later, Anton von Freund (Tószeghi), a Budapest brewer, doctor of philosophy, and patient and friend of Freud's, who became a patron of the analytic movement, joined the group. Thus Budapest stole a march on Zurich, although the contest for analytic preeminence between these rival cities was never definitively settled.

The activities of the Hungarian analysts were to all intents and purposes suspended during World War I. Yet each member went on with his work; training and research continued as much as possible. The correspondence between Freud and Ferenczi is full of reflections on the war, politics, and their disappointment in "Mrs. A." (their way of talking about Austria to avoid censorship), but also about issues of therapy, theory, analytic training, and organization. Because Ferenczi was serving as a military physician with the Hussars in the small garrison town of Pápa, he had ample time to read, write, and conduct analyses.

During wartime came two noteworthy requests for membership, those of Géza Róheim, an anthropologist, and Elizabeth Révész, a medical doctor. Others followed in 1918: Ernest Pfeiffer, also a physician, and Manó Dick, a publisher. There were also clinical developments. Ferenczi reported to Freud on February 22, 1915, the "first recorded analysis on horseback" with his army commander, and on May 5 an analysis of someone suffering from traumatic neurosis after a grenade explosion. The material gathered during this period helped to develop the theory and therapy of shellshock, the theme of Ferenczi's paper at the 1918 Budapest Congress.

Ferenczi's training analysis was also a key event, especially given its importance for later thinking about this topic, which has always been given a particular emphasis in Hungary. Ferenczi was so sure that he wanted to undertake this analysis that he asked Freud several times to take him on before Freud eventually agreed. Ferenczi's analysis took place during three very brief periods in 1914 and 1916 and cost him, according to his letter of October 22, 1916, a total of 1,245 crowns.[5] Ferenczi even wished to contract "a slight typhoid so that he could get leave" from his army duties, as he confessed to Freud on April 4, 1915, and thus begin the second phase of the analysis as soon as possible.

The Hungarian group, although formally paralyzed, was teeming intellectually. The idea emerged of founding a polyclinic specializing in war neuroses, which created a new field of analytic investigation. Ferenczi also pursued a new ambition—securing a position at the university. Doubtless, when Freud went to see Ferenczi in Pápa on September 29, 1915, these projects were among those they discussed.

The meetings of the Hungarian group, recommenced in January 1917, despite continued mobilization and fatigue on the part of the analysts, but it was only on March 24, 1918, that the society was fully reconstituted and functioning. Monthly meetings were held with presentations by Ferenczi, Róheim, and Márton Jellinek. In all likelihood these were rough drafts of their respective papers at the 1918 Budapest Congress—"The Psychoanalysis of War Neuroses," "The Self: A Study in Folk Psychology," and "On Friendship." These meetings were attended by colleagues on leave in Budapest, including Max Eitingon from Berlin.

When objections by members from the victorious powers caused the planned postwar congress to be moved from Breslau to Budapest, the Hungarian analysts took charge of it. The mayor of Budapest, István Barczy, was there, as were other representatives of the government, as well as leading figures of the medical and popular media, including the cinema. This was the moment of triumph for psychoanalysis in Hungary. In a letter of September 30, 1918, Freud thanked Ferenczi for his efforts, declaring that "his baby" would in the future be safe in Ferenczi's hands and those of a few others.

When the Minister of Health for the army suggested to Ferenczi that he open a center for psychoanalysis in Budapest, he agreed, but on the condition that he could have two assistants: Eitingon as a specialist in hypnosis, and Hollós as a psychiatrist. The actual analytic cases, as he wrote to Freud on October 8, 1918, he kept for himself. Although scientific work was difficult in postwar conditions, especially given the frequency of general strikes, the Hungarian Association continued its activities.

Other cultural and political societies started up under the newly installed republic. Ferenczi became increasingly involved. Impressed by the organization of the trade unions, he joined a social democratic union of doctors, explaining to Freud on November 7, 1918, that analysis would gain from belonging to an "association of creative artists and scientific researchers." He was nominated to head the scientific section. Gradually, Hollós, Jenő Harnik, Pfeiffer, and Radó returned from the front. Ferenczi even invited Freud to settle in Budapest, which he regarded as the true homeland of psychoanalysis.

Then the Royal Medical School at the University of Budapest opened its doors to psychoanalysis. This was the first time that an analytic institute and a university had been formally brought together (Moreau-Ricaud 1990). The idea of teaching psychoanalysis at a university finally became a reality. Medical students sought courses on the theory of analysis. They met with the rector and signed petitions, first in 1918 and then again in 1919. At first 180, soon 1,000 students demanded that analysis be taught.

The Hungarian Association prepared a memorandum in response to this opportunity. Freud weighed in by writing "On the Teaching of Psycho-Analysis at Universities" (1919), which first appeared in Hungarian in *Gyógyászat*. Ferenczi counted on the support of Mihály Károlyi's ministers, who, except for Zsigmond Kunfi, the Minister of Education, had expressed an interest in psychoanalysis. The petition of January 28, 1919, sent to Kunfi, reads as follows:[6]

> We, the undersigned, students of the Medical Faculty of the Hungarian University of Science in Budapest, call your attention to the fact that, until now *psychoanalysis* has not been taught at our university.

This science is relevant not only for specific medical practice, but also to pure and applied psychology (sociology, pedagogy, criminology), which makes its *regular teaching at the university* an unavoidable necessity.

The fact that the introduction of psychoanalysis has been so far been rejected can be explained—in our opinion—not only by the alleged scientific objections of the official university circles, but also by personal and political hostilities.

In the interest of science, we think it should not be allowed that any consideration whatsoever block the free development of a new discipline.

We refer to the fact that psychoanalysis has been taught for years at the following universities abroad: in Vienna: Prof. Freud, in London: Prof. Jones, in Leyden: Prof. Hlyerman [Heymans], in Boston (Harvard University): Prof. James Putman [sic], in Zurich: Prof. Bleuler.

We think that the most appropriate person for lecturing in psychoanalysis at the University of Budapest is *Doctor Sándor Ferenczi,* neurologist, the most devoted cultivator of psychoanalysis in our country, whose name is acknowledged abroad as well.

We ask and hope that our request will be taken into consideration and that the measures to be taken in this direction will be realized this semester.

Contrary to the impression created by the students' desire, however, there was no formal chair of psychoanalysis at any other universities at this time. Even Freud was only an "Extraordinary Professor" (i.e., one without any right to vote in faculty affairs).

Ferenczi and his allies were forced to wait. During this time Freud, in a letter of February 13, 1919, advised Ferenczi about more personal matters, including his marriage and moving to more suitable quarters. He also warned him about the risk of a dishonest compromise between analysis and power, reminding Ferenczi that his first task was to conduct research and help people.

Kunfi commissioned Ernő Jendrassik, a professor of neurology, to provide an expert opinion concerning psychoanalysis. His report concluded that it was not scientific and spread "immorality and pornography." He declared the petition invalid because a majority of the signatories were women! Ferenczi's nomination was rejected on March 25, 1919, by the Republic of Councils; but finally, on April 25, thanks to Radó or perhaps to Gyömrői, one of the People's Commissioners in the Commune government and the husband of analyst Edit Ludowyk-Gyömrői, Ferenczi's candidacy was approved by the government and he was made a professor. He became simultaneously the director of the newly established psychoanalytic clinic. The decree was signed by Lukács, People's Commissioner at the Ministry of Education and Culture and Kunfi's deputy.

Ferenczi began teaching on June 20 and delivered some twenty lectures, which took place on Tuesdays and Fridays and ran for ninety minutes, on "Psychoanalytic Psychology for Doctors." A mark of his success was the overflowing hall. The Budapest analysts as a whole had a strong presence in the University: Hollós became "demonstrator in psychiatry"; Harnik gave classes on the work of Freud and Breuer; Radó, Révész, and Róheim also lectured. The Psychoanalytic Society of Medical Students was founded. "Analysis is being sought after everywhere," Ferenczi exulted to Freud on April 12, 1919. All went well until the fall of the Republic of Councils.

After the summer of 1919, the official life of psychoanalysis in Hungary was brought to an end. The reactionary White Terror ruthlessly invaded everything, even the university. Jewish students were beaten and expelled and Jewish professors dismissed. Not only did Ferenczi lose his university post, but his confrères expelled him from the Medical Society. He had to retreat into the background and distance himself from politics. His friends at *Nyugat,* particularly Ignotus, became his only institutional support. Ferenczi was forced to abandon his projects, first the polyclinic commissioned by the ministry, then a clinic that was to be privately funded by Anton von Freund but, because of von Freund's death and the difficulty of transferring funds, could not be founded.[7]

The first emigrants departed. Gifted trainees who would have qualified in Budapest—including Alice and Michael Bálint and Franz Alexander—left for Berlin. Ferenczi himself, faced with mounting political and financial problems, also considered emigrating. Over the next few years, he was frequently tempted to go to the United States, Vienna, or Berlin, but in a letter of March 15, 1920, Freud advised him to stay in Budapest, because otherwise analysis would collapse in Hungary.

Despite being endangered, the Association continued to work under Ferenczi's direction and, because of his dynamism, even managed to expand. New members joined, including Sándor Feldmann in 1919 and Aurél Kolnai in 1920. Eugenia Sokolnicka and Melanie Klein were also involved for a brief period. Klein worked with Anton von Freund in the "Association for Infant Research." László Révész and Vilma Kovács became members in 1924, and Sándor Lóránd and Alice Bálint in 1925.[8] The following year saw the election of Michael Bálint and Géza Dukes; Hermann became secretary following Radó's departure for Berlin. At the end of 1924, the members numbered some twenty-four people, who, like an extended family, would get together at Ferenczi's house for Christmas. Others were invited to attend its meetings—August Aichhorn, Georg Groddeck, Wilhelm Reich, and Anna Freud.

As for Ferenczi himself, "Psychoanalysis and Social Policy" (1922) shows how far he had moved away from politics. He still believed in progress but now sought to promote it only indirectly by trying to improve interpersonal and social relations through healing the inner world of fantasy. Since he had ceded the presidency of the International Psychoanalytic Association in favor of Jones in 1919, he also began to distance himself from the politics of the analytic movement. As early as 1910, when he proposed the founding of the International Psychoanalytic Association, he warned against "the excrescences that grow from organized groups" when "childish megalomania, vanity, admiration of empty formalities, blind obedience, or personal egoism prevail instead of quiet, honest work in the general interest" (Ferenczi 1911, 302).

In 1924 Ferenczi published *Thalassa,* which Freud considered "perhaps the boldest application of psycho-analysis that was ever attempted" (1933, 228). After 1925, Ferenczi devoted what proved to be his last years to refining and defending his theories. He attracted a following of patients and students and, as his meetings with Freud became increasingly intermittent, he was forced to become more independent intellectually.

The Budapest analysts continued to produce original work. In letters to Freud of 1926 Ferenczi mentioned Dukes's *Psychoanalysis and Criminality* (1920), Bálint's case study of a heart condition caused by somatic transference, and biographical essays by Hermann on Fechner, Darwin, and Bólyai. Róheim had been awarded a literary prize in 1921.[9] A pioneering psychoanalytic anthropologist, he opposed "consulting room analysis" and in 1929 went to Australia to do field work. He wrote to his analyst, Vilma Kovács: "It requires infinite patience to do ethnographic work; it's much more tiring than analysis" (1929, 30).

Until 1925, the composition of the fledgling society had been quite mixed. But Ferenczi now decreed that henceforth it would admit only those who had undergone analysis and completed both theoretical and practical training. Vilma Kovács gave a regular seminar on analytic technique, and she became the arbiter for the training of analysts at Budapest and elsewhere. Her 1935 article, "Training Analysis and Control Analysis," explains the Hungarian approach. It is based on the candidate's own personal analysis and the training analyst's assessment of the candidate's handling of a case. The idea that the training analyst is best suited to help neophytes with their first cases is grounded on the theoretical emphasis given to countertransference. This form of assessment has provoked numerous arguments, but it has the merit of having been the first attempt to establish the principles governing qualification as an analyst, in contrast to Berlin, where admission to membership remained a formality.

In 1927, Hollós published *My Farewell to the Yellow House*.[10] The Yellow House was (and still remains) an asylum at Lipótmező (Leopold's field), in Budapest, which Hollós, who had been its chief doctor, had reformed. This memoir formed part of his campaign against the widespread prejudices regarding mental illness—the poor treatment and even violence to which institutionalized patients were often subjected and the stigmas they had to endure for the rest of their lives. Hollós drew attention to the fact that some mental patients recovered from their illnesses, while those near to the patient—and even the caregivers themselves—often refused to accept this as a possibility. *My Farewell to the Yellow House,* which is still relevant today, impressed Freud, who concluded that he himself was an "inadequate psychiatrist" and intolerant toward psychotics. It led him to wonder whether, in his dealing with such patients, he wasn't "actually behaving as doctors did in the past toward those suffering from hysteria" (Sabourin 1985, 167). Other Hungarians took up Hollós' approach, including Lajos Lévy, Lilly Hajdu, Endre Almássy, and Robert Bak.

In addition to the innovations introduced by Hollós, Lóránd experimented with hypnosis to promote painless childbirth and wrote an article on this subject in *Gyógyászat* in 1923. Alice Bálint, Melanie Klein, Kata Lévy, and Elizabeth Révész all started working with children and developing research, based on Ferenczi's ideas. They unanimously rejected the notion of primary narcissism in favor of theories about object relationships and primary bonding between mother and child. Hermann started the work that led to his theory of the filial instinct and the concept of clinging. At the same time, Michael Bálint, who was interested in psychosomatic problems, launched his introductory analytic seminars for doctors. His theoretical work on the relationship between doctors and patients resulted in the "Bálint Groups" that are still active in many parts of the world today.

Budapest analysts increasingly turned their attention to practical and clinical problems. A Polyclinic for children was in operation by 1930, and in December 1931, a Polyclinic for adults was finally opened at Mészáros Street 12, in an apartment block built by Frigyes Kovács—the husband of Vilma Kovács and patron of the Budapest group—who loaned them the premises. "It is always the private sector that supports just causes," Ferenczi commented to Freud on May 31, 1931. These events were the most notable since the creation of the society. However, the Polyclinic constantly confronted difficulties created by the university and the medical and political authorities, which Vilma Kovács and Michael Bálint tried energetically to resolve. Ferenczi was the first director, to be replaced after his death by Bálint.

From the time it opened, the Polyclinic operated at full throttle. In part it was a training institute, a meeting place every Friday for analysts and students; but it was also a full-fledged therapeutic clinic. However, by 1937, it became too dangerous to keep working there; at each of the seminars, a policeman was present taking notes. In 1942 the Polyclinic was closed. The Hungarian Psychoanalytic Association was almost purged by the Nazi-allied Pointed Cross, before being officially proscribed in 1948 by the Stalinist regime. Nonetheless, even during the darkest years, Hermann continued to train analysts secretly.

Only in 1983, as a harbinger of other political changes, did the Hungarian Association begin to reorganize, achieving provisional recognition from the International Psychoanalytic Association. Its status in Hungary was first that of an approved society within the Society of Psychiatry (Nemes 1986); but since 1988, it has been independent of psychiatry. At the meeting of the International Psychoanalytic Association in Rome in 1989, the Association received full recognition.

An inventory of the work of Hungarian analysts as different as Alice and

Michael Bálint, Hermann, Kovács, and Róheim—among many others—shows that the Budapest School was not dominated by a single school of thought. But all of these masters were Ferenczi's pupils and extended his legacy through their experiments in diverse fields of practice and theory. It is above all thanks to Ferenczi that psychoanalysis experienced a freedom in Budapest that was, perhaps, never found in the schools of Vienna or Berlin.

NOTES

1. For this historical overview, I have consulted Haynal (1988), Molnar (1987), and relevant articles in the *Encyclopedia Universalis,* and benefited from personal communications from André Haynal and Joseph Gabel.

2. For the influence of psychoanalysis on Hungarian literature, see Moreau-Ricaud (1992). Further useful material about Ferenczi's relations with the *Nyugat* circle is in Lórand (1966).

3. These works have been translated into French by Péter Adam and Maurice Regnaut as *Cinéma muet avec battements de coeur* (1988) and *Le traducteur cléptomane* (1985).

4. On the contacts between Ferenczi, Stein, and Jung, see the following chapter by György Vikár.

5. Due to the inflation of the period, it is difficult to convert this amount into contemporary terms.

6. This document was rediscovered by Patrizia Giampieri-Deutsch and is quoted here from the translation in Erős and Giampieri (1987, 23–24). My account of Ferenczi's appointment to a university professorship closely follows theirs.

7. The mayor of Budapest attempted to get his hands on this money, but wanted to invest it in a general hospital rather than in a psychoanalytic institute. See Ferenczi's letters to Freud of December 18 and 26, 1919.

8. The election of Dr. László Révész, brother of Elizabeth Radó-Révécz, allows us to deduce the criteria for nomination to membership that had been imposed. Candidates were required to undergo a personal analysis, conduct several analyses under supervision, and present a case study.

9. It was on this occasion that the "Budapest Freud Society" sent a birthday card to Freud. Its signers included István and Olga Hollós, Radó, Elizabeth Radó-Révész, Feldmann, Ernst Pfeiffer, Mrs. Imre Hermann, Ferenczi and his wife Gizella, and Róheim.

10. A French translation by Judith Dupont, *Mes adieux à la maison jaune,* has been published in *Le Coq-Héron,* 100 (1986). The work remains untranslated into English.

REFERENCES

Brabant, E., E. Falzeder, and P. Giampieri-Deutsch, eds. 1992. *The Correspondence of Sigmund Freud and Sándor Ferenczi. Volume 1, 1908–1914.* Supervised by A. Haynal. Trans. P. T. Hoffer. Cambridge, Mass.: Harvard University Press, 1993.

Erős, F., and P. Giampieri. 1987. The Beginnings of the Reception of Psychoanalysis in Hungary, 1900–1920. *Sigmund Freud House Bulletin,* 11–2:13–27.

Ferenczi, S. 1901. Lecture et santé. In *Le jeune Ferenczi: Premiers écrits, 1899–1906.* Ed. and trans. C. Lorin, pp. 176–82. Paris: Aubier, 1983.

———. 1911. On the Organization of the Psycho-Analytic Movement. In *Final Contributions to the Methods and Problems of Psycho-Analysis.* Ed. M. Bálint. Trans. E. Mosbacher et al., pp. 299–307. New York: Brunner/Mazel 1980.

Freud, S. 1901. *The Psychopathology of Everyday Life.* In *The Standard Edition of the Complete Psychological Works.* 24 vols. Ed. and trans. J. Strachey et al. Vol. 6. London: Hogarth Press, 1953–74.

———. 1914. On the History of the Psycho-Analytic Movement. *S.E., 14:7–66.*

———. 1923. Dr. Sándor Ferenczi (On His Fiftieth Birthday). *S.E., 19:267–69.*

———. 1933. Sándor Ferenczi. *S.E., 22:227–29.*

Haynal, A. 1988. *The Technique at Issue: Controversies in Psychoanalytic Method from Freud and Ferenczi to Michael Bálint.* Trans. E. Holder. London: Karnac, 1989.

Lóránd, S. 1966. Sándor Ferenczi: Pioneer of Pioneers. In S. Eisenstein, F. Alexander, and M. Grotjahn, eds. *Psychoanalytic Pioneers,* pp. 14–35. New York: Basic Books.

Molnár, S. 1987. *De Béla Kun à János Kádár.* Paris: Presses de la fondation nationale des Sciences Politiques.

Moreau-Ricaud, M. 1990. La psychanalyse à l'université: histoire de la première chaire. Budapest avril 1919–juillet 1919. *Psychanalyse à l'université,* 15–60:111–27.

———, ed. 1992. *Cure d'ennui. Écrivains hongrois autour de Ferenczi.* Paris: Gallimard.

Nemes, L. 1986. Le destin des psychanalystes hongrois pendant les années du fascism. *Le Coq-Héron,* 98:3–12.

Róheim, G. 1929. Letter to Vilma Kovács. *Le Coq-Héron,* 70 (1978):28–30.

Sabourin, P. 1985. *Ferenczi: Paladin et grand-vizir secret.* Paris: Éditions Universitaires.

Three

The Budapest School of Psychoanalysis

■

G Y Ö R G Y   V I K Á R

It is characteristic of old stories to be continuations of even earlier ones. The beginning of Hungarian psychoanalysis is interwoven with the world-famous name of Sándor Ferenczi. But he himself inevitably also had a forerunner.

An international antialcoholism conference took place in Budapest in 1905. There, one of the leading figures of the Hungarian temperance movement, the neurologist Fülöp Stein, met Eugen Bleuler, director of the Burghölzli mental hospital in Zurich and a pioneer in modern psychiatry. As a result of this acquaintance Stein traveled a year later to the Burghölzli and took part in C. G. Jung's word association experiments. In 1907 Jung and his wife visited Stein in Budapest. Jung reported the event to Freud in a letter, adding that Stein and another neurologist, Dr. Ferenczi, hoped to meet Freud and had asked him to serve as their "mediator." Thus, strange though it may seem, it was through Jung that psychoanalysis first reached Hungary. Jung's effect on Hungarian psychoanalysis proved minimal (although he greatly influenced Hungarian literature of the age). Ferenczi's daring concepts, however, set forth in *Thalassa* (1924), are built on the notion of phylogenetic memory traces, which might owe something to his former "mediator." On the other hand, Ferenczi's strong biological orientation clearly separates him from Jung.[1]

Stein introduced Ferenczi to Freud on February 2, 1908, and then, as if

An earlier French version of this chapter, " 'L'école de Budapest' d'après un témoignage hongrois," was published in *Critique*, 32 (1974), 237–52.

having fulfilled his historical mission, gradually faded from the Hungarian psychoanalytic scene. He attended the first international psychoanalytic congress, held in Salzburg in April 1908, without reading a paper. He continued to practice psychoanalysis until 1913, but then ceased and did not join the Hungarian Psychoanalytic Association that was founded that year. He became the director of an institute for alcoholics, to whom he devoted the rest of his life.

In contrast to Stein's, the life of Ferenczi became one with the psychoanalytic movement from that time on. Ferenczi had read all of Freud's works as they appeared, but he had initially felt a strong resistance to them. He found the hypotheses of Breuer and Freud's "Preliminary Communication" (1893) too sophisticated and unrealistic. Not even *The Interpretation of Dreams* (1900) had a profound effect on him. It was only some years later that he began to realize the vastness of the perspective on understanding psychological diseases that had been opened up by Freud's method. Once convinced of the truth of the new science, however, he became a passionate follower. At the Salzburg conference he gave a paper, "Psychoanalysis and Pedagogy," which was infused with optimism and faith that the penetration of psychoanalytic knowledge into pedagogy would prevent many forms of neurotic suffering. By 1909 he grew to be an intimate friend of Freud's and, with Jung, accompanied him on his trip to America. The plan of the lectures that Freud gave at Clark University took shape during morning conversations with Ferenczi. It was Ferenczi who proposed the establishment of the International Psychoanalytic Association. He was likewise a member of the "Committee" that united Freud's closest colleagues following the defection of Jung. In 1913 Ferenczi founded the Hungarian Psychoanalytic Association. In the meantime, he published one paper after another, including the pathbreaking "Introjection and Transference" (1909) and "Stages in the Development of the Sense of Reality" (1913).

Anyone familiar with the training procedures and scientific protocol of psychoanalysis today must be astonished by this chronology of events. What explains the astounding speed of Ferenczi's development? How could he become one of the masters of the new science almost within months and how could the Hungarian psychoanalytic movement grow up around him within several years?

True, Ferenczi was already thirty-five years old in 1908, with extensive neurological and psychiatric experience behind him. But such training alone doesn't make a good psychoanalyst. It is also true that there were problematic features in his personality. Because Ferenczi himself realized this, he thrice spent a few weeks in psychoanalysis with Freud, in 1914 and 1916. As Ernest Jones has suggested, the first clinical example in Freud's late paper, "Analysis Terminable and Interminable," is about Ferenczi. Freud writes:

A certain man, who had himself practiced analysis with great success, came to the conclusion that his relations both to men and to women—to the men who were his competitors and to the woman whom he has loved—were nevertheless not free from neurotic impediments; and he therefore made himself the subject of an analysis by someone else whom he regarded as superior to himself. This critical illumination of his personality had a completely successful result. He has married the woman he loved and turned into a friend and teacher of his supposed rivals. Many years passed in this way, during which his relations with his former analyst remained unclouded. But then, for no assignable external reason, trouble arose. The man who had been analyzed became antagonistic to the analyst and reproached him for having failed to give him a complete analysis. (1937, 221)

I break off the quotation here. It is possible that the experience of his own treatment led Ferenczi to the conclusion that a training analysis should not be shorter but longer and more profound than the treatment of patients. He was the first one to proclaim this.

Medical experience and some weeks of psychoanalysis—we would hardly consider this to constitute sufficient training. But we cannot deny that Sándor Ferenczi became not only a great teacher and psychoanalytic theorist but also an excellent healer. Imre Hermann has emphasized his moral values, love of justice, and modesty, which made him treat his patients as equal partners, as well as his readiness to help others, which at times bordered on self-sacrifice.[2] Despite being critical of Ferenczi, moreover, Jones acknowledged his special gift for analytic work. It is likely that the greatness of the historical task had a ripening effect on the developing talents of Ferenczi and his first colleagues. The creation of a new science, which revealed the unknown sides of human psychological functioning, galvanized their energy. And perhaps there was something in the air of the age . . . because a question immediately arises: why was it precisely in

Hungary that psychoanalysis first took root outside the German-speaking areas? Was the proximity to Vienna just an accident?

The development of the ideas and movement of psychoanalysis was not at all independent of the historical and social conditions of the age. Several contradictory theories have been proposed to account for these connections. But the part played by the unique conditions and atmosphere in turn-of-the-century Budapest has been neglected by historians. Only recently has extensive research been undertaken on the reception of psychoanalysis in Hungary. A paper by Ferenc Erős and Patrizia Giampieri (1987), although still only a preliminary study, sheds valuable light on the social and cultural conditions of the age, and I shall summarize some of their findings.

The beginning of the twentieth century was a period of unsurpassed prosperity in Hungarian intellectual life. Both the fine arts and music discarded provincialism and the slavish cultivation of national traditions and moved into the forefront of modern European culture. In music it suffices to mention the names of Béla Bartók and Zoltán Kodály, who are famous throughout the world. But because of the immediate psychological aspects, the development of literature is more interesting here. It was in 1906—that is, two years before Ferenczi started his career as an analyst—that Endre Ady's volume, *New Poems (Új versek),* was published. This was a declaration of war against Hungarian literary traditions. Self-complacent patriotism and idyllic love poetry at once became a thing of the past. Ady's confessional style presents a realistic picture of twentieth-century man. We hear in his poetry the sounds of sensual love, carnal desire, and the longing for money and power. These are mixed with the cruel exposure of social contradictions, or what Oscar Wilde termed "Caliban's anger at not seeing his reflection in the mirror." Ady's style was influenced by the French symbolists; he expressed himself by means of presentiments, dreams, and symbols. Ady was a literary leader, and many of the writers who gathered around him became celebrated figures of Hungarian literature in their own right. They were often rivals, but they shared a common interest in psychology; all of them were capable of observing the subtle vibrations in the human psyche, its self-deceptions and self-revelations, and they fought against pseudo-moralistic prejudices. The great indignation they elicited in many layers of society was a natural consequence of their work.

The Hungarian society of that age had already been stretched by great conflicting forces. Hungary had theoretically been an independent state since 1867, an equal partner of Austria in the Habsburg monarchy. In reality, however, Hungary only played second fiddle. The constitution reflected the principles of bourgeois liberalism, while feudalistic privileges remained more or less intact. By the turn of the century, however, a wealthy and influential upper-middle class also emerged and began to exert great influence. The workers' movement, too, was gaining in strength. The image that this society created and maintained about itself became increasingly remote from reality. As János Paál has written in his study of the history of Hungarian psychoanalysis, "The spirit of the age was a peculiar mixture of wealth, technical development, and economic prosperity combined with malaise, a premonition of the cataclysms to come" (1976, 103). Budapest became a cosmopolitan European city with all the advantages and disadvantages of urbanization. The colorful press and the vivid life in literary cafés led to a rapid exchange of information. The progressive intellectuals put question marks to everything that had heretofore been considered "truth" and were susceptible to all kinds of novelty. Psychoanalysis soon became popular among them, while the conservative forces of the society, especially official medicine, reacted with great resistance.

The journal *Nyugat (West)*, founded in 1908, was a forum for the new Hungarian literature and progressive ideas. Hugo Ignotus was the chief editor and at the same time one of the founders of the Hungarian Psychoanalytic Association. So the columns of this journal of historical importance were open also to reports of public interest written by psychoanalysts.

It is worth enumerating the first members of the Hungarian Psychoanalytic Association because their fame has persisted. István Hollós was a leading psychiatrist, one of the apostles of a more humane and freer treatment of the mentally ill. He wrote a novel, *My Farewell to the Yellow House* (1927), which arose out of his observations made in a large mental hospital. The novel was a great success and has been translated into several languages. Lajos Lévy was an internist of great reputation and later the director of a hospital. Freud asked him for a consultation because of his heart problems. Lévy's entry into the Association increased the weight of psychoanalysis within the society of Hungarian physicians. Sándor Radó became famous for his studies on depression and drug abuse. In the 1920s he emigrated, first to Berlin, then to the United States, where his strong biological orientation and idiosyncratic ideas were the subject of fierce debates. During his stay in Berlin he initiated Heinz Hartmann's psychoanalytic training. I have already mentioned the name of Ignotus. His joining the Association was a sign of the degree to which psychoanalysis became an integral part of the prosperity of Hungarian intellectual life at the beginning of the twentieth century.

It is Sándor Ferenczi, however, who has had by far the greatest importance in the history of Hungarian psychoanalysis. His studies were always influenced by Freud's brilliant work, but they contained something distinctive from the beginning. Let us consider his paper, "Stages in the Development of the Sense of Reality" (1913). Freud states that the pleasure principle that completely rules the child's life at the start has to give way gradually to the reality principle, due to the pressure of external conditions. Giving up the feeling of omnipotence in infancy is a part of this process. Ferenczi describes in detail how each step of this process occurs, as if he were unfolding the content of Freud's statement. The basic idea of the paper, however, is entirely characteristic of Ferenczi: the omnipotence of thoughts, which is present in the child's fantasy and in the symptom-formation of the adult suffering from obsessional neurosis, was once a reality. All of us have been omnipotent inside the mother's womb, where all of our desires were gratified. The child experiences the illusion of omnipotence even after birth for a certain time, since it is able to control the parents by its gestures and first words. Only gradually does the painful confrontation with reality take place, as a result of which the child realizes that the world does not immediately depend on its will. Ferenczi finds a phylogenetic parallel here and introduces the concept of the "erotic sense of reality": autoeroticism corresponds to the childhood feeling of omnipotence, while the heterosexual relationship parallels the reality principle. This paper contains the germ of Ferenczi's masterwork, *Thalassa*, which was published eleven years later.

Ferenczi was drafted for military service during World War I, during the quiet intervals of which he worked on the outline for his book. From 1916 he was assigned to a Budapest military hospital, so that it was possible to continue his psychoanalytic practice. Melanie Klein and Géza Róheim started their analytic training with him at this time. Both are important figures in the history of psychoanalysis. Klein was admitted to the Hungarian Psychoanalytic Association in 1919. She began to develop her technique of play therapy in Hungary, but she soon left Budapest and continued her analysis with Karl Abraham in Berlin. After 1926 she lived in London. Her influence on British psychoanalysis is well known, and her innovations in child psychoanalysis are epoch making. Ferenczi's effect on her can only be measured indirectly.

Róheim, on the other hand, belonged to the Budapest School. He was one of the first psychoanalysts who supported Freud's ideas by the direct anthropological observation of primitive cultures. His book, *The People of Churunga* (1932), was written in Hungarian, and Róheim extended these studies to Hungarian popular customs as well. He noted the phenomenon of "collective trauma" in the course of his journey to Australia. Children of the same culture experience similar traumatic events, although there are individual differences. The effect of these traumas can be demonstrated in the characteristic myths and rituals of the given culture. (This insight is crucial to the later ethnopsychological work of Erik H. Erikson.) Róheim emigrated to the United States in the late 1930s and wrote his books in English from then on. His affection for his mother country, however, remained undiminished.

The fifth International Psychoanalytic Congress took place in Budapest in September 1918. Shortly thereafter, from October 23 to October 30, followed the so-called Michaelmas-day revolution that subverted the reign of the Habsburg dynasty and led to the proclamation of the Hungarian republic. The revolutionary winds could be felt at the congress, which was devoted to war neuroses. Freud declared at the end of his lecture on the development of psychoanalytic treatment that the psychotherapy of neuroses ought not to remain the privilege of the rich. There had to come a time when poor people, too, could receive adequate treatment for their troubles. In keeping with this ideal, Anton von Freund, a wealthy Hungarian brewer (whose charitable benefactions have had an enduring effect), established a foundation to support a psychoanalytic publishing house and a polyclinic. The latter plan could be realized only much later due to the tumultuous historical events that followed each other very rapidly. At the news of this initiative, however, the first psychoanalytic outpatient clinic opened in Berlin.

During the period of the Hungarian Soviet Republic, student petitions led to Ferenczi's receiving a professorship at the University of Budapest. This was the first psychoanalytic chair at any university. But unfortunately it didn't last long. After the 133 days of the Hungarian Soviet Republic, the white terror commenced with the entry of Miklós Horthy. Ferenczi was not allowed to leave his flat for a long time, and his relations with his foreign colleagues were very restricted. The waves of white terror abated slowly and were followed by so-called consolidation, that is, the partial restoration of the parliamentary government and Hungarian constitutionalism. Hungary was one of the most peculiar states in Europe between the two world wars: a kingless kingdom with a conservative government and gradually increasing influence of the extreme right, it still preserved certain liberal conventions. Thanks to the latter, the Psychoanalytic Association remained able to function, though it was sharply attacked by right-wing nationalists. Not only did the Association endure, it was a place of fertile scientific and pedagogic work. What we call the "Budapest School" took shape in this period.

Hungarian psychoanalysis has an external history—how it spread, how its organizational forms took shape and fell apart, and how its members lived and met their historical destinies. I shall return to this aspect soon. But it has an internal history as well—the story of the formation of the distinctive way of thinking that constitutes an analytic school. Let us follow the path of this internal history.

Ferenczi started to experiment with therapy at the beginning of the 1920s. He wanted to increase the efficiency of treatment and to improve his method for the sake of patients who were considered untreatable or stuck at a certain point in therapy. He first elaborated the "active technique." By this he meant not that the analyst should be active but that the patient should follow instructions to expose himself to the situations that elicited his symptoms and to observe on the spot his immediate feelings and thoughts that emerged. (For example, someone suffering from agoraphobia should go out in the street.) But Ferenczi soon revised these experiments, and the instructions became much milder forms of advice. In the meantime he worked on the theoretical study he had started during the war. It was published in 1924 under the title *Versuch einer Genitaltheorie*. The book became famous in English and French translations under the title *Thalassa*, the Greek word for "sea." I cannot review the book in depth here, but will mention the basic ideas.

In *Thalassa*, Ferenczi examines the developmental process of genital sexuality. He argues that human existence begins with a catastrophe—the trauma of birth and the separation from the mother. The desire to "return to the mother" accompanies the individual throughout life. Autoeroticism realizes this desire on a low level of the sense of reality, that is to say, in a hallucinatory way. The penis, in a sexual relationship, gets transitorily back to the womb while the sperm does the same literally, corresponding to a higher degree of erotic sense of reality. Ferenczi compares this developmental process to phylogenesis: breaking out of the mother's body corresponds to being cast out of the primal sea. Ferenczi also reviews the way the genitals of animals and their forms of copulation develop in the course of phylogenesis and draws a parallel between these and the developmental stages of infantile sexuality. This is why copulation is a return to the ancient sea, a "thalassal regression."

Let us not pose the question of how much truth there is to this fantastic scientific hypothesis, since it cannot be answered on the basis of our present knowledge. Let us rather consider two of its key features: (1) the Oedipus complex, which had hitherto been the center of psychoanalytic research, decreases in importance in favor of the separation of the child from the mother; and (2) infantile sexuality, including autoeroticism, becomes linked to the mother-infant relationship more tightly than ever. Both statements imply a theoretical turning point in the history of psychoanalysis, though this was not at all clear at the time the book was published.

This change was characteristic of Ferenczi's healing activity as well. That is, from this point on there was a sort of "maternal" element in his therapeutic behavior. He did not consider to be generally valid Freud's advice that the analyst should remain neutral and frustrate transferential desires. He had often found, in treating difficult cases, that indulgence—providing some gratification of the infantile desires emerging in the transference situation—led to a considerable diminution of the patient's tension and accelerated progress in the analysis. He treated some of his adult patients in analysis as if they were children. His last studies—"The Principle of Relaxation and Neocatharsis" (1930), "Child Analysis in the Analyses of Adults" (1931), and "Confusion of Tongues between Adults and the Child" (1933)—elicited resistance within the psychoanalytic movement and spoiled his relationship with Freud. After Ferenczi died of pernicious anaemia in 1933, Freud wrote of these experiments: "He had probably set himself aims which, with our therapeutic means, are altogether out of reach today" (1933, 229).

Today, when "symbolic wish-fulfillment" has become a psychotherapeutic tool in the treatment of the mentally ill and borderline cases, these healing experiments of Ferenczi's do not seem nearly as strange as they did at that time. It is not by accident that one of his followers was the first to experiment with psychoanalysis with patients suffering from schizophrenia. Lilian Hajdu, a psychiatrist and psychoanalyst, published her study on the subject in 1933. According to Ferenczi, the analyst has to put himself on the patient's level of regression in order to understand his communications. Franz Alexander was greatly influenced by these ideas. (Alexander was Hungarian by birth but received his analytic training in Germany.) Alexander believed that the essence of the healing effect of psychoanalysis lay in providing a corrective emotional experience. Ferenczi also influenced Béla Grünberger, a Hungarian psychoanalyst living in Paris who received his training in Germany and France. Grünberger has put the narcissistic fantasy of omnipotence at the center of his theories. He attributes the "narcissistic monad," which has been sealed off from the disturbing effects of the external world and the instinctual drives, to experience within the womb. Thus he follows Ferenczi's train of thought in "Stages in the Development of the Sense of Reality."

Now I shall deal with two of Ferenczi's most extraordinary followers, both of whom were extremely influential in their own right: Mihály Bálint and Imre Hermann. Bálint played a prominent role in Hungarian scientific life but had to leave the country because of the threat of fascism; he gained his worldwide fame abroad. Hermann stayed at home, and his presence maintained the continuity of psychoanalysis in Hungary.

Bálint was born in Budapest in 1896. He obtained his medical degree in 1920, his studies having been interrupted by military service during World War I. Originally he was a physician interested in biology. In the 1920s he worked in the Department of Biochemistry of the Kaiser Wilhelm Institute in Berlin, and later at the Berlin Clinic for Internal Diseases. After returning to Budapest, he started his analysis with Ferenczi, who had a great influence on him throughout his life. From that time on Bálint felt psychoanalysis to be his calling, but he never lost interest in general medical practice. His earliest writings dealt with the connections between general medical practice and psychology. The Budapest Psychoanalytic Polyclinic, which had been planned since 1918, opened in 1931. Bálint was originally the deputy director, but after Ferenczi's death he took over the leadership. In 1939 he emigrated to England with his wife and son. Bálint published a series of important books, including *Primary Love and Psychoanalytic Technique* (1952), *The Doctor, His Patient and the Illness* (1957), and *The Basic Fault: Therapeutic Aspects of Regression* (1968).

Bálint always searched for ways in which analytic knowledge could be utilized in general medical practice. The famous case seminars or "Bálint groups" he held for general practitioners served this goal, as did his elaboration of a method of brief therapy directed toward one goal, known as "focal therapy." His theoretical works are characterized by a dynamic contemplation. He considered the first relationship, that between mother and infant, to have enormous importance. Bálint stresses that this relationship is interpersonal and mutual in its character from the first moment on and cannot sufficiently be described by the notion of "oral dependency." The breakdown of this relationship creates the basic fault, which cannot be dissolved by interpretation, as can a neurotic conflict. This early state of deficiency leads to one of two opposing character types: the ocnophil, who reacts with anxiety to any moving away of the love object; or the philobat, who becomes anxious because of the extreme proximity of the object. Both attitudes are maintained throughout life. The basic fault can only be overcome if the therapist creates an atmosphere in which the patient is able to regress to the emotional world of the first love object. At this point, with the help of transference, a "new beginning" becomes possible. The analytic and comparative ethnological studies of Bálint's first wife, Alice, on mother-infant relationships are likewise integral features of the profile of the Budapest School.

Hermann was born in 1889 and, after receiving his medical degree in 1913, worked as a psychiatrist for two years. He took up experimental psychology in his youth and preserved this interest throughout his career. He built a bridge between psychoanalysis and general psychology and biology. Ferenczi became known to him in 1911 during his university years. His first analytic studies dealt with the psychology of reasoning: "Intelligence and Deep Thought" (1920), "Psychoanalysis and Logic" (1924), "The Ego and Reasoning" (1929). In "On Formal Tendencies of Choice" (1921) Hermann reported on a series of experiments in which he found that out of a row of similar elements—matches, coins, etc.—adults tended to choose from the middle, whereas children chose from one of the edges, as did individuals in regressive states. In "Preference for Edges as a Primary Process" (1923), he argued that this pattern possessed a general psychological validity and that it explained why dreams take their content from the two "edges" of memory traces of the previous day and from childhood. His book, *Psychoanalysis as a Method* (1933), remains a classic and has been reprinted both in German and Hungarian.

Hermann's greatest scientific achievement, however, is to have identified and described the clinging instinct. From the early 1920s he followed the studies that were being carried out on anthropoid apes, the primates closest to humans in the evolutionary chain. Simultaneously he took note of the importance of the eroticism of the hand in the development of instincts. He recognized that the instinctual clinging of the young ape to its mother's hair was preserved in modified form in the human infant as an innate tendency with reflexological bases. Its individual psychological, cultural, and pathological effects can be amply demonstrated. At the beginning of life, clinging is an independent instinctual need. Later on it fuses with the libidinal instincts, but can emerge again in regressive states. Mother and infant create a biological unit that only dissolves step by step and is replaced by "clinging at a distance"—that is, love. Hermann's key paper, "Sich-Anklammern, Auf-Suche-Gehen," was published in 1936 in the *Internationale Zeitschrift für Psychoanalyse,* and again in English in *Psychoanalytic Quarterly* in 1976 as "Clinging—Going-in-Search." The repression of going-in-search—that is, hiding—is the counterpart of the instinct of clinging. These phenomena can be observed embedded in interpersonal relationships and interwoven with different cultural models in the behavior of all little children.

Hermann again dealt with the issue of clinging in detail in his comprehensive 1943 Hungarian work, *The Ancient Instincts of Man*. (A French translation, *L'instinct filial*, appeared in 1970.) He elaborated several important ramifications of the syndrome of clinging that can be fully understood only today. One of the main primary sources of anxiety in the infant is the fear of losing the mother, getting torn from her body. For the male, this fear flows into the castration anxiety of the oedipal period. Losing the genital also means losing the chance of returning to the woman (or mother). The feeling of shame is a kind of anxiety that makes clinging impossible; the command to be ashamed comes from the child's educator. This is the person to whom the child would like to cling, and the shaming involves the exclusion of the child from the larger community as well. Here we can see the theoretical contribution of clinging to social psychology, which is especially fertile with respect to aggression. The aggressive instinct, Hermann argues, doesn't exist by itself, but is called forth by different instinctual situations. Aggression has varied sources in humans, such as the frustration of clinging (the clinging hand begins to clutch), sibling rivalry, starvation, and acts of injustice. Social institutions can exacerbate aggression—for example, by persecuting racial or religious minorities. By driving out an assimilated minority, a nation that has been injured in its integrity abreacts the separation trauma in a self-aggrandizing way.

Hermann also dealt with numerous other issues. He studied the psychology of artistic creation and scientific invention, the connection between spatial experience and different emotional states, and that between the perversions and music. The restoration of a disturbed psychic continuity stands at the center of his methodological ideas. János Paál (1976) rightly observes that continuity was characteristic both of Hermann's way of life and his work until his death in 1984. He wrote his works and carried on his analytic practice with inexhaustible patience and a firm inner independence.

Besides Bálint and Hermann, many other superb psychoanalysts have worked in Hungary, though I cannot include everyone who is deserving of mention here. I should note that there have been talented representatives in Hungary also of Stekelian active analysis and Adlerian individual psychology. A new school of depth psychology has also arisen — Lipót Szondi's fate analysis. Szondi closely linked his own theory of instincts to genetics. In the course of his research on pedigrees he assumed that there are latent genetic factors behind a person's manifest instinctual constitution. These do not reveal themselves openly but influence the choice of vocation and partner as well as medical history and the manner of death. The test he worked out in Hungary has since spread all over the world. Szondi had a good relationship to the Hungarian analytic school and gave a prominent place to the clinging instinct in his theory. He worked in Zurich from the end of World War II, and the majority of his books were published in Switzerland.

I have spoken about the leading Hungarian analysts and the different directions of their investigations. Do they have any common features that allow us to speak of a "Budapest School"?

Bálint (1937) tried to answer this question at the Four Nation Conference, the meeting of Czechoslovakian, Austrian, German, and Hungarian analysts held in Budapest in 1937. He compared the outlook of the Hungarian school to that of the Vienna and London (i.e., Kleinian) analytic schools on the importance of the psychological development in the first years of life. In Bálint's view, the characteristic of the Hungarian school is its refusal to accept the concept of "primary narcissism." Because the mother and infant form a biological unit in the first months of life, one cannot speak of an independent self in the infant. As this dyad slowly breaks apart, the child directs its libido toward the mother. This is not merely a passive narcissistic expectation, but an active endeavor to cling. The libido is not only directed to the breasts, as partial objects, but to the whole maternal body. This is why Bálint speaks of "primary object love." He traces his ideas back to Ferenczi, who emphasized the interpersonal aspect of the mother–infant relationship.

Although Bálint's notion of "primary object love" has not been generally accepted by the psychoanalytic world, the outlook of the Budapest School has exerted a great influence on later theories and therapies. It has shed valuable light on the preoedipal period and on the importance of interpersonal relationships. These views have been corroborated by numerous studies throughout the last decades (e.g., Harlow's experiments with monkeys, René Spitz's observations of infants, etc.). It can hardly be denied that the works of Hungarian psychoanalysts who emigrated both before and after World War II inspired these studies. The view of the analyst as a passive mirror has been increasingly replaced by one of analysis as a mutual relationship, in which transference and countertransference are intertwined. Bálint greatly influenced these new therapeutic endeavors, and many analysts today regard Ferenczi as their earliest forerunner.

In Hungary itself, the Hungarian Psychoanalytic Association was allowed to function even during World War II, although its meetings took place under the control of the political police. The spirit of freedom and the attraction psychoanalysis exercised on left-wing youth elicited distrust in the government. Many members of the Association suffered under the Jewish Law imposed in 1939 and the increasing fascist pressure; their public appearances were restricted and they were not allowed to play a leading role within the Association. Nevertheless, the Association was not forced to compromise its principles. Hermann's book, *The Ancient Instincts of Man,* was published in 1943 even though it contained critical analyses of militarism and anti-Semitism. (This was perhaps due to the contradictions of the Hungarian "see-saw" politics at that time. There were opponents of the Germans in the leading social classes who sought a reconciliation with the Allies.) But after the German army invaded Hungary on the March 19, 1944, the Association was not allowed to hold any more meetings. The majority of its members were persecuted, and Lívia Nemes (1985) has written about their fate. It is not only my reverence for them that makes me mention their names, but their outstanding talent, which was cut off before it could be fully developed. Géza Dukes, a lawyer, was killed in a German concentration camp. He studied issues of criminology from a psychoanalytic point of view. József M. Eisler was a neurologist, art critic, art collector, and writer of aphorisms. Zsigmond Pfeifer wrote significant studies on the theory of games and the psychology of music and anxiety. Erzsébet Kardos, a child analyst (and the first wife of Endre Pető, a famous analyst who later lived in New York), and László Révész and his family were shot in Budapest. Many others disappeared during the war and their fate is still unknown.

In the spring of 1945, after the war, the members of the Association met again, full of hope. The new democratic government seemed for a time to offer a large scope for psychoanalysis. Hermann was invited to be a lecturer at the University of Budapest. Analysts took part in the mental hygiene movement and in building up the socialistic health care service. Alice Hermann was employed by the Trade Union Association as a consultant. Tibor Rajka got a role as an organizer of health care. Lilian Rotter was the consultant for psychohygienics in the capital. But in 1949, when the "cult of personality" began to dominate the Communist world, psychoanalysis became an ideologically condemned science; the Psychoanalytic Association was disbanded for many years, and no analytic lectures could be given or reports published. Analytic therapy barely survived in Hungary because the Health Ministry permitted doctors to choose the most adequate treatment method in a given case. In the late 1950s Hermann and Rajka began training new analytic candidates. After the 1956 invasion the condemnation of psychoanalysis decreased gradually, and beginning in 1958 Hermann's papers and other analytic writings could be published. Further important changes occurred at the end of the 1960s. While maintaining its ideological reservations, the government gave a green light to the practice of analysis. In 1969 Hermann's eightieth birthday was officially celebrated by old followers and new pupils alike. The papers all pertained to Hermann's lifework. So, for example, Robert Bak, who visited his homeland from the United States, spoke about clinging theory, sadism, and domination; Lívia Nemes spoke about the role of cognitive psychology in the theory of clinging; I summarized the psychology of invention; Gábor Paneth discussed the role of thermal and olfactory sensations in paranoia; Adorján Linczényi examined perversions and the world of music; György Hidas outlined the dynamic structure of the psychoanalytic situation; and Tibor Rajka spoke about the pathological dynamics of obsessive-compulsive people.

Five years later, in 1974, the one-hundredth anniversary of Ferenczi's birth was celebrated in a solemn style. On this occasion the leaders of the Hungarian Neurological and Psychiatric Societies officially took part. The increasing reputation of Hungarian psychoanalysts is marked by the fact that five of Hermann's followers who received their training after World War II (Hidas, Linczényi, Nemes, Paneth, and I) were admitted to the International Psychoanalytic Association at the 1975 London Congress. The Hungarian psychoanalytic movement has developed further ever since and made efforts to overcome the disadvantages of its protracted isolation. In 1989 the renewed Hungarian Psychoanalytic Society became an accredited member of the International Psychoanalytic Association. But this is another story.

NOTES

1. On Fülöp Stein and his relationship to Jung, see Hermann (1974a).
2. Hermann's memorial lecture (1974b) was read in 1974 at the meeting held in memory of Ferenczi.

REFERENCES

Bálint, M. 1937. Early Development of the Ego. Primary Object Love. In *Primary Love and Psycho-Analytic Technique*, pp. 90–108. London: Maresfield Library, 1985.

Erős, F., and P. Giampieri. 1987. The Beginnings of the Reception of Psychoanalysis in Hungary, 1900–1920. *Sigmund Freud House Bulletin*, 11:12–27.

Freud, S. 1933. Sándor Ferenczi. In *The Standard Edition of the Complete Psychological Works*. Ed. and trans. J. Strachey et al. 24 vols., 22:227–29. London: Hogarth Press, 1953–74.

———. 1937. Analysis Terminable and Interminable. *S.E.*, 23:216–53.

Hermann, I. 1974a. A magyar pszichoanalitikai és individualpszichológiai mozgalom kezdete a Freud-Jung levelezés tükrében. [The Beginning of the Hungarian Psychoanalytic and Individual Psychology Movements in the Mirror of the Freud-Jung Correspondence.] *Orvosi Hetilap*, 115:2099–3002.

———. 1974b. Ferenczi Sándor személyiségének néhány vonása. [Some Personality Traits of Sándor Ferenczi.] Unpublished manuscript.

Nemes, L. 1985. The Fate of the Hungarian Psychoanalysts during the Time of Fascism. *Sigmund Freud House Bulletin*, 9:20–28.

Paál, J. 1976. Psychoanalyse in Ungarn. In D. Eicke, ed., *Die Psychologie des 20. Jahrhunderts*, 3:103–15. Zurich: Kindler.

Four

O, Patria Mia

■

J O H N   E .   G E D O

What has been the impact of psychoanalysts of Hungarian origin on America? It is a difficult question to answer. Certainly, it has been nothing like the effect of Hungarian actors, movie moguls, comedians, steel workers, football coaches, physicists, mathematicians, socialites, or musicians— conductors above all. (Every time Georg Solti conducts the Chicago Symphony, I am tempted to yell out, "Éljen a magyar hadsereg!" [Long live the Hungarian Army!] But my very American wife would be mortified . . .) Actually, it would be easier to write about the effect America has had on Hungarian psychoanalysts. It has turned them into bourgeois cosmopolites (as they used to say a few decades ago in Moscow), art collectors, political conservatives, and Anglophiles.

I am certain only about the fact that America was easier to influence over two generations ago, when Sándor Ferenczi inaugurated the influx of Hungarian psychoanalysts to our shores, than it is today. For the last several decades, American society has gradually turned away from the great traditions of Europe. The widely known difficulties of psychoanalysis in the United States of the 1990s are but one minor aspect of this repudiation of "Eurocentrism." Insofar as it continues to muddle on, American psychoanalysis has acquired an indigenous flavor. Its pragmatism, empiricism, optimism, and adherence to a civic religion partly egalitarian, partly moralistic, would probably make it unrecognizable to Sigmund Freud—or, better, these mutations justify Freud's skepticism about the possibility that *his* creation would really take root in American soil (Gedo 1991, 147–58).

When Ferenczi came to America in 1926, to teach and to initiate some analyses, he attracted many adherents. Although his stay was relatively brief, it was followed by the formation of a steady American clientele who traveled to Budapest, including some who subsequently became psychoanalysts themselves. Among these pilgrims, by far the most influential was Clara Thompson, for she was to serve as a conduit between Ferenczi and her close friend Harry Stack Sullivan, the *chef d'école* of an important movement within American psychiatry.

As a consequence of Thompson's subsequent activities in New York and Sullivan's in Washington (including the latter's very great impact on the psychological treatment of severely impaired patients, often in hospital settings), an "interpersonal school" of psychoanalysis has become one of the major voices on the American scene for more than fifty years. Although to my knowledge this large group did not include any Hungarian émigrés, nor did it emphasize the role Ferenczi had played in its genesis,[1] this was the American school that adopted his daring experimental program to develop technical modifications of psychoanalysis suitable for persons who suffer from conditions more severe than neuroses. However, the Hungarian flavor of this movement was soon overshadowed by the leading roles within it of the German-born Frieda Fromm-Reichmann and Erich Fromm.

The first Hungarian analysts who transplanted themselves to America as actual immigrants were two faculty members of the Berlin Psychoanalytic Institute (the first formal analytic training institution, established shortly after World War I). Both Franz Alexander (*nota bene:* Franz, not Ferenc) and Sándor Radó were more or less imported in order to employ their experience as psychoanalytic educators to assist in the organization of psychoanalytic institutes on the Berlin model in the New World. Although Radó had become secretary of the Hungarian Psychoanalytic Association in 1913 and did not move to Berlin until 1922, he was analyzed by Karl Abraham. Alexander, who was the first candidate ever to enroll in a psychoanalytic training program, does not appear to have had significant contact with the Ferenczi circle before his departure to Berlin. He was also an analysand of Abraham's. Thus it would not be justified to classify either man as a representative of a "Budapest School" of psychoanalysis.

Nonetheless, both brought a specifically Hungarian influence to bear on their organizational activities.

Radó was invited to New York in 1931 by A. A. Brill to organize the New York Psychoanalytic Institute. About a dozen years later, when his support within the New York group declined, he founded the first university-based psychoanalytic program within the Department of Psychiatry at Columbia University.[2] He was head of this new enterprise from 1944 to 1957. Alexander reigned over the Chicago Institute for Psychoanalysis he created in 1933 until he was overthrown by a palace coup in 1955; thereupon he moved to Los Angeles (with a cadre of loyal followers) and organized the Southern California Psychoanalytic Institute. In other words, both Radó and Alexander moved from being young pillars of the Establishment to positions as middle-aged revolutionaries. Or counterrevolutionaries. Talpra magyar! Most vagy soha! [On your feet, Hungarians! Now or never!]

Of course, I am quoting the motto of the wrong Hungarian revolution: these Freudian proconsuls did not represent the progressive spirit of 1848, however much they presented themselves in the guise of Freedom Fighters. Rather, they battled in the tradition of the aristocratic rebels against the Habsburg yoke ca. 1700: the party of the "kuruc." For them the psychoanalytic establishment always represented Vienna—paternal authority to be overthrown precisely because it is admired. If the Rákóczy March could be heard in the background, so much the better!

In their intellectual contributions, Alexander and Radó were equally adventuresome. Alexander's interest in psychosomatic medicine and Radó's biologically based effort to enunciate a schema of "adaptational psychodynamics" anchored them within a medical framework, so that even these aspects of their departures from orthodoxy maintained an aura of conservatism. (Incidentally, they were prime movers in organizing the Academy of Psychoanalysis, a professional body of *medical* psychoanalysts that also provides a home for Sullivanians trained outside the aegis of the American Psychoanalytic Association.) Both Alexander and Radó committed themselves to devising psychoanalytically based psychotherapies briefer and simpler than psychoanalysis proper—efforts that, in their excessive optimism, largely depended on the charisma of their proponents. It reminds one of the Revolution of 1956 . . .

The decade that followed the arrival of these pioneers saw the gathering of a growing stream of Hungarian refugees in America. These analysts fled the menace of Hitlerism—not so much in Hungary proper, where German hegemony only became complete in 1944, but in the various countries of Mittel-Europa successively taken over by the Nazis. Analysts of Hungarian origin were forced to flee Germany, Austria, and Czechoslovakia before it became obvious that all of continental Europe would become an arena for the Holocaust. Some refugees made intermediate stops before they reached America, so that my information about the movements of specific persons is incomplete. Suffice it to state now that such prominent colleagues as Therese Benedek, George Gerő, and Susan Déri came here from Germany; Emmanuel Windholz and Jan Frank from Prague; Margaret Mahler from Vienna; and René Spitz from Paris. To what degree they maintained sentimental ties to Hungary, after spending their adult years elsewhere, I do not know. As psychoanalysts, however, they had no direct connection to Budapest (although Benedek and Mahler had contact with Ferenczi before they left Hungary as young professionals-in-training).

Eminent though these refugees became in America, none was destined to match the intellectual influence of David Rapaport, who left Budapest just before the outbreak of war and reached the United States by way of Palestine. Rapaport had barely obtained his doctorate in psychology when he emigrated, and he never did have clinical training in psychoanalysis. As a theoretician and an expositor of theory he has had few peers in psychoanalysis, and his reputation as a teacher in Topeka and Stockbridge (where he was chief psychologist for the Menninger and Austen Riggs Foundations, respectively) became legendary. A whole cohort of influential analytic thinkers—Roy Schafer, Robert Holt, Merton Gill, George Klein, Robert Wallerstein, Herbert Schlesinger, to name a few—developed under his tutelage, and his publications (even notes made during his lectures) have guided generations of students.

Rapaport's theoretical allegiance was to the ego psychology that prevailed in America during World War II and for more than two decades thereafter. He espoused the metapsychology proposed by Heinz Hartmann, which he tried to refine and systematize. If he can be said to have had links to psychoanalytic heterodoxy at all, these extended no further than to the psychological theories of Erik Erikson, which Rapaport tried to integrate into the analytic mainstream by lending them conceptual rigor under the umbrella of Hartmann's adaptive viewpoint. One cannot find any trace of a Budapest influence on these ideological commitments—if anything, Rapaport (like Margaret Mahler) was a firm partisan of the Viennese tradition.

Despite this analytic conservatism, Rapaport brought something unique to American psychoanalysis from his university training in Budapest. His intellectual focus as a psychologist was specifically historical: he wrote his dissertation on the underpinnings behind the development of scientific psychology formed by the successive advances in Western philosophy. Although this work (1974) was published in English only after his death, in his lifetime he brought to bear on all of his work an epistemological sophistication then unknown in American analytic circles. (In this connection, it is relevant to recall that psychoanalysis in the United States was then almost exclusively medical; its practitioners were consequently impregnated with the naive pragmatism characteristic of much of medical practice.)

In my judgment, Rapaport's profound impact on his students and readers, for which he is widely remembered, was due not only to his superior intellect and his admirable scientific ideals, important and rare though these qualities may have been. Beyond these personal considerations, Rapaport carried much of the analytic community with him because his own epistemological position was more solidly grounded than those of his contemporaries in America, including the other exiles from continental Europe. To be more specific, Rapaport actively used *both* traditions within modern philosophy, those of empiricism and rationalism, in the manner characteristic of Kant. Although in this sense Freud himself was a Kantian, his policy of refusing to discuss the philosophical background of his work obscured this fact for the analytic community. The United States is still ruled by the empiricism of seventeenth- and eighteenth-century British science, so that Rapaport's brilliant emphasis on the use of reason (what he called the need for systematization) had a tremendous effect on analytic scholarship. This influence survives to this day in the form of the intellectually rigorous monograph series, *Psychological Issues,* edited by his disciples.

Although Rapaport was alone in leading the cause of rationalism in American psychoanalysis, in his insistence on the imperative need for empirical research he was only one of many influential contributors. It is probably not a coincidence, however, that a very large proportion of the Hungarian-American analytic community had prominent roles in these efforts. (I have no explanation for this phenomenon, but I have no doubt that it must have had roots in the *ambiance* of prewar Hungary.) The only one of these investigative programs that was initiated in Europe was the anthropological field work of Géza Róheim, who was professor of anthropology at Budapest, an analysand of Ferenczi's, and a training analyst of the Hungarian Association. He conducted field work in Africa, Australia, and Melanesia from 1928 through 1931. Although his combativeness on behalf of psychoanalysis apparently impaired his reception in American anthropological circles, the tradition he initiated of interdisciplinary work at the frontier of the two domains has continued to gain adherents in this country. One of these was another Hungarian émigré, George Devereux. (I have always envied his solution for the transliteration of his name, Deverő; I wish I had thought of writing mine "Guedeux"!)

The earliest research program in psychoanalysis initiated in the United States was the psychosomatic investigation carried on under Alexander's aegis at the Chicago Institute. It is true that Georg Groddeck's activities in his private sanatorium in the Black Forest constitute what one might call a "prescientific" precedent for these efforts. However, Alexander's attention to research methodology, his success in gaining financial support for the investigation, and his enlistment of many colleagues for a collaborative enterprise marked the beginning of a new era in psychoanalytic scientific endeavors. Perhaps the most fruitful of the many projects that formed part of this research was Therese Benedek's effort (in collaboration with endocrinologists) to study the effects of the menstrual cycle on the inner world of women. Incidentally, a third Hungarian, Thomas Szász, eventually joined the Alexander team; after Alexander's departure for Los Angeles, Szász became professor of psychiatry at Syracuse University, where he made a *succès de scandale* as a leader of the antipsychiatry movement.

A second major domain of American empirical research in psychoanalysis was opened in the 1940s: the field of the direct observation of children.

The analytic pioneers of this expanding scientific movement included the Hungarians René Spitz and Margaret Mahler. Their achievements in this area were, in their lifetime, only matched by the work of the Hampstead Clinic in London. Among his other findings, Spitz's discovery of the devastating effects of institutionalization in infancy—the syndrome he named "hospitalism"—revolutionized pediatric practice in much of the Western world. (As a medical student in New York ca. 1950, I still saw dying babies who suffered only from a lack of opportunity to form human bonds.) Spitz ultimately ended his career in Denver, where Robert Emde continues the tradition of psychoanalytic infant observation established by his mentor. Margaret Mahler's influential research projects, first on the psychoses of young children, later on what she called the "separation-individuation process," have not had the uniformly favorable reception that greeted the work of Spitz; at the same time, Mahler's theories created a sizable partisan following (particularly in New York and Philadelphia) that has only recently lost its sectarian flavor as the result of further observations of infants and toddlers have begun to resolve the controversial issues of Mahler's era.[3]

If my account of the diaspora gives the misleading impression that the specific qualities of the "Budapest School" (the ideas that Imre Hermann perpetuated in the psychoanalysis that survived in Budapest through the dark decades of fascism and communism) never reached America, this distortion probably results from the fact that Ferenczi's most direct heir among the émigrés was Michael Bálint, who settled in London and was only an occasional visitor in the United States. (These visits were most frequent in Cincinnati, where they were organized by Paul Ornstein, a young analyst trained in this country who left Hungary after the events of 1944–45. Ornstein had a period as the American proponent of Bálint's method of brief therapy; after Bálint's death, however, he became interested in self-psychology. Anna Ornstein, his wife and a fellow-Hungarian, has followed a similar course.)

None of the other Hungarian exiles had the same commitment as Bálint to carry the banners of Ferenczi into battle, although some did rise to the occasion when, in his biography of Freud, Ernest Jones alleged that Ferenczi's dissension from analytic orthodoxy was a consequence of a psychotic illness. Notable among these was Sándor Lóránd, who had become a leading figure at the New York Psychoanalytic Institute. However, Lóránd is best remembered for an organizational achievement: he led the establishment of a third training institution in New York affiliated with the American Psychoanalytic Association—the Institute now located at the New York University Medical Center.

The analyst whose American work is closest in spirit to the tradition established in Budapest was Robert Bak. Interestingly enough, he was an influential member of that supposed bastion of conservatism, the New York Institute. He wrote extensively on the problem of perversions, particularly on fetishism, clarifying some of their pregenital determinants. This was a line of investigation extending Ferenczi's experiments with the analysis of conditions previously thought not to be analyzable. Perhaps Bak succeeded in making himself heard on these matters because he also had unchallenged prestige as a bon vivant, an intellectual, and a man of the world.

Hungarian chauvinists may be tempted to claim that "self-psychology," the dissident viewpoint developed by Heinz Kohut, is an American variant of the ideas promulgated by Ferenczi and his Budapest successors. In the narrower sense, this notion is clearly mistaken: Kohut was self-consciously Austrian, he was analyzed by Viennese analysts, his allegiances within Chicago psychoanalysis were to the intellectual opponents of Alexander, and he long considered himself to be destined to succeed Hartmann as the leading theoretician of ego psychology. In a broader sense, of course, when he began to struggle with problems of the primitive sectors of personality he may have been influenced by Ferenczi's writings: I can certainly attest to the fact that I found these radical testaments of Ferenczi's last years to be highly suggestive for my own thinking about such matters.

As someone who had the opportunity to witness Kohut's evolution toward self-psychology at first hand, I formed the opinion that his views changed only on the basis of his personal experiences—particularly as a result of his efforts to understand himself. He was singularly incapable of profiting from what colleagues said or wrote. Hence I do not believe that he was swayed by the publications of Ferenczi—or, for that matter, those of Winnicott, whose views he knew to be more akin to his own. In fact, in my judgment, Kohut's clinical theory (i.e., his delineation of a series of archaic transference constellations) was entirely original, and only his emphasis on the supreme technical importance of empathy leads some readers to believe that his work is a continuation of the Hungarian tradition: they assume that this viewpoint implies an endorsement of Bálint's idea of a "new beginning" or Winnicott's concept of a "holding environment." Yet it is well to remember that Kohut kept reiterating that empathy is merely an observational tool; its therapeutic usefulness depends on the manner in which the analyst is able to make use of the information it produces. For all I know, Paul Ornstein may look upon self-psychology as the successor of the Budapest School, but I regard this idea as mistaken.

There were doubtless many other analysts in America who had roots in Hungary: Sándor Feldmann in Rochester, Endre Pető and Nicholas Young in New York, and probably some I have overlooked or whose names do not clearly sound a magyar note. At any rate, this is not the place to list a complete roster; suffice it to say that those living who had analytic training in Europe before World War II are now in their eighties and no longer active professionally. As far as I know, the Ornsteins and I now constitute the older generation of practicing Hungarian-American analysts, and I suspect I am alone among us in having left Europe before 1940. In recent years, younger colleagues with Hungarian names have cropped up on the roster of the American Psychoanalytic Association. I have never met any of them in person. I assume most represent the exodus of 1956, although, of course, some could be descendants of earlier immigrants.[4]

Instead of tracing these relatively recent developments, I should like to end on a more personal note, by making some remarks about what it has meant to me, as an *American* psychoanalyst (and I have some right to claim that my work would have been unthinkable outside of an American context), to be reminded of my ties to Hungary. When I became a candidate at the Chicago Institute, both Alexander and Benedek spoke to me about our shared heritage. I was then still trying to put European experience behind me, so that their friendly overtures merely annoyed me. Nonetheless, Benedek became my first supervisor and, without ever mentioning Ferenczi's name, taught me some of the technical precepts embodied in the latter's writings: *analyse à l'hongroise!*

To be more precise, Benedek did not teach the controversial technical modifications Ferenczi introduced in the last few years of his life; she advocated the analytic position enunciated in Ferenczi's 1924 monograph, coauthored with Rank, *The Development of Psycho-Analysis*. (Benedek's own analysis with Ferenczi had taken place just a short time before, following his discharge from military service in World War I.) This technical viewpoint stressed the primacy of affective reliving in the analytic here-and-now; it decried any overemphasis on genetic reconstruction at the expense of concrete *experiencing*. Although tolerant of my evident fascination with theoretical understanding, Benedek tried to minimize my juvenile enthusiasm for abstractions by focusing much of her attention on what I seemed to feel about my patient. ("Vatch ze countertransference," she would say. "Gee Dr. Benedek, how do I do that?" I replied. "I told you: VATCH IT!")

I learned about the origins of Ferenczi's precepts when, in 1966, I was asked to write a review article for *Psyche* (Frankfurt) on the occasion of the reissue in German of Ferenczi's corpus of writings. In the course of this project, I had to acknowledge that I am also a *Hungarian* psychoanalyst (albeit one with a motor aphasia for his native tongue). When, a few years later, I was for the first time asked to be a panelist at a national meeting in the United States, Emmanuel Windholz and Jan Frank sought me out on the platform and spoke to me about having been medical school classmates of my father. By that time, their embrace felt to me like a homecoming.

Yet it would be incorrect to characterize my feelings about my emigration as the nostalgia of an Ovidian exile: I do not see Budapest as the metropolis, and Lake Michigan is not the Black Sea. I am confident that in this respect my attitudes are fairly representative of those prevalent among other colleagues of Hungarian origin. Whether they were forced out of their homeland by religious persecution or political convictions (or both), none could have been left without bitterness about Hungary. I can never forget that my passport, when I left the country, was stamped with a large capital K, in red, for "Kivándorló" (emigrant): no reentry was permitted, and I did not return for fifty years. Another way to put this matter is that when I echo Aida's *la patria mia* in the title of this essay, I am also identified with the ambivalence of her exile. I prefer my American identity. Nonetheless, I continue to cherish bits of the old culture preserved in the diaspora, such as the psychoanalytic heritage of the Budapest School.

NOTES

1. To do her justice, in 1950 Thompson wrote an enthusiastic Introduction for the English translation of the three volumes of Ferenczi's papers published in the United States (Ferenczi 1916, 1926, 1955). In my judgment, however, this essay did not serve Ferenczi well because it was so polemical that it could only provoke those who felt themselves to be part of the Freudian "mainstream." See also the reprint (1988) of Thompson's obituary of Ferenczi.

2. Although the reasons for this loss of allegiance were complex, and Radó doubtless felt that the ethos of the New York Institute was intellectually too conservative and discouraging of free inquiry, it is also likely that many colleagues found Radó's style of leadership to be too authoritarian to suit them. In this sense, both Radó and Alexander were unable to become American enough: they were indelibly stamped with the "K. und K." label ("Kaiserliche und Königliche," i.e., "imperial and royal," was the designation of the Austro-Hungarian "dual monarchy").

3. It is conceivable that Mahler's readiness to attribute crucial significance in emotional development to the vicissitudes of the "separation-individuation process" (climaxing around the end of the second year of life) were a legacy of her admiration for Ferenczi during her Budapest years as an adolescent. Much of the resistance to Mahler's ideas came from Freudian traditionalists who mistrusted her relative shift of emphasis to such a preoedipal phase of development. In my judgment, however, the influence of Mahler's work is destined to diminish because she did not dare to be radical enough to abandon Freud's metapsychology, which was poorly suited to encompass her challenging observations.

4. Of the varied sources of information I have collected for this essay, most came by way of direct contact with the persons involved; in some cases this was supplemented or reaffirmed by the concurrence of survivors (Alexander's daughter Kiki, Benedek's niece Eva Sandberg, Rapaport's widow Elvira.) Dr. Paul Stepansky kindly shared with me his knowledge about Margaret Mahler, whose memoirs (1988) he prepared for publication. Radó and Róheim are described in the volume *Psychoanalytic Pioneers* (Alexander, Eisenstein, and Grotjahn 1966). For a list of the principal publications of the contributors I mention—one happily too massive to include here—readers should consult Grinstein's Index (1956–75). My own views on the significance of the respective contributions of Ferenczi and Rapaport are spelled out in *Conceptual Issues in Psychoanalysis* (1986).

REFERENCES

Alexander, F., S. Eisenstein, and M. Grotjahn, eds. 1966. *Psychoanalytic Pioneers.* New York: Basic Books.
Ferenczi, S. 1916. *Sex in Psycho-Analysis.* Trans. E. Jones. New York: Basic Books, 1950.

Ferenczi, S. 1926. *Further Contributions to the Theory and Technique of Psycho-Analysis.* Ed. J. Rickman. Trans. J. Suttie et al. New York: Basic Books, 1952.

————. 1955. *Final Contributions to the Problems and Methods of Psycho-Analysis.* Ed. M. Bálint. Trans. E. Mosbacher et al. New York: Basic Books.

Gedo, J. 1986. *Conceptual Issues in Psychoanalysis.* Hillsdale, N.J.: Analytic Press.

————. 1991. *Toward the Biology of Clinical Encounters.* Hillsdale, N.J.: Analytic Press.

Grinstein, A. 1956–1975. *The Index of Psychoanalytic Writings.* New York: International Universities Press.

Mahler, M. 1988. *The Memoirs of Margaret S. Mahler.* Ed. P. E. Stepansky. New York: Free Press.

Rapaport, D. 1974. *The History of the Concept of Association of Ideas.* New York: International Universities Press.

Thompson, C. M. 1988. Sándor Ferenczi. *Contemp. Psychoanal.*, 24:182–95.

Five

Ferenczi's Early Impact on Washington, D.C.

■

ANN-LOUISE S. SILVER

This chapter outlines the four principal avenues by which Ferenczi initially influenced the Washington, D.C., analytic community. These are: (1) his writings, as made available by William Alanson White and Smith Ely Jelliffe (Burnham 1983); (2) his visit to Washington in 1927; (3) his treatment of Harry Stack Sullivan's close friend and colleague, Clara Thompson (Perry 1982); and (4) perhaps most importantly, his and Georg Groddeck's impact on their junior colleague, Frieda Fromm-Reichmann (Grossman and Grossman 1965; Fromm-Reichmann 1989). The more I learn about Ferenczi and Groddeck, and about how closely Fromm-Reichmann (1889–1957) worked with Groddeck, the more I recognize the enormous debt of gratitude that Chestnut Lodge Hospital, a private psychiatric and psychoanalytic institution in Rockville, Maryland, owes to Ferenczi and Groddeck. Their enthusiastic belief in the power of psychoanalysis to benefit even the sickest patients, and their courage in flexible experimentation, have inspired many people at Chestnut Lodge over the ensuing years and decades. Their approaches to this work shaped the style and attitudes of Fromm-Reichmann, who agreed with Ferenczi on some points and disagreed with him on others.

A version of this chapter was presented at the Fourth International Conference of the Sándor Ferenczi Society in Budapest in July 1993. For an exploration of related issues, see my "Countertransference, Ferenczi, and Washington D.C.," *Journal of American Academy of Psychoanalysis,* 21 (1993), 637–54.

As has been widely recognized, Ferenczi wrote presciently on many controversial topics: childhood sexual abuse and other traumata, the emotional involvement of the therapist, and physical contact between doctor and patient. I will emphasize his delineations of the patient's need to cure the doctor so that the doctor can then cure the patient. He developed clear notions of analytic *activity*, which include playfulness, mutual cueing, and staying with the patient's regression so that it can be understood. He realized that his own affects were vital clues to understanding the patient's difficulties:

I may remind you that patients do not react to theatrical phrases, but only to real sincere sympathy. Whether they recognize the truth by the intonation or colour of our voice or by the words we use or in some other way, I cannot tell. In any case, they show a remarkable, almost clairvoyant knowledge about the thoughts and emotions that go on in their analyst's mind. To deceive a patient in this respect seems to be hardly possible and if one tries to do so, it leads only to bad consequences. (Ferenczi 1933, 161)

In words especially resonant for Chestnut Lodge, Ferenczi said:

I have had a kind of fanatical belief in the efficacy of depth-psychology, and this has led me to attribute occasional failures not so much to the patient's "incurability" as to our own lack of skill, a supposition which necessarily led me to try altering the usual technique in severe cases with which it proved unable to cope successfully.

It is thus only with the utmost reluctance that I ever bring myself to give up even the most obstinate case, and I have come to be a specialist in peculiarly difficult cases, with which I go on for very many years. (1931, 128)

These were also Fromm-Reichmann's messages and her legacy. She worked at Chestnut Lodge from 1935 until her death in 1957, was a training and supervising analyst and a president of the Washington Psychoanalytic Society, and taught at the Washington School of Psychiatry, where one of her courses resulted in her classic text, *The Principles of Intensive Psychotherapy* (1950). Her comments in the Lodge's staff conferences (Silver and Feuer 1989) and in her supervisory work always focused on the therapist's anxieties and his or her ways of defending against them; meanwhile she resolutely opposed passivity. People who did not know the Lodge would sometimes jeer at their imagined ludicrous image of analysts sitting silently behind couches while patients with florid psychoses free-associated. In contrast,

Fromm-Reichmann counseled a supervisee working with a chronically schizophrenic patient, "You must make each hour with this woman a memorable experience" (Fort 1989, 250).

William Alanson White (1870–1937) and Smith Ely Jelliffe (1866–1945) also deserve our thanks. The two of them, along with Jelliffe's wife, Helena Dewey Leeming Jelliffe, did more than perhaps any other Americans to bring early psychoanalytic information to the United States. They made frequent trips to Europe, where they attended analytic meetings and visited with participants. The two men had met in Binghamton, New York, when Jelliffe came to the State Hospital there as a summer intern in 1896 while White was serving as an assistant psychiatrist. Some twenty-five years later, in 1921, when White was superintendent of Washington D.C.'s federal mental hospital, St. Elizabeths Hospital, he gave Harry Stack Sullivan his first job in Washington (Perry 1982, 179). Coincidentally, Sullivan grew up only thirty miles from Binghamton.

White credited Jelliffe with launching his writing career (1938, 174–76). He wrote the extremely popular *Outlines of Psychiatry* (1921), whose royalties funded their monograph series, which brought many German analytic works to the rapid attention of an eager American audience (Burnham 1983, 194–96). With White, Jelliffe, based in New York City, founded and edited *The Psychoanalytic Review,* the first American analytic journal. As White recalled, "In 1913, Dr. Jelliffe and I, after a great deal of preliminary consultation with various people—historians, anthropologists, psychologists, etc.—launched *The Psychoanalytic Review*" (1938, 56). (The scope and agenda of this journal would reappear in Sullivan's journal *Psychiatry,* which was inaugurated in 1937.) The first Washington Psychoanalytic Society was founded on July 6, 1914, with White as its chairman, and met at St. Elizabeths Hospital.

White's professional identity was based on scrupulous and fervent attention to nuances and details in his patients' discourses. In his role as superintendent, he taught this skill to his staff and looked for a similar orientation in those he hired. His staff member, Edward Kempf, for example, wrote *Psychopathology* (1920), the first American psychiatric text to apply psychoanalytic ideas to the description and treatment of people suffering from psychosis, and dedicated the book to White. In White's words:

I was ready for these psychoanalytic concepts because of the work that I had done with [Boris] Sidis in studying the problems of mental dissociation and double personality. I was accustomed to sit by the patient's bedside with pencil and paper and take down religiously everything that he said, hoping to find among these broken fragments of his discourse some leading line that would be of significance and importance. I was accustomed to listening to these delirioid utterances and expecting to be able to hitch them up with actual occurrences in the life of the patient, and I even expected that this was, theoretically at least, possible to the minutest detail. I had perhaps never formulated definitely the theory of psychic determinism but I acted as if I had, and the concept was therefore not alien to my way of thinking and acting. (1933, 57)

Recalling her own preanalytic career, Fromm-Reichmann concurred: "When I was an intern at the psychiatric hospital of the medical school of the University in Königsberg, nobody knew yet what psychotherapy was. But I knew it could be done. What I did was sit with the psychotics. Day and night, and night and day, and listen to them and just say a few kind things so that they went on. I got furious when they were mistreated" (1989, 474). White resolutely protected the patients in his hospital, especially when they had been harmed by attendants (Grob 1985, 89–94). While White's and Fromm-Reichmann's careers overlapped for only two years (he died two years after Fromm-Reichmann's arrival in Washington), their common vision and uncommon leadership created an ambience in Washington characterized by a unique combination of humanism and scientific productivity.

Sullivan worked at St. Elizabeths Hospital from 1921 to 1922, when he began work at the Sheppard and Enoch Pratt Hospital in Towson, Maryland (Perry 1982, 179–88). He remained active in the Washington psychoanalytic community and stayed in touch with White. As Helen Perry has chronicled:

In the fall of 1926, Ferenczi came to the United States for eight months, his second trip to the U.S., lecturing that winter in the New School for Social Research in New York City. On December 9, 1926, Sullivan wrote to White, suggesting that he invite Ferenczi, "the genius of the psychoanalytic movement," to come to Washington for three or four months. Two days later, White wrote denying the request; as usual, he was shrewd in avoiding, for himself and the hospital, financial obligations and intellectual disputes. Without White's sponsorship, Ferenczi gave several lectures in Washington in the spring of 1927. (1982, 228).

Ferenczi delivered five lectures under the auspices of the Washington Psychoanalytic Association.[1]

Fortunately for us, White and Jelliffe lived far enough from each other that they communicated by frequent and casual letters, and Jelliffe, formerly a systematic botanist whose first publication was a cataloguing of the flora of Brooklyn's Prospect Park, meticulously kept his correspondence. Their letters from the spring of 1926 contain discussions of the business of translating and publishing Ferenczi's "Genital Theory" (1930), the résumé of *Thalassa* (1924) he provided at the Washington Psychopathologic Society the following April. White commented on May 28, 1926: "His stuff ought to be good material. He is one of the brilliant men of Europe and it is the kind of material of course which we want to get in the Series for the benefit of the American readers."[2] On June 17, 1926, White wrote, "I have looked over the Ferenczi manuscript and I really think it is [an] exceedingly interesting piece of work and as I like to say provocative, and I think we ought to use it." About a year later, May 9, 1927, Jelliffe reported to White:

Among other things we have had a seminar—about 20, for 10 weeks with Ferenczi. It was quite entertaining and illuminating. He is very clear and stimulating and for myself helped a lot towards getting my notions into a better state of security. I did not learn anything new—conceited ass as I am—but notwithstanding it was helpful. We started at the 23rd Street joint but it was uncomfortable so I got them to foregather in my front room and we had a grand time. I blew them to a buffet supper at the end having supplied them cigars for 8 weeks—cheap ones I will admit. The only things I myself brought up, organic situations, and theoretical views of libido dynamics in dreams, F. dodged quite nicely—but the discussions were entertaining. F. tried to smoke out the Rankians but got nowhere.

In New York, Ferenczi was welcomed enthusiastically; he was a charismatic speaker who always drew large crowds to his lectures. But, according to Ernest Jones, when he began organizing a psychoanalytic society of his own analysands who were not medical doctors, he was ostracized by the New York analysts (1957, 134).

Ferenczi's Influence in the Washington, D.C., Area

When Ferenczi presented "The Genital Theory" at the Washington Psychopathological Society on April 11, 1927, the formal discussants were

William A. White, Nolan D. C. Lewis, Harry Stack Sullivan, and Philip Graven. The talk was published in *The Psychoanalytic Review*, but copies of the discussions do not seem to have survived (Noble and Burnham 1989, 544).

Ferenczi's point of view was "in harmony with Harry Stack Sullivan's evolving concepts of interpersonal relationships both as the causes of psychiatric problems and as the major tools for treating them" (Chapman 1976, 53). Sullivan had begun work in psychiatry in 1920, treating people suffering from psychosis. His close friend, Clara Thompson, has commented, "When Ferenczi was in the United States in 1926, Sullivan met him and found his thinking the most congenial to his own way of thinking of any of the analysts. At the same time, it would be an exaggeration to say that they influenced each other to any extent. Their contact was too brief, and each continued to develop without further communication with the other" (1952, 105).

Clara Thompson became the first elected president of the Washington-Baltimore Psychoanalytic Society, serving for two years, from 1930 to 1932, when she left for Budapest. At that time, Sullivan was vice president of the American Psychoanalytic Association. Thompson has remarked, "I would not have gone to Ferenczi [for my personal analysis] if Sullivan hadn't insisted that this was the only analyst in Europe he had any confidence in; and therefore, if I was going to go to Europe and get analyzed, I had just better go there. So I went" (Perry 1982, 202). The plan was that, on her return, she would analyze Sullivan, which she did for a relatively short time, stopping after about three hundred treatment hours because Thompson "had such awe of Sullivan's intellectual capacities that she could not effectively go on with it" (Chapman 1976, 53). Sullivan seems to have been referring to her when he commented that he had proposed to a woman, and she had accepted, but the next morning they each had raced to the phone to call the other and call it off (Perry 1982, 201–2). Neither married or had children. Thompson was treated by Ferenczi in the summers of 1928 and 1929, and then for two years continuously from 1931 until Ferenczi's death in 1933. She was one of Ferenczi's patients in his experiment with mutual analysis, and she later commented on his theories and practice:

In contrast to Freud's idea that the neurotic problems of childhood develop from the child's struggle with his instincts, Ferenczi believed that the child became ill as a result of the neurosis of his parents. "There are no bad children. There are only bad parents," he said. He firmly believed that a person became ill because of what had happened to him. (1944, 246–47)

His orientation may have contributed to Fromm-Reichmann's notions, later revised, of the schizophrenogenic mother.

Thompson seems to figure in Ferenczi's *Clinical Diary* as Dm, the patient who brought down Freud's wrath on Ferenczi. Ferenczi wrote on January 7, 1932:

See the case of Dm., a lady who, "complying" with my passivity, had allowed herself to take more and more liberties, and occasionally even kissed me. Since this behavior met with no resistance, since it was treated as something permissible in analysis and at most commented on theoretically, she remarked quite casually in the company of other patients, who were undergoing analysis elsewhere: "I am allowed to kiss Papa Ferenczi, as often as I like." I first reacted to the unpleasantness that ensued with the complete impassivity with which I was conducting this analysis. But then the patient began to make herself ridiculous, ostentatiously as it were, in her sexual conduct (for example at social gatherings, while dancing). It was only through the insight and admission that my passivity had been unnatural that she was brought back to real life, so to speak, as insight does have to reckon with social opposition. Simultaneously it became evident that here again was a case of repetition of the father-child situation. As a child, Dm. had been grossly abused sexually by her father, who was out of control; later, obviously because of the father's bad conscience and social anxiety, he reviled her, so to speak. The daughter had to take revenge on her father indirectly by failing in her own life. (1985, 2)

Here we have a fascinating vignette in which a woman, abused by her father, takes revenge on him indirectly, in the transference, when she sounds the alarm of *potential* metaphorical incest, a sequence that is hardly rare in the treatment of those who have suffered childhood abuse. Ferenczi was rebuked by Freud, who had been his analyst and was aware of Ferenczi's difficulties (Stanton 1991, 48–49). Ferenczi's work has languished for over fifty years, a heavy price to pay for his having inadequately maintained physical boundaries and thus passively encouraged a potential seduction. This illustrates the principle, emphasized by Fromm-Reichmann, that countertransference involves containing our reactive impulses. Ferenczi had been actively passive, imprudently refraining from setting limits on physical contact.

This episode raises the issue of confidentiality, the revealing of secrets to those not clinically involved in a particular treatment. In a footnote to the *Clinical Diary,* Judith Dupont (in Ferenczi 1985, 3n. 2) officially broke through the confidentiality that Ferenczi attempted to protect even in his private journal and identified Thompson as Dm. Dupont has revealed a secret that Thompson may have told only Ferenczi and possibly Sullivan, who then would have made an astute clinically based referral when he sent her to Ferenczi.

On her return from Budapest, Thompson moved from Washington to New York City, but continued to collaborate with Sullivan as well as with Fromm-Reichmann and their associates, who taught in the Washington School of Psychiatry and its New York City branch, which would become the William Alanson White Institute; they all commuted between Washington and New York as often as once a week.

A dramatic clinical event highlights the teamwork among these analysts, which allowed for hostile rivalry. Thompson once had a patient who developed a paranoid reaction and bought a gun for the purpose of killing her. On the way to her session, the gun in her purse, the patient fell on the sidewalk, having developed a hysterical paralysis. The police discovered the pistol. Thompson directed the patient to Fromm-Reichmann at Chestnut Lodge.[3] As Sue A. Shapiro notes, "In her college yearbook Thompson described her future plans to be a doctor and . . . stated that her goal was 'To murder people in the most refined manner possible' " (1993, 165). This was the only time that Thompson referred a patient not simply to Chestnut Lodge but specifically to Fromm-Reichmann.

Ferenczi's impact on psychoanalytically oriented work with the severely mentally ill has been too little acknowledged. I had expected to find frequent references to Ferenczi in the transcripts of the nearly one hundred lectures that Sullivan gave at Chestnut Lodge, but was astounded to discover that he at no time discussed, and only rarely alluded to, Ferenczi or anyone else who had contributed to his thinking (Sullivan 1940, 178).

Ferenczi's Influence on Fromm-Reichmann

I believe that Ferenczi's major impact on the Washington area occurred with the arrival of Fromm-Reichmann at Chestnut Lodge in 1935. Fromm-

Reichmann had had a close and longstanding collaboration with Georg Groddeck. In 1920, Ferenczi met Groddeck at the sixth International Psychoanalytical Association Congress in The Hague, Holland. They were to become close friends, and Ferenczi frequently visited Groddeck's sanatorium in Baden-Baden. Edith Weigert notes that Groddeck likewise "played a stimulating role in the group of Heidelberg psychoanalysts to which Frieda Fromm-Reichmann belonged" (1959, v). Fromm-Reichmann dedicated her *Principles of Intensive Psychotherapy* "To my teachers: Sigmund Freud, Kurt Goldstein, Georg Groddeck and Harry Stack Sullivan."

Fromm-Reichmann was hardly a novice at the time she met Groddeck in the mid-1920s. She had worked closely with Kurt Goldstein treating brain-injured soldiers and had administered a hospital specializing in this area during World War I. From Goldstein, Fromm-Reichmann gained the following benefits: (1) a thorough grounding in neurology, with a special emphasis on aphasia and its treatment; (2) experience in writing scientific papers, some coauthored with him (Goldstein and Reichmann 1914, 1916, 1919, 1920); (3) an opportunity to work in hospital administration and to lead men in a men's world during wartime (she was a major in the Prussian Army); and (4) a holistic orientation, which released her from the mind-body duality. Goldstein regarded the zeal of psychoanalysts with outspoken skepticism and articulately outlined how theoreticians have a tendency to comb their data for support of their pet theories rather than to look for objective knowledge; this resonates with Ferenczi's lifelong orientation as a researcher. Goldstein's most widely known work, *The Organism: A Holistic Approach to Biology Derived from Pathological Data in Man* (1939), sets forth his thesis. The Chestnut Lodge Staff Library houses Fromm-Reichmann's personal copy, which is inscribed by Goldstein: "Frieda, In alter, erneueter Zuneigung [in old, renewed affection]. Aug. 1946 Santa Fe, Kurt."

In addition to her experience with Goldstein, Fromm-Reichmann had worked at the Weisser Hirsch sanatorium in the mountains near Dresden with I. H. Schultz, whom she identified as the only person doing psychotherapy in hospitals immediately after the war. Still based in Dresden, she started her psychoanalytic training in 1923, at the age of thirty-four, in Munich with Wilhelm Wittenberg, whom Daniel Burston characterizes as "a zealous Freudian" (1991, 15). Fromm-Reichmann said, "My first analyst was Wittenberg, somebody in Munich whom nobody knows. A very decent fellow. Later, Erich [Fromm] went to him. We had decided when we both would be through, we wanted to take him out for champagne and he should teach us how to eat oysters. But, unfortunately, he died of cancer before that. An awfully nice fellow" (1989, 479). Later she underwent a training analysis with Hans Sachs in Berlin (1989, 480). Thus, she was Sachs's analysand at the time that he, Karl Abraham, and Max Eitingon vehemently opposed Rank and Ferenczi when they brought out their coauthored book, *The Development of Psycho-Analysis* (1924).

This complex grounding prepared Fromm-Reichmann to be receptive to and immediately conversant with Groddeck's and Ferenczi's ideas and efforts, while remaining keenly aware of their ideological ramifications. In her 1924 paper, "On Psychoanalysis," which was read at the Society for Natural and Medical Sciences in Dresden, she emphasized the unity of mind and body. Probably she was already working closely with Groddeck, who was twenty-three years her senior. Later, she opened her own sanatorium, with a kosher kitchen, which was nicknamed the "torah-peuticum." [4] There, she met, briefly treated, and in 1926 married and arranged clinical training for the Zionist sociologist, Erich Fromm, who was ten years her junior. That year, they organized a group of nine Frankfurt analysts, who formed an institute in 1929. "By contrast to other psychoanalytic institutes, the one in Frankfurt did not train psychoanalysts, but tried to influence the social sciences by taking part in the university teaching program" (Hoffmann, personal communication). As World War II closed in, and two years after Ferenczi's death in 1933, it was Fromm-Reichmann who arranged for Groddeck's hospitalization, thus saving him from his delusional plan personally to warn Hitler that his men were being unfair to the Jews (Grossman and Grossman 1965, 195–98).

Leslie Farber has described one aspect of Fromm-Reichmann's support of her colleague and teacher:

Anyone who knew Dr. Fromm-Reichmann knew that she was a well-brought-up, refined, upper middle-class, German-Jewish lady. During Georg Groddeck's last years, prior to his commitment to an institution, she performed the offices of his hostess with fastidious skill. Once or twice a year, she helped Groddeck to assemble at his estate a group of distinguished European psychiatrists. It was her duty to arrange for food, wine, and cigars and in general to put these guests (many of whom did not know one another) at their ease, to ensure a comfortable social atmosphere out of which might come the sort of conversation Groddeck wished about matters psychoanalytic. Once the group had gathered, and following all her work of arrangement and preparations, she was required, as the only woman present, to assist in setting the scene and maintaining the appropriate tone to the occasion, but always without calling attention either to her assistance or to the novelty of her presence. Of course, it might happen that in the consideration of some question of feminine psychology, Groddeck would suddenly turn to her and say, "Frieda, we men cannot really know about these things. As a woman, Frieda, you must instruct us." At such moments, I am sure, she was more than rewarded for the physical and emotional labor of these occasions, not to mention the irritations involved in dealing with a person as crotchety and difficult as Groddeck became in his later years. (1976, 192)

In taped interviews, Fromm-Reichmann said, "I've had a life where I always had to be the muse, because I thought what they [the men] will do will be of greater significance. And what I could do was just to take off their jobs so that they could do their special work" (1989, 475). Thus, despite her distinguished career and resolutely independent views on the practice of psychoanalysis, Fromm-Reichmann conformed to the conventional attitudes toward gender roles that prevailed in her social milieu.

In 1931, Dexter Bullard, Sr., took over management of Chestnut Lodge, which had been founded by his father in 1912. He gave himself five years to determine the direction of the place, and at the four-and-a-half-year mark, he reluctantly brought in the German-Jewish immigrant, since he needed summer coverage. He had decided the hospital would have a psychoanalytic orientation, since he was struck by the similarity between psychotic communications and the life of the mind in dreaming. He often said it was love at first sight when he met Frieda. Actually, she was just what he needed, since she had vast experience in actualizing what he had only dimly imagined. She stayed, and put his hospital on the world map (Silver 1989a).

On rereading the transcripts of the meetings held at the Lodge, either the Wednesday staff conferences (Silver and Feuer 1989) or of the voluminous year-long "Schizophrenia Seminar" held in 1952 (unpublished), I am struck by the congruence between the participants' orientation regarding countertransference and that expressed in Ferenczi's papers. I shall quote one such example, from the open discussion of a case presentation. Fromm-Reichmann, who was four feet, ten inches tall, commented to a large athletic male therapist: "What we hear is that you made contact with her [the patient] and that she talks to you, but I have a hard time hearing what other directives you have in conducting this treatment, other than 'Thank God, we talk to each other,' not using the talking to each other for any *purpose* and it could be that you haven't been active or positively aggressive there for the reason you just mentioned, that you are afraid" (Silver and Feuer 1989, 25–26).

However, I find no instance where Fromm-Reichmann mentioned Ferenczi or Groddeck in those settings. The "Schizophrenia Seminar" culminated in a 1953 panel presentation at the American Psychoanalytic Association, "Intuitive Processes in the Psychotherapy of Schizophrenics," with contributions by Fromm-Reichmann (1955a, 1955b), Alberta Szalita-Pemow (1955), Harold Searles (1955), Donald Burnham (1955), and Marvin Adland (unpublished). The transcript of the seminar, which is being prepared for publication, is redolent with the same brutal self-honesty and clinical dedication that infuse Ferenczi's *Clinical Diary*.

I believe that Fromm-Reichmann brought the spirit of Groddeck's, Ferenczi's, and certainly her own work to the United States at Chestnut Lodge; however, like Sullivan, she did not expatiate about the specific contributions of colleagues who had shaped her views. During her years in Washington, Ferenczi's and Groddeck's names had become anathema; their ideas about how to use psychoanalysis in the treatment of severely ill patients were often heavily attacked.

Fromm-Reichmann became a popular and inspiring teacher, both locally and nationally. However, we do Fromm-Reichmann herself and our patients a disservice if we consider her a miracle worker with superhuman empathic abilities and meteoric brilliance. By making her seem so grand, we risk missing her message, which is that with training and self-honesty, the majority of therapists can work intensively with patients suffering from psychosis and borderline disorders. She had mastered skills, as had others in her European analytic community. She was the carrier, the vector for their infectious optimism, curiosity, humanism, and relative egalitarianism. She brought these qualities and their accumulated clinical expertise with her. The Lodge became her substitute for Groddeck's and her own sanatorium; the small group meetings and the staff conferences replicated the discussions at Baden-Baden and the Southwest German Psychoanalytic Institute in

Heidelberg. The community of colleagues supported each other so that once again the patients' therapeutic strivings could be recognized.

The key difference between Ferenczi's style of work and that at the Lodge is the latter's far more rigorous structuring of the treatment situation. As Fromm-Reichmann has summarized:

> Ferenczi, one of the most impressive leaders in the early years of psychoanalysis, followed a different course. He was convinced, as are all psychoanalysts, that the clarification of early infantile and childhood experiences are of paramount significance to patients. He invited patients to re-enact their experiences with him, believing that these transferred reactivations would speed therapeutic experiences. My objection to this suggestion stems predominantly from the danger implicit for many psychiatrists of losing track of their role as participant observer by becoming a gratified participant co-actor in relation to the patient's infantile needs. I feel more strongly opposed to it from this standpoint than from anything else that has been said for verbalization versus action. This objection is similar to those discussed later regarding sexual experiences with patients. (1950, 123)

I wonder whether Fromm-Reichmann's concluding demurrals allude to possible remarks by Thompson about her treatment with Ferenczi.

The Patient as Therapist to His Analyst

Harold Searles's paper, "The Patient as Therapist to His Analyst" (1972), delineates phenomena closely related to those observed by Ferenczi. Lewis Aron has recently commented that "Searles may be the contemporary American answer to Ferenczi" (1992, 183). Although Aron draws parallels between Searles's and Ferenczi's dedication to working with severely ill patients, he does not consider their treatment approaches, which contrast in many ways. Searles is alert to patients' therapeutic strivings, but does not act upon their unconscious invitations to reverse roles. He writes: "I am focusing upon the situation of psychoanalytic therapy, wishing to highlight both the irony and the technical importance of the (to my mind) fact that the more ill a patient is, the more does his successful treatment require that he become, and be implicitly acknowledged as having become, a therapist to his officially designated therapist, the analyst" (1972, 381). Ferenczi made this acknowledgment of the patient's therapeutic function explicit, as his *Clinical Diary* testifies, while Searles elaborates on the importance of maintaining this dimension of the work implicit.

Intriguingly, Searles finds Groddeck in 1923 to be the first who "explicitly describes the patient's functioning as therapist to the doctor." He quotes Groddeck as having said: " 'And now I was confronted by the strange fact that I was not treating the patient, but that the patient was treating me' " (1972, 446). While Ferenczi's writings are currently undergoing rediscovery, I think we should also resuscitate the works of Groddeck, who published his observation of how the patient becomes a therapist to the doctor in *The Book of the It* (1923, 262–23) some ten years before Ferenczi confided similar thoughts to his *Clinical Diary*.

In closing, I want to stress the importance of this Ferenczian tradition for contemporary clinicians, since we as a professional group are under unprecedented stress. In the current climate, in which external forces regiment our treatment approaches, it is vital that we understand ourselves as patients. Without such self-scrutiny, we run the risk of counteridentifying with our patients—that is, resonating with and mirroring their states of tension, rather than empathizing with them—and thus failing to use our countertransference constructively as we grapple with the emotional stresses of treating those with severe illnesses.

NOTES

1. For a listing of all the papers read before the Washington Psychoanalytic Association between 1924 and 1929, see Karpman (1930, 103).

2. This and the following quotations from the correspondence between White and Jelliffe are taken from the Manuscript Division of the Library of Congress.

3. This information is derived from medical records at Chestnut Lodge. Confidentiality precludes further access.

4. I am indebted for this and other information about Fromm-Reichmann's years in Germany to personal communications from Klaus Hoffman, M.D., a psychoanalyst from Reichnau, Germany. He and I are preparing a book on this period in Fromm-Reichmann's life, which will include a translation of her early papers.

REFERENCES

Aron, L. 1992. From Ferenczi to Searles and Contemporary Relational Approaches: Commentary on Mark Blechner's "Working in the Countertransference." *Psa. Dialogues,* 2:181–90.

Burnham, D. 1955. Some Problems in Communication with Schizophrenic Patients. *J. Amer. Psa. Assn.*, 3:67–81.

Burnham, J., ed. 1983. *Smith Ely Jelliffe: American Psychoanalyst and Physician and His Correspondence with Sigmund Freud and C. G. Jung*. Chicago: University of Chicago Press.

Burston, D. 1991. *The Legacy of Erich Fromm*. Cambridge, Mass.: Harvard University Press.

Chapman, A. H. 1976. *Harry Stack Sullivan: His Life and His Work*. New York: Putnam.

Farber, L. 1976. Schizophrenia and the Mad Psychotherapist. In *The Ways of the Will: Essays toward a Psychology and Psychopathology of Will*, pp. 184–208. New York: Basic Books.

Ferenczi, S. 1930. Masculine and Feminine: Psychoanalytic Observations on the 'Genital Theory' and on Secondary and Tertiary Sex Characteristics. *Psychoanal. Rev.*, 17:105–13.

———. 1931. Child Analysis in the Analyses of Adults. In Ferenczi 1955, pp. 126–42.

———. 1933. Confusion of Tongues between Adults and the Child: The Language of Tenderness and of Passion. In Ferenczi 1955, pp. 156–67.

———. 1955. *Final Contributions to the Problems and Methods of Psycho-Analysis*. Ed. M. Bálint. Trans. E. Mosbacher et al. New York: Brunner/Mazel.

———. 1985. *The Clinical Diary of Sándor Ferenczi*. Ed. J. Dupont. Trans. M. Bálint and N. Z. Jackson. Cambridge, Mass.: Harvard University Press, 1988.

Fort, J. 1989. Present-day Treatment of Schizophrenia. In Silver 1989b, pp. 249–70.

[Fromm-]Reichmann, F. 1924. Über Psychoanalyse. *Deutsche Med. Wochenschr.*, 50:758–61.

———. 1950. *Principles of Intensive Psychotherapy*. Chicago: University of Chicago Press.

———. 1955a. Introduction. Panel on Intuitive Processes in the Psychotherapy of Schizophrenia. *J. Amer. Psa. Assn.*, 3:5–6.

———. 1955b. Clinical Significance of Intuitive Process of the Psychoanalyst. *J. Amer. Psa. Assn.*, 3:82–88.

———. 1989. Reminiscences of Europe. In Silver 1989b, pp. 469–81.

Goldstein, K., and F. Reichmann. 1914. Über die körperlichen Störungen bei der Dementia Praecox. *Neurol. Zentralbl.*, 33:343–50.

———. 1916. Beiträge zur Kasuistik und Symptomatologie der Kleinhirnerkrankungen. *Arch. f. Psychiat. u. Nervenkrankh.*, 56:466–521.

———. 1919. Über corticale Sensibilitätsstörungen, besonders am Kopfe. *Ergebn. d. Ges. Neurol. u. Psychiat.*, 53:49–79.

———. 1920. Über praktische und theoretische Ergebnisse aus den Erfahrungen an Hirnschussverletzten. *Ergebn. d. Inn. Med. u. Kinderh.*, 18:405–530.

Grob, G. 1985. *The Inner World of American Psychiatry. 1890–1940: Selected Correspondence*. New Brunswick, N.J.: Rutgers University Press.

Groddeck, G. 1923. *The Book of the It*. Trans. V. M. E. Collins. New York: Mentor, 1961.

Grossman, C., and S. Grossman. 1965. *The Wild Analyst: The Life and Work of Georg Groddeck.* New York: Braziller.

Jones, E. 1957. *The Life and Work of Sigmund Freud.* Vol. 3. New York: Basic Books.

Karpman, B. 1930. The Washington Psychoanalytic Association, 1924–1929. *Psychoanal. Rev.,* 17:101–4.

Noble, D., and D. Burnham. 1989. A History of the Washington Psychoanalytic Institute and Society. In Silver 1989b, pp. 537–73.

Perry, H. 1982. *Psychiatrist of America: The Life of Harry Stack Sullivan.* Cambridge, Mass.: Harvard University Press.

Searles, H. 1955. Dependency Processes in the Psychotherapy of Schizophrenia. *J. Amer. Psa. Assn.,* 3:19–66.

———. 1972. The Patient as Therapist to His Analyst. In P. Giovacchini, ed., *Tactics and Techniques in Psychoanalytic Therapy, Vol. II: Countertransference,* pp. 95–151. New York: Aronson, 1975.

Shapiro, S. A. 1993. Clara Thompson. Ferenczi's Messenger with Half a Message. In L. Aron and A. Harris, eds., *The Legacy of Sándor Ferenczi,* pp. 159–74. Hillsdale, N.J.: Analytic Press.

Silver, A.-L. 1989a. Introduction. In Silver 1989b, pp. 1–12.

———, ed. 1989b. *Psychoanalysis and Psychosis.* Madison, Conn.: International Universities Press.

Silver, A.-L., and P. C. Feuer. 1989. Fromm-Reichmann's Contributions at Staff Conferences. In Silver 1989b, pp. 23–45.

Stanton, M. 1991. *Sándor Ferenczi: Reconsidering Active Intervention.* Northvale, N.J.: Aronson.

Sullivan, H. S. 1940. *Conceptions of Modern Psychiatry: The First William Alanson White Memorial Lectures.* New York: Norton.

Szalita-Pemow, A. 1955. The "Intuitive Process" and Its Relation to Work with Schizophrenics. *J. Amer. Psa. Assn.,* 3:7–18.

Thompson, C. 1944. Ferenczi's Contribution to Psychoanalysis. *Psychiatry,* 7:245–52.

———. 1952. Sullivan and Psychoanalysis. In P. Mullahy, ed., *The Contributions of Harry Stack Sullivan: A Symposium on Interpersonal Theory in Psychiatry and Social Science,* pp. 101–16. New York: Hermitage House.

Weigert, E. 1959. Foreword to D. Bullard, Sr., ed., *Psychoanalysis and Psychotherapy: Selected Papers of Frieda Fromm-Reichmann,* pp. v–x. Chicago: University of Chicago Press.

White, W. A. 1921. *Outlines of Psychiatry.* Washington: Nervous and Mental Disease Publishing Co.

———. 1933. *Forty Years of Psychiatry.* New York: Nervous and Mental Disease Publishing Co.

———. 1938. *The Autobiography of a Purpose.* Garden City, N.Y.: Doubleday.

PART II

Disciple and Dissident

Six

Asymmetry and Mutuality in the Analytic Relationship: Contemporary Lessons from the Freud-Ferenczi Dialogue

■

AXEL HOFFER

In this paper I shall view the historical disagreements and tensions between Sigmund Freud and Sándor Ferenczi as metaphors for the conflicts, dilemmas, and tensions experienced by contemporary psychoanalysts in each analytic hour. I shall focus on the third of three areas of disagreement between them. The first area, and probably the best known, finds Freud on the side of abstinence and frustration and Ferenczi on the side of gratification and indulgence. In the second area, Freud's orientation is more toward the head and intellect while Ferenczi's is clearly toward the heart and feelings. Finally, the third area reveals Freud to be more inclined to an authoritarian, asymmetrical analytic relationship; Ferenczi, by contrast, passionately seeks a mutual and equal relationship with Freud, his former analyst.

I want to suggest that we analysts constantly experience an inevitable, necessary tension between these analytic—indeed human—polarities. We are riding with our analysand on a bicycle built for two. We must always move the handlebars first in one direction, then in the other. Should we move too far in either direction, or become paralyzed into rigid immobility, we will fall off the path. We must deal with that tension by oscillating (Fenichel 1941; quoted by Gardner 1991, 851). How each of us deals with that necessary tension—how we oscillate—determines what kind of analysts we are, what paths we follow, and whether we fall into the ditch. My aim is to become better acquainted with the Freud and Ferenczi within each of us. My question is: "How—and why—is a psychoanalytic relationship different from other relationships?" An examination of asymmetry and mutuality will help us to answer those questions.

Ferenczi's *Clinical Diary* (1932) and the extensive Freud-Ferenczi correspondence now becoming available to us together reveal that Ferenczi's third and final challenge to Freud reaches to the heart of the psychoanalytic relationship. I shall now examine the implications for our practice of that challenge—namely, Ferenczi's passionate insistence on an egalitarian rather than an authoritarian analytic relationship, culminating in his experiments with "mutual analysis." From the perspective of a study of the fascinating twenty-five-year personal, professional, and analytic relationship of Freud and Ferenczi, I shall show how the opposing tendencies toward asymmetry and mutuality create an inevitable tension in the analytic relationship. Finally, I shall elucidate how an analyst's self-awareness can help to maintain a level of tension necessary for optimal therapeutic benefit.

A brief historical review begins with Freud's fundamental principle of abstinence summarized in his highly influential papers on technique, which even now remain the standard against which modifications are judged. Freud states:

Analytic technique requires of the physician that he should deny to the patient who is craving for love that satisfaction she demands. The treatment must be carried out in abstinence. By this I do not mean physical abstinence alone, nor yet the deprivation of everything that the patient desires, for perhaps no sick person could tolerate this. Instead, I shall state it as *a fundamental principle* that the patient's need and longing should be allowed to persist in her, in order that they may serve as forces impelling her to do work and make changes, and that we must beware of appeasing those forces by means of surrogates. And what we could offer would never by anything else than a surrogate, for the patient's condition is such that, until her repressions are removed, she is incapable of real satisfaction. (1914, 165)

Elsewhere Freud emphasizes:

You will remember that it was a frustration that made the patient ill. . . . Cruel though it may sound, we must see to it that the patient's suffering . . . does not come to an end prematurely. If . . . his suffering becomes mitigated, *we* must re-instate it elsewhere in the form of some appreciable *privation:* otherwise we run the danger of never achieving any improvements except quite insignificant and transitory ones. (1919, 162)

Freud's advocacy of abstinence and frustration (in an implicitly asymmetrical authoritarian relationship) contrasts with Ferenczi's description of "mutual analysis" where the emphasis is on safety and symmetry. Initially, in the early 1920s, Ferenczi wholeheartedly embraced Freud's technical principle of abstinence. Indeed, Ferenczi is well known for his "active technique," which consisted of tension-heightening demands and prohibitions that he imposed on patients in stalemated analyses. After renouncing his "active technique" in the mid-1920s, however, Ferenczi went to the opposite extreme by adopting what he called the "relaxation technique" (1930). With this approach—less often discussed than his "active technique"—Ferenczi tried to gratify the patient's longings while minimizing his own demands. He tried to create a "safe" atmosphere in which the patient felt totally accepted and trusting, hoping thereby to enable the patient to reexperience the emotions originating in traumatic childhood experiences. Ferenczi's technique of "relaxation" contained an implicit reenactment of his conception of the idealized early mother-infant bond, characterized by an ambience of total acceptance and indulgence of the help-seeking, traumatized child-within-the-analysand (Hoffer 1991).

Because of its relevance to our inquiry into asymmetry and mutuality, I shall now consider the problem of whether feelings in the analytic relationship—for example, transferential and countertransferential feelings of love—are real. The questions to ponder include: How is a psychoanalytic relationship different from an ordinary relationship? Is an ordinary relationship real and an analytic relationship—with its analysis of transferential feelings—unreal? Are transferential feelings unreal? In contrast to transferential feelings, are feelings in the therapeutic alliance, like those in an ordinary relationship, real?

In the last decade, psychoanalysts have asked: "Whose reality is it?" (Modell 1991; Schwaber 1992). They have thereby placed a renewed emphasis on understanding the patient's psychic reality and on the construction of reality during the therapeutic process by the analyst as well as by the analysand. A brief review of the shifts in psychoanalytic theory and technique will put our questions about asymmetry and mutuality into sharper focus. As we identify recent shifts in psychoanalytic practice, we recognize that they also correspond to broader shifts in Western societies away from authoritarianism and certainty toward egalitarianism and relativity. I shall illustrate these shifts by comparing Ralph Greenson's analytic attitude in the 1960s first with that of Ferenczi in the 1930s and then with contemporary practice (Hoffer 1985).

According to Greenson, "Transference reactions are always inappropriate. They may be so in the quality, quantity or duration of the reaction." He continues by offering the following clinical example:

A young woman patient reacts to my keeping her waiting for two or three minutes by becoming tearful and angry, fantasizing that I must be giving extra time to my favorite woman patient. This is an inappropriate reaction in a thirty-five-year-old intelligent and cultured woman, but her associations lead to a past situation where this set of feelings and fantasies fit. She recalls her reactions as a child of five waiting for her father to come to her room to kiss her goodnight. She always had to wait a few minutes because he made it a rule to kiss her younger sister goodnight first. Then she reacted by tears, anger and jealousy fantasies—precisely what she is now experiencing with me. Her reactions are appropriate for a five-year-old girl, but obviously not fitting for a thirty-five-year-old-woman. The key to understanding this behavior is recognizing that it is a repetition of the past, i.e., a transference reaction. (1967, 152–53)

I can agree with part of what Greenson says here, specifically with the usefulness of pursuing the patient's associations to the analyst's lateness to deepen understanding of the psychic reality of the past. But Greenson's description of the "inappropriateness" of the transference reaction brings to mind Ferenczi's objections to the analyst's condescending attitudes. It is difficult enough, it seems to me, to be an analytic patient without having to bear the potential humiliation of the analyst's judging which of her reactions to him are "childish and inappropriate" and which are "reasonable." Furthermore, such judgments as to whether or not a particular response to him is unrealistic, childish, and inappropriate—and hence transferential—distract the analyst from wholeheartedly attending to the analysand's psychic reality. I am, therefore, in sympathy with Ferenczi, who, as early as 1931, expressed his commitment to a focused exploration of the patient's psychic reality:

It is advantageous to consider for a time *every one,* even the most improbable, of the communications as is some way possible, even to accept an obvious delusion. Two reasons for this: thus, by leaving aside the "reality" question, one can feel one's way more completely into the patient's mental life. (Here something should be said about the disadvantages of contrasting "reality" and "unreality." The latter must be taken equally seriously as a *psychic* reality; hence above all one must become fully absorbed in all that the patient says and feels.) (1931, 235)

Since analytic attention is again being focused on psychic reality, I want to suggest that transference and countertransference—the latter defined by James McLaughlin (1981) as the analyst's transference to the patient—are as real and genuine as any other feelings. Furthermore, the analyst's efforts to distinguish between "real" and "transferential," "appropriate" and "inappropriate," or "childish" and "mature" feelings are distractions from and resistances to deepening our understanding of where the analyst and the analysand live—namely, in the latter's psychic reality.

I want to proceed now from the discussion of psychic reality and the reality of transferential feelings—for example, love—to two conditions that distinguish such feelings from their counterparts in ordinary relationships: inequality and asymmetry. I have already touched on the issue of inequality that arises when the analyst views himself as the judge, arbiter of reality, or one who knows. In the following vignette, Greenson's comment calls our attention to the asymmetry created by traditional analytic anonymity (non-self-disclosure) and nonreciprocity. This analytic example highlights how self-disclosure and reciprocity are natural ingredients of an ordinary relationship that is equal and mutual:

A young woman, shy and timid, begins in the third month of her analysis to evince unmistakable signs of believing she had fallen in love with me. Finally, after some days of struggling with her feelings, she tearfully confesses her love. Then she begs me not to treat this state of affairs in the same cold, analytic way I had treated her other emotions. She pleads with me not to remain silent and aloof. I should please say something, anything—it is so humiliating for her to be in such a position. She weeps and sobs and becomes silent. After a while I say, "I know this is very hard for you, but it is important for us that you express exactly how you feel." The patient is silent a moment and then says pleadingly and angrily: "It's not fair, you can hide behind the analytic couch, and I have to expose all. I know you don't love me, but at least tell me if you like me; admit you care a little, tell me I'm not just a number to you—the eleven o'clock patient." She weeps and sobs and is silent again. I too keep silent for a time and then say: "It's *true,* it is not fair; the analytic situation is not an equal one; it is your task to let your feelings come out and it is my job to understand you, to analyze what comes up. Yes, it's not fair." (Greenson 1967, 226–27)

In analyzing this patient, in my view, it would be more useful to explore the ways in which she experienced the analyst as unfair than to comment on the truth or falsity of her perception. Specifically, I might continue to investigate the analysand's psychic reality of the experience of "unfairness" (Hoffer 1993).

For purposes of this discussion, however, Greenson gives us a vivid (although otherwise unremarkable) example of the one-sidedness and asymmetry in the analytic relationship. If we look at the psychic reality not only of the analysand but also of the analyst, what do we find? Are the analyst's feelings less "real" than the analysand's? To judge the feelings in an analytic relationship as less "real" than those in an ordinary relationship posits, in my view, a false dichotomy. The thesis of this paper is that the analytic situation creates a pull—exemplified by this paradigmatic vignette—away from the asymmetry inherent in the analytic relationship and toward mutuality. This pull in turn generates an inevitable tension with which every analyst must come to terms. Freud recommended to Jung in 1909 that he develop a "thick skin" to protect against countertransferential sexual behavior with analysands (McGuire 1974, 230). Ferenczi, by contrast, devoted himself to removing any emotional wall that separated him from his analysands, which led to the extreme decision to reverse roles in his experiment with "mutual analysis." Can one be an effective analyst with a thin skin? With a thick skin? How thick should the good analyst's skin be?

Having discussed Ferenczi's challenge to Freud's principle of abstinence, the renewed emphasis on psychic reality, and the asymmetry inherent in the analytic relationship and the tension this creates in the analyst, I turn now to the topic of mutuality. I shall begin by reviewing the history of the relationship between Freud and Ferenczi and highlighting the polarity of asymmetry and mutuality, which is often referred to as that of authoritarianism and egalitarianism.

As late as 1930, Freud expressed dismay at Ferenczi's effort to push him into resuming Ferenczi's analysis in order to complete it. Freud had no interest in trying to make up for what had been missed in the past, urging that it be left to Ferenczi's self-analysis. Ferenczi's response in February 1930 conveys the flavor of their dialogue:

> The analytically open exchange in no way means that I want to push you into the role of analyst again and thereby give you up as a tried-and-tested, proven friend. My hope—which I believe is not unjustified—is that an analytically free exchange is also possible between reliable friends. I must confess that I would no longer feel right in the one-sided role of analysand. Do you think that such a mutual openness would be impossible? [1]

Indeed, as Judith Dupont points out (1994; see also Hoffer 1994), Ferenczi offered to analyze Freud in 1926, but Freud declined.

I want here to question Ferenczi's hope that an *analytically* free exchange is also possible between reliable friends. In my view, whereas a mutual openness is certainly desirable and possible between friends, true analytic openness requires a professional relationship that is necessarily asymmetrical because both parties must be committed to the analysis of the analysand. To attempt in a relationship to be simultaneously the analyst and analysand compromises both roles. When we come to consider Ferenczi's description of mutual analysis, we must wonder whether this represents an actual deep analytic process on his part or a countertransferential confession—a very different phenomenon. I seriously doubt whether truly free associations are possible in a mutual analysis (Rizzuto 1992) and submit that an authentic analysis requires an asymmetrical focus on the analysand.

Thus, although an analytic relationship can be similar to an ordinary relationship in the genuineness of the feelings as well as in its intimacy and uniqueness, it differs from the latter in its overriding purpose. Hence, what I consider to be the analysand's "real" relationship with the analyst promotes his or her self-inquiry and self-understanding. The inherent asymmetry follows from the *raison d'être* of the relationship, which exists for the analysand's benefit. However, that inherent asymmetry stimulates within the analyst a countervailing inclination toward a more symmetrical, more mutual relationship.

As noted above, the inclination of the analyst toward a mutual relationship with the analysand is taken to its logical extreme in Ferenczi's *Clinical Diary* (Hoffer 1990). In one notable case, he was pressed by a severely traumatized patient (who is referred to by the initials R.N., but was in fact Elizabeth Severn; Fortune 1993) in a stalemated analysis openly to acknowledge to her his unresolved countertransferential difficulties. Ferenczi was aware of his hidden hatred toward her. R.N. insisted that the only honest way to free the analysis from their impasse would be for Ferenczi to agree to be analyzed by her. With his characteristic candor and egalitarian tendencies, along with a willingness to experiment and take personal risks—and out of desperation—Ferenczi consented to reverse roles and positions. For a period of several months, he and R.N. took turns sitting behind the couch in a procedure that Ferenczi dubbed "mutual analysis." If we recall Freud's (1914) statement about the analyst's obligation to see to it that the patient's suffering not come to an end prematurely, we may contrast the following passage from Ferenczi's *Diary*:

Certain phases of mutual analysis represent the complete renunciation of all compulsion and of all authority on both sides: they give the impression of two equally terrified children who compare their experiences, and because of their common fate understand each other completely and instinctively try to comfort each other. Awareness of this shared fate allows the partner to appear as completely harmless, therefore as someone whom one can trust with confidence. (1932, 56)

The pull to mutuality that Ferenczi describes is familiar to all clinicians. In fact, his description of mutual analysis reminds me of the fairy tale of Hansel and Gretel with its two terrified children, bad witch, and eliminated parents. Ferenczi feels that such mutuality may be required to create a feeling of safety in the analysand. The sincerity of his efforts and the candor with which he reports them deserve our respect. In my opinion, however, a countertransference problem is one for which the analyst must take responsibility while attending to its impact on the patient. It is not a shared problem, and the purpose of analysis is not to provide mutual comfort; furthermore, I am convinced that the patient does not require this type of mutuality to feel safe with the analyst.

But if we step back and view Ferenczi's pull toward mutual analysis as a metaphor, we can acknowledge our wishes to comfort our patients and to be comforted by them by sharing the painful and frightening feelings that have arisen from parallel experiences. To recognize that pull while choosing not to act on it creates tension within the analyst. It is important that the analyst be aware of that tension and its sources.

Having considered the pull on the analyst to turn the asymmetrical analytic relationship into a mutual one, we can now pursue further the comparison between the nature of the "reality" in analytic and ordinary relationships. In "Observations on Transference Love," Freud declares: "It is therefore just as disastrous for the analysis if the patient's craving for love is gratified as if its suppressed. The course the analyst must pursue is neither of these; it is one for which there is *no model in real life*" (1914, 166). Freud here distinguishes the analytic relationship from all others; furthermore, he holds that it is so unprecedented that no model exists for it in real life. A strong statement! Could it be true? It is ironic that whereas the analyst is experienced in the transference as though he were a number of people—and hence models—in the patient's life, there is no model for what the analyst does. But Freud's statement is convincing because by being many people for the patient, the analyst is also *none* of them. He remains only the analyst in real life. And here again lies the source of the tension within the analyst. He is real, in a real relationship with the analysand, and yet there is no prototype for him in real life.

It is puzzling that Freud, after asserting that the love in the transference is indisputably genuine and real, advises the analyst to "keep firm hold of the transference love, but treat it as something *unreal*" (1914, 166). What does it mean to keep firm hold on something real, yet treat it as unreal? These contradictory statements reveal to us Freud's struggle with an unresolved—and perhaps unresolvable—paradox (Modell 1990). Is the analytic relationship real?

It is my thesis that in analysis the feelings and the relationship are as real as in an ordinary relationship. To pass judgments on what are "real" and "unreal" or transferential and nontransferential feelings distracts the analyst (and consequently the analysand) from the primary analytic goal of fully exploring the analysand's psychic reality. Such judgments may easily serve to create unwitting resistances to the analysis. To reiterate, what defines the analytic relationship is its unique purpose. The analytic relationship has an inherently unidirectional therapeutic aim that is lost if it becomes equal and mutual—that is, if it becomes "ordinary."

I am in essential agreement with the position advanced by Modell: "The psychoanalytic setting is designed to maximize the analysand's communication to the analyst but not the reverse. The analyst's emotional position vis-à-vis the analysand follows this asymmetry of communication in that the analyst reveals to the analysand only what is judged to be in the best interests of the analysis" (1990, 39). Modell elaborates:

Although this experiment [with mutual analysis] now strikes us as naive and imprudent, Ferenczi was struggling with therapeutic dilemmas which are still very much with us. For example, Ferenczi was confronted with the problem that it was hypocritical to withhold information regarding a negative countertransference; psychoanalysts had not yet discovered how a negative countertransference could be placed at the service of the patient's treatment. One of the patients with whom he experimented was someone whom he disliked but who, at the same time, had the transference illusion that Ferenczi was in love with her. By means of this mutual analysis Ferenczi was able to reveal to this patient certain antipathetic countertransference attitudes that were hindering the progress of treatment, and following his confession, the treatment did in fact move forward. (143)

Modell's conclusion recognizes the contemporary relevance of Ferenczi's struggles:

The matter of equality between analyst and analysand is still a current therapeutic issue. . . . This dilemma reflects the presence of two different levels of reality: the necessary inequality within the frame, which coexists with the equality outside of the frame. Echoes of Ferenczi's egalitarian concerns can be heard in Kohut's advice that the analyst acknowledge his own empathic failures, and Gill's objection to the concept that transference distorts, which assumes that it is the *analyst* who is the judge of what is real. (143)

Thus, the universal tendency to symmetry and mutuality *within* the analytic frame poses a continual temptation to the analyst to transform the analytic relationship into an ordinary relationship such as exists *outside* the frame. On a broader theoretical level, some schools of analytic thought that in my view advocate excessive self-disclosure attenuate the unique analytic relationship by turning it into a more ordinary one, which (while it may be mutually gratifying) lacks the therapeutic power of an asymmetrical analytic relationship. That power is most available when both participants can freely attend, with all the resources available, to a full exploration of the *analysand's* psychic reality.

In conclusion, the analysand's free association and the analyst's evenly hovering or "free" attention (Gardner 1991, 865) create a genuine, intimate, real, and unique relationship—one that is inherently asymmetrical because it is primarily for the benefit of only one of the participants. Judging whether transferential and countertransferential feelings are real or distorted distracts the analyst from helping the analysand to explore fully his or her psychic reality. My thesis is that there is a natural—indeed universal—pull toward symmetry and mutuality in the intimacy of the analytic relationship just as there is in all other relationships. Awareness of the tension that that pull creates alerts the analyst to the temptation to convert the analytic relationship into an ordinary relationship.

Unwittingly, the analyst may relieve that necessary and normal tension in the analytic relationship in two contrasting ways: (1) by increasing the asymmetry and distance through a withdrawal into a state of intellectualized detachment; or (2) by eliminating the asymmetry by making the relationship a mutual, ordinary one. I believe, however, that, like a rider on a bicycle built for two, the analyst should lean first in one direction, then in the other, to maintain the equilibrium necessary to keep the therapeutic process moving forward.[2] Awareness of the therapeutic value of this tension helps the analyst first to tolerate it, then to take notice of it, and ultimately to wonder self-analytically about it—especially if it should suddenly disappear. The *absence* of that predictable tension thus serves as a signal that the analyst has moved too far in one direction or another. My advice to analysts may then be a disheartening one—stay tense (but neither too much nor too little)!

In historical retrospect, the long-standing tension in the Freud-Ferenczi relationship can be seen to have arisen out of Ferenczi's struggle against its inherent asymmetry. Freud, on the authoritarian side, continuously maintained his seniority and authority as the father of psychoanalysis. On the egalitarian side, Ferenczi, in his wish to analyze Freud and in his experiments with mutual analysis, carried to an extreme the wish—present in both the analyst and analysand—to form a symmetrical relationship. If taken too far, however, both the positions of Freud and Ferenczi eliminate the tension necessary to propel the analytic process.

Recognition of the tension in the Freud-Ferenczi relationship, which I have elaborated as a metaphor for the inevitable tension in every analytic relationship, heightens the contemporary analyst's awareness of the dilemmas he or she confronts in each analytic hour. The analyst must be prepared to contain that level of tension internally in order to provide the analysand with an optimally therapeutic analytic experience. Because the analytic relationship is unique in its method, purpose, and ambience, we need self-awareness to avoid falling in the ditches of either intellectualized detachment or emotional overinvolvement.

NOTES

1. Quoted by permission of Dr. Judith Dupont. My translation.
2. To answer the question of who steers and who supplies the power would require another chapter.

REFERENCES

Dupont, J. 1994. Freud's Analysis of Ferenczi as Revealed by Their Correspondence. *Int. J. Psycho-Anal.*, 75:301–20.
Fenichel, O. 1941. *Problems of Psychoanalytic Technique.* New York: Psychoanalytic Quarterly.
Ferenczi, S. 1930. The Principles of Relaxation and Neocatharsis. In Ferenczi 1955, pp. 108–25.
———. 1931. On the Patient's Initiative. In Ferenczi 1955, p. 235.
———. 1932. *Clinical Diary.* Ed. J. Dupont. Trans. M. Bálint and N. Z. Jackson. Cambridge, Mass.: Harvard University Press. 1988.
———. 1955. *Final Contributions to the Problems and Methods of Psycho-Analysis.* Ed. M. Bálint. Trans. E. Mosbacher et al. London: Karnac.
Fortune, C. 1993. The Case of "RN": Sándor Ferenczi's Radical Experiment in Psychoanalysis. In L. Aron and A. Harris, eds., *The Legacy of Sándor Ferenczi*, pp. 101–20. Hillsdale, N.J.: Analytic Press.
Freud, S. 1914. Observations on Transference Love. In *The Standard Edition of the Complete Psychological Works.* Ed. and trans. J. Strachey et al. 24 vols., 12:157–71. London: Hogarth Press, 1953–73.
———. 1919. Lines of Advance in Psycho-Analytic Therapy. *S.E.,* 17:157–68.
Gardner, M. R. 1991. The Art of Psychoanalysis: On Oscillation and Other Matters. *J. Am. Psychoanal. Assn.,* 39:851–70.
Greenson, R. 1967. *The Technique and Practice of Psychoanalysis.* New York: International Universities Press.
Hoffer, A. 1985. Toward a Definition of Psychoanalytic Neutrality. *J. Am. Psychoanal. Assn.,* 33:771–95.
———. 1990. Review of *The Clinical Diary of Sándor Ferenczi.* Ed. J. Dupont. *Int. J. Psycho-Anal.,* 71:723–27.
———. 1991. The Freud-Ferenczi Controversy—A Living Legacy. *Int. Rev. Psycho-Anal.,* 18:465–72.

————. 1993. Is Love in the Analytic Relationship "Real"? *Psychoanal. Inq.,* 13:344–56.

————. 1994. Ferenczi's Search for Mutuality: Implications for the Free Association Method. An Introduction. In A. Haynal and E. Falzeder, eds., *100 Years of Psychoanalysis. Cahiers Psychiatriques Genevois,* Special Issue, pp. 199–204.

McGuire, W., ed. 1974. *The Freud-Jung Letters.* Trans. R. Manheim and R. F. C. Hull. Princeton: Princeton University Press.

McLaughlin, J. 1981. Transference, Psychic Reality and Countertransference. *Psychoanal. Q.,* 50:639–64.

Modell, A. 1990. *Other Times, Other Realities.* Cambridge, Mass.: Harvard University Press.

————. 1991. A Confusion of Tongues, or Whose Reality is It? *Psychoanal. Q.,* 60:227–44.

Rizzuto, A.-M. 1992. Personal communication.

Schwaber, E. A. 1992. Countertransference: The Analyst's Retreat from the Patient's Vantage Point. *Int. J. Psycho-Anal.,* 73:349–62.

Seven

Sándor Ferenczi: Negative Transference and Transference Depression

■

T H I E R R Y   M .   B O K A N O W S K I

(*Translated by David Alcorn*)

> My own position in the psycho-analytical move-
> ment has made me a kind of cross between a pupil
> and teacher.
> — Ferenczi, "The Principle of Relaxation
> and Neocatharsis"

In 1937, at eighty-one years of age and still possessing boundless intellectual curiosity, Freud wrote a monograph in which he attempted to define the principal obstacles to the successful completion of psychoanalytic treatment. Drawing on theory as well as more than forty years' experience as an analyst, Freud strove to elucidate the psychic forces that can give rise to deadlock or failure in these disastrous "interminable" analyses.

Among the examples Freud adduces to illustrate his hypotheses is the following analytic narrative:

A certain man, who had himself practised analysis with great success, came to the conclusion that his relations both to men and women — to the men who were his competitors and to the woman whom he loved — were nevertheless not free from

An earlier French version of this chapter, "Ensuite survient un trouble: Sándor Ferenczi, le transfert négatif et la dépression de transfert," appeared in Michèle Bertrand et al., *Ferenczi, patient et psychanalyste* (Paris: Harmattan, 1994), pp. 9–52.

neurotic impediments; and he therefore made himself the subject of an analysis by someone else whom he regarded as superior to himself. This critical illumination of his own self had a completely successful result. He married the woman he loved and turned into a friend and teacher of his supposed rivals. Many years passed in this way, during which his relations with his former analyst also remained unclouded. But then, for no assignable external reason, trouble arose. The man who had been analyzed became antagonistic to the analyst and reproached him for having failed to give him a complete analysis. The analyst, he said, ought to have known and taken into account the fact that a transference-relation can never be purely positive; he should have given his attention to the possibilities of a negative transference. The analyst defended himself by saying that, at the time of the analysis, there was no sign of a negative transference. (1937, 221)

As we know, Freud here refers to Ferenczi, and he is himself the analyst who is "regarded as superior." This is Freud's way of posthumously continuing the dialogue with his friend who had died four years earlier, in May 1933. Freud appears to be asking how it could be that Ferenczi, whose therapeutic skill was held in great respect by his contemporaries, should have come to reproach him with not having analyzed his *negative transference*. Indeed, Freud wonders further, how could this former patient and close friend have come to suspect that he himself had had *a negative countertransference response?* Are these complaints to be read as the deferred effects of a *negative therapeutic reaction?* How is one to categorize this residual hatred provoked by the analysis and the analyst, which remained undetected at the time? Ought he to have adopted a hostile "active" technique, so that Ferenczi's negative affect could have been made available for analysis? At the very least, Freud's compulsion publicly to narrate his analytic history with Ferenczi in "Analysis Terminable and Interminable" indicates that this misadventure had left a considerable impact on him and that he was still trying to think through its implications.

In spite of the inconclusive and even tragic end to the relationship between the founder of psychoanalysis and the man he once looked upon as his "Paladin and secret Grand Vizier," there can be no doubt about Ferenczi's exceptional importance to the history of the psychoanalytic movement. From the first years of his psychoanalytic vocation, Ferenczi's outstanding clinical gifts and his grasp of theoretical matters made him one of the few truly original thinkers of the time. Furthermore, the place he occupied beside Freud for the twenty-five years between 1908 and 1933 —

by turns pupil, disciple, patient, and close and trusted friend—meant that his authority was recognized throughout the psychoanalytic community. However, his standing with Freud changed almost imperceptibly during the last five years of his life until it became "exceptional"—in the sense that "the exception proves the rule." The technical modifications Ferenczi began to introduce in 1928 and the theoretical formulations to which they gave rise were deemed unacceptable by Freud, who saw them as subversive. From then on, disagreement and disharmony reigned, and the estrangement that ensued in the year before Ferenczi died was distressing to both men.

In 1920, a year that marks a turning point for psychoanalysis, first Freud and then Ferenczi began to appreciate the diabolical character of the repetition compulsion, which caused so many analyses—such as that of the Wolf Man—to become bogged down or end in failure. Faced with the clinical consequences of this compulsion, psychoanalysts wondered how it could be overcome or at least mitigated.

Ferenczi tried to find an answer through his own experience with "difficult" cases and the theoretical challenges they posed. In doing so, he put into practice some new variations in technique. From 1918 to 1933, he became increasingly involved in attempts to reevaluate and then modify the clinical setting, partly through what would nowadays be called "putting it on trial" (Cahn 1983). He began by proposing what he called the *active technique*. This failed, so he abandoned it in favor of the *relaxation technique* or *neocatharsis*. Freud remained suspicious of this trend because he regarded it as a step backwards that revived ways of thinking by which he had himself been tempted before discarding his seduction theory in 1897.

In this second phase of technical innovation, Ferenczi was confronted with complex transference situations, which cast doubt on the received metapsychology of the time. He interpreted them as a pure repetition of childhood trauma, and this led him to question the concept of trauma. He widened Freud's theoretical hypothesis about seduction and made a remarkable breakthrough. The etiology of trauma in Ferenczi's view is the *emotional rape* of the child by an adult, a *confusion of tongues* between them, due to the adult's *denial* of the child's *despair*. Ferenczi saw the essential question in his patients to be one not of the natural destiny of the libido but of extreme states of mental (and sometimes physical) pain—*the agony of mental life.*

As Ferenczi's thinking evolved between 1928 and 1933, a conflict with Freud became inevitable. A theoretical gulf opened up between them around the concept of infantile trauma. In Freud's view, to claim that the compulsion to repeat stemmed from a traumatic situation mistakenly rendered the object responsible and underestimated the resources of the mind to transform trauma and the mental pain associated with it. He voiced his objections to Ferenczi's theoretical regression in a letter of October 2, 1932: "I no longer believe you will correct yourself as I corrected myself a generation ago. . . . For a couple of years you have systematically turned away from me. . . . Objectively I think I could point out to you the technical errors in your conclusions, but why do so? I am convinced that you would not be accessible to any doubts" (Dupont 1985, xvii).

As Michael Bálint has pointed out, "the historic disagreement between Freud and Ferenczi acted as a trauma on the psychoanalytic world" (1967, 152). When Ferenczi died, a discreet veil was thrown over the matter, which was not lifted for over thirty years. This veil brought with it silence with respect to Ferenczi the man, reticence with respect to his work, and even a partial loss of memory about his importance to Freud. Above all, this attitude is symptomatic of the difficulty felt by both his contemporaries and successors in comprehending his prescient clinical and theoretical intuitions. Ferenczi was one of the founders of modern clinical practice, but it was necessary to await the passing of several generations of analysts before there could be a "return to Ferenczi" and a renewal of interest in the questions he raised long ago.

"From Unexhausted Springs of Emotion"

In the days following Ferenczi's death in May 1933, Freud wrote an obituary. He recalled the major role that his friend had played in the psychoanalytic movement and the tribute he had paid to him ten years before on his fiftieth birthday. But after reiterating his admiration for Ferenczi's "versatility and originality and the richness of his gifts" (1933, 227), and singling out *Thalassa* (1924) as Ferenczi's masterpiece, he added:

After this summit of achievement, it came about that our friend slowly drifted away from us. On his return from a period of work in America he seemed to withdraw more and more into solitary work, though he had previously taken the liveliest share in all that happened in analytic circles. We learnt that one single problem had monopolised his interest. The need to cure and to help had become paramount in him. He had probably set himself aims which, with our therapeutic means, are altogether out of reach today. From unexhausted springs of emotion the conviction was borne in upon him that one could effect far more with one's patients if one gave them enough of the love which they had longed for as children. He wanted to discover how this could be carried out within the framework of the psychoanalytic situation; and so long as he had not succeeded in this, he kept apart, no longer certain, perhaps, of agreement with his friends. Wherever it may have been that the road he had started along would have led him, he could not pursue it to the end. (229)

This note, quite different in tone from the previous one, clearly indicates that there had been prolonged difficulties in the relationship between the two men. These were due both to their theoretical differences and to Ferenczi's complaint to Freud about his *unanalyzed negative transference*. In his letter of January 17, 1930, Ferenczi claimed that this omission was at the root of the difficulties he had encountered in his own analytic practice:

What happens in the relationship between you and me (at least in me) is an entanglement of various conflicts of emotions and positions. At first you were my revered mentor and unattainable model, for whom I nourished the feelings of a pupil—always somewhat mixed, as we know. Then you became my analyst, but as a result of unfortunate circumstances my analysis could not be completed. I particularly regretted that, in the course of the analysis, you did not perceive in me and bring to abreaction negative feelings and fantasies that were only partly transferred. It is well known that no analysand—not even I, with all the years of experience I had acquired with others—could accomplish this without assistance. Painstaking self-analysis was therefore required, which I subsequently undertook and carried out quite methodically. Naturally this was also linked to the fact that I was able to abandon my somewhat puerile attitude and realize that I must not depend quite so *completely* on your favor—that is, that I must not overestimate my importance to you. (Dupont 1985, xiii)

Freud replied on January 20, 1930, that he was "amused to read certain passages," particularly those in which Ferenczi reproached him for not having analyzed the negative transference. It was, he observed, as though Ferenczi had forgotten that at the time nobody—not even the two of

them—knew that negative transference reactions were always to be expected. In addition, Freud went on, given the excellent relationship between them, it would have taken quite some time before that became
clear.[1]

At this key point in his relationship with Freud, Ferenczi clearly adopted
a different point of view from the one he confided to Georg Groddeck
eight years earlier, after a visit to Vienna, in a letter of February 27, 1922:

Pr. Fr. occupied himself 1–2 hours with my conditions; he adhered to his earlier
opinion that the main thing in my case is the hatred toward *him,* who (just like the
father at one time) had interfered with my marriage to a younger bride (now
daughter-in-law). Hence therefore my murderous intentions toward him, which
express themselves in nocturnal death-scenes (growing cold, moaning). These
symptoms are overdetermined by reminiscences of witnessing parental intercourse.—I must admit that it did me good to be able to talk for once about these
feelings of hate with the beloved father. (Ferenczi and Groddeck 1982, 41)

In view of this letter, how are we to read Ferenczi's 1930 complaint that
his negative transference was not analyzed? Is it a simple memory lapse on
his part? Or is it a more extreme form of repression based on a hard core of
negation and denial? A form of splitting? If such were the case, what would
be the effect of the destiny of the transference neurosis that at that moment
gave rise to such apparently unjustified complaints?

There is in fact neither contradiction nor paradox in these statements. If
we follow Ferenczi's thinking and his technical and theoretical formulations
from 1920 to 1930, it becomes apparent that *what Freud and Ferenczi meant
by the negative transference is of a qualitatively different order.* Negative transference in Freud's view develops through the vicissitudes of an essentially
paternal dynamic, while for Ferenczi it is *maternal* (Bokanowski 1979, 1988).
Their use of the same term inevitably gave rise to conceptual vagueness and
confusion. What is more, the negative maternal transference based on
primitive narcissistic conflicts and consequent difficulties with symbolformation had not yet been conceptualized. Ferenczi deserves credit for
having been the first to outline its metapsychological characteristics and to
attempt to describe what was at issue in the transference-countertransference situation.

Technical and Theoretical Issues in Ferenczi's Analytic Work

We can understand the importance of Ferenczi's developments only if we recall his analytic background and the context in which he began to practice. His career falls into two main periods. The first, from 1908 to 1918, represents his years of apprenticeship and training. With them came a particular type of relationship to Freud, which was all the more complicated because almost from the beginning Ferenczi was not only a disciple and heir to a body of doctrine, but he was also Freud's trusted friend and confidant. Yet after the masterstroke of "Introjection and Transference" (1909), Ferenczi put himself in the position of an apparently immature hopeful waiting for Freud to take him into analysis.

Despite the increasing urgency of his appeals, compounded by his romantic entanglements of 1911–12, Ferenczi had to wait two and a half years until, in 1914 and 1916, he received three periods of analysis, each of which lasted a few weeks. But the circumstances were awkward, and neither Freud nor Ferenczi felt that the latter gained very much from this experience, though both agreed that it was not to be dismissed out of hand.

The second period of Ferenczi's career spans the fifteen years of technical experiment, from 1918 to 1933. With hindsight we can see that he attempted to disengage from the transference to Freud and sublimate what he felt had been left unanalyzed in him. His innovations are also, as I have indicated, a response to the challenges that the repetition compulsion posed for analysts in the aftermath of World War I. Freud attempted to formulate ways of dealing with this issue in such key texts as *Beyond the Pleasure Principle* (1920), *The Ego and the Id* (1923), "The Economic Problem of Masochism" (1924), *Civilization and Its Discontents* (1930), and "Splitting of the Ego in the Process of Defence" (1938). Like Freud's, Ferenczi's solutions to the riddle of repetition took shape only gradually, but they differed radically in that they were primarily concerned with technique.

Ferenczi was a brilliant and indefatigable clinician. From his first years as a practitioner, he set himself the task of comprehending the limitations he came up against in treating the most intractable patients. His contemporaries regarded him as a "savior" and did not hesitate to send him patients with whom they had failed. A man of independent temperament, Ferenczi was bold, creative, undogmatic, and determined to maintain his freedom of thought and action. After a decade of analytic practice, he came to the conclusion that *clinical observation* and *experience (Erlebnis)* were inseparable. Insofar as technique was the indispensable offshoot of theory, Ferenczi thought that it should be shaped according to the demands of the treatment situation. The difficulties he encountered in his analyses—negative transference, resistance to and by means of the transference, narcissistic and masochistic attitudes, actings-in and actings-out—were regularly connected to the psychological configurations of his patients—severe character disorders, "as-if" and narcissistic personalities, borderline cases, etc.—and they led him over time to envisage a series of conceptions fundamentally different from the technique recommended by Freud and that had been practiced hitherto. Ferenczi's technical innovations can be read not only as modifications of the setting but also as *countertransference reactions.* Reaching deadlock in some cases, he was on the lookout for a different theoretical and practical perspective in his work.

Three distinct subphases in the development of his technique can be outlined: (1) the phase of *active technique* (1918–26); (2) the phase of *technical flexibility* (1926–29); and (3) the phase of *neocatharsis and mutual analysis* (1929–33), both of which were directly related to his concurrent thinking on trauma.

In the active technique, Ferenczi's technical innovations sprang from his realization that the difficulties met with in analysis derived from the way that patients sometimes cut themselves off mentally from their symptoms even though these were quite visible. Such patients could be regarded as partly "absent" from themselves; they had no self-representation of their symptoms. Ferenczi thought it essential to draw back into the transference character traits and even mental processes that, in spite of progress in the treatment, remained split off and encrypted; his aim was to weaken resistance and reignite analyses that had become bogged down.

Contrary to the received impression, Ferenczi intended that the patient and not the analyst should be the active party. By means of injunctions *(Gebote)* and prohibitions *(Verbote),* the analyst encouraged the patient to adopt an active stance, that is, to do or stop doing something. Thus, in contrast to the cathartic method, in which the lifting of repression caused a memory to emerge and stimulated an affect, the active technique facilitated the return of the repressed by inducing both action and the advent of the corresponding affect.

However, the unpredictability of the results and limitations inherent in the method rapidly convinced Ferenczi that the technique had little to recommend it. It considerably amplified the patient's resistance without bringing in its wake an increase in frustration or in deprivation, and indeed some patients seemed to welcome this heightened tension in order to satisfy their masochism within the analysis itself. The result was stalemate. "Contra-indication to the 'Active' Psycho-Analytical Technique" (1926) marks the end of this period of research. In this paper, Ferenczi criticizes both the method and its results. He observed that the increase in tension induced by the active technique represented for the patient a repetition of earlier traumatic situations that lay at the root of the neurosis. The change in perspective in this paper was the prelude to a completely different approach.

Having tried to shorten analysis through the application of the active technique, Ferenczi in his period of flexibility and experiment now proposed to lengthen it. His idea was to allow insecure patients time to develop a stronger narcissistic base that would not clash with the limits prescribed by the analytic process. The main technical feature, articulated in "The Elasticity of Psycho-Analytic Technique" (1928), was "benevolence," which implied a "countercathexis" of hatred. For Ferenczi this was a new approach to the countertransference; the analyst made himself available to the demands of the patient and flexibly changed his technique to meet the patient's needs.

Abandoning the gentler forms of active intervention, Ferenczi concentrated on what the patient appeared to be expecting from him as an analyst. His aim was to have empathy *(Einfühlung)* for his patient, thanks to the psychological flair that should enable the analyst to appreciate when and how to communicate something to the patient. Empathy joined with "kindness" was meant to convince the patient of the analyst's sympathetic attentiveness. "The analyst, like an elastic band, must yield to the patient's pull, but without ceasing to pull in his own direction" (1928, 95).

The problem remained of determining the limits of this "elastic" technique. How far should the analyst go with his patient? How could an appropriate atmosphere be promoted without repeating in the treatment situation the conditions that might have presided over the initial childhood trauma? In Ferenczi's view, an overly dogmatic adherence to "classical" technique might well do just that. By contrast, the analyst's unshakable benevolence toward his patient, regardless of the extremes of language or actions to which the latter might go, fostered the growth of trust because the analyst was felt to be reliable and not tarnished by "professional hypocrisy" (1933, 159). This in turn made possible an authentic and personal relationship between patient and analyst.

Such considerations led Ferenczi to envisage a permissive method of *relaxation* or *neocatharsis,* and he even went so far as to condone mutual expressions of physical tenderness similar to those between a mother and child. A new conception of trauma took shape in the years that followed. The four works that together form the main corpus of this innovative theory bear witness to Ferenczi's thinking during his final period. Two papers—"Child Analysis in the Analyses of Adults" (1931) and "Confusion of Tongues between Adults and the Child: The Language of Tenderness and of Passion" (1933)—were published during his lifetime; the other two texts—the *Clinical Diary* (1985) that he conducted from January through October of 1932 and "Thoughts on Trauma" (1934)—were posthumous.

Extrapolating from what he observed during psychoanalytic therapy, Ferenczi (1933) concluded that trauma was caused by the *passionate impulses* in adults, which arose in response to the child's search for tenderness and truth, and of adults' refusal to acknowledge the child's mental suffering. This is experienced by the child as a form of terrorism that hampers the development of independent thought. Trauma is augmented by the child's introjecting of the adult's (unconscious) feelings of guilt, which alter the loved object and turn it into a hated one. All these traumas can be reactivated and amplified by the analyst's rigidity during treatment.

The child who experiences aggression is overwhelmed by his defenses and resigns himself to his inevitable fate; he withdraws from himself and observes the traumatic event. In this state he may perhaps look on the aggressor as mentally ill, a madman whom he must attempt to cure. In this way, the child becomes a "wise baby" and his parent's psychiatrist. Excited and destitute, the child is overwhelmed by an excess of both external and, above all, internal stimuli. He has neither the means of discharge nor the capacity to think the situation through, and therefore finds himself plunged into deep distress. The child, Ferenczi hypothesizes, *identifies with the aggressor* and *introjects the adult's guilt feelings,* which augments his confusion. Superimposed on the *passionate love and punishments* inflicted by the adult is the child's *terrorism of suffering.* In this dynamic likewise lie the seeds of *passionate transference.*

With *mutual analysis,* his final technique, Ferenczi intended to improve the comprehension and resolution of all these problems created by "passionate" clinical situations. The technique is closely related to Ferenczi's conception of trauma (Janin 1988). Trauma results from a splitting of the ego. The split-off part, which is difficult to reach in analysis, exists in both analyst and patient and comes to function as a traumatic zone common to both. The goal of mutual analysis is to obtain release from this blind spot.

Yet once more Ferenczi had to yield to hard facts. This final technique ironically resulted in reinforcing the situation it had been designed to alleviate — the patient's being "seduced" by the analyst and the analysis. It was also unclear what meaning could be ascribed to such unfamiliar and obscurely organized material. To whom, patient or analyst, could it be referred? Ferenczi concluded that the countertransference predicaments he found himself facing in mutual analysis with difficult patients proved the *insufficiency of his personal analysis.* Hence his painful and bitter comment in his *Clinical Diary:* "Mutual analysis: only a last resort! Proper analysis by a stranger, without any obligation, would be better" (1985, 115).

Ferenczi's Transference Depression

The exemplary humility and analytic honesty in his *Clinical Diary* are tributes to Ferenczi's desperate attempts to explore as thoroughly as possible the experiences of countertransference and psychoanalysis. This document, originally intended only for his private consultation, contains a digest of notes Ferenczi made each day. But it can also be read as Ferenczi's *accusation* against Freud, the acme of his negative transference to and idealizing of the latter, with Ferenczi, a disciple of genius, demanding a *maternal form of reparation* through his technical innovations.[2]

From this perspective, "mutual analysis" appears to originate in Ferenczi's desire to situate Freud in fantasy in a preambivalent maternal role and receive from him something akin to *primary love*. The implication is that Ferenczi was in the throes of a *primary depression* that could neither find a proper outlet nor even be designated as such; therein lay the real source of his *transference depression* reactivated and buttressed by his relationship with Freud.[3] It could not be properly unmasked or allowed to develop—much less analyzed—simply because at the time the necessary conceptual tools were not available. But it was at the root of Ferenczi's need to try to work through what he regarded as an "unanalyzed" residue; and it is also what induced him in the 1920s to begin to put forward innovative conceptual developments that made Freud fear that he was being sidetracked into something far removed from orthodox practice.

What Ferenczi described as *negative transference* did not refer merely to the paternal imago. In using such a designation—he had no other available—he probably attempted to account for *a primary depression that Freud did not recognize*, which was transformed into a *transference depression* once his powerful affects were galvanized by the encounter with Freud, psychoanalysis, and the psychoanalytic process.[4]

Transference depression reveals, usually after several years of analysis, a particular kind of depression that repeats an *infantile depression*. The latter results from an abrupt abandonment by the caretaking object that the subject experiences as a calamity. The essential feature of infantile depression is that it occurs in the presence of an object that is itself engulfed by a mourning process. Up to that point, the infant possesses authentic mental vitality, but then is faced with a sudden cessation of the object's affective cathexis; a dramatic alteration—a mutation—of the maternal imago ensues. The happy relationship with the mother is brought to a halt and remains paralyzed. When the mother enters into mourning and decathects her child, mental life is transformed in a way that is experienced by the infant as *catastrophic*.

As the letters make clear, from the very beginning of their relationship

Ferenczi was involved in an intense idealized transference to Freud. No-body ever remained indifferent where Freud was concerned! This transference was accompanied by an immediate transference to psychoanalysis and its doctrine, which at that time were indistinguishable from Freud himself. In return, Ferenczi's remarkable capacity to turn to account the Freudian ferment was certain to attract Freud. From then on, an exceptional bond linked both men.

This dual encounter was truly a case of "love at first sight," reinforced by the many interests shared by the two partners. Freud realized that Ferenczi had an immense talent that would make him both a first-class practitioner and an eminent theoretician of psychoanalysis, and he could see also that Ferenczi was ready to devote everything to the battle for the cause. Ferenczi found in Freud a father who apparently would not hesitate to seek the support of a son and seemed able to endorse the latter's ongoing struggle for self-assertion and independence. However, Ferenczi—enthusiastic, sensitive, generous, hungry for recognition and affection, with his prodigious outbursts of spontaneity—sometimes came up against a lack of reciprocity on Freud's part. Although communicative and warm-hearted, Freud often withdrew behind a mask of aloofness, all the more because he hoped to find in Ferenczi a son who had *already* resolved a fair number of problems.

Their different ways of coming to terms with their sensitivity are echoed in their modes of thought. The relationship was such that at certain crucial moments a high degree of ambivalence was aroused in both protagonists. It was often in *moments of tension* that Ferenczi would seek Freud's help. He attempted *analysis by correspondence* and informed Freud regularly of the progress of his *self-analysis* in order to try to untie the transferential knots that he supposed to be the source of his difficulties with Freud.

Until October 1914, when Freud agreed to analyze him, Ferenczi's epistolary self-analysis was a substitute for an analysis that did not declare itself as such. Ferenczi's letters were really an urgent and repeated request for analysis by Freud. His use of correspondence for self-analysis reached its climax between 1914 and 1917, when it took over from the analysis he had had with Freud in 1914 and 1916. Yet for the first six years of their relationship, faced with the transference responses of this pupil who had become a friend, Freud did all he could to postpone the analysis, sometimes using their friendship as a justification. A combination of factors seems to have motivated his determination.

Dazzled by his disciple's clinical ability and exceptional capacity for introjecting theory, Freud seemed convinced that a mere *transference to theory* would be an adequate substitute for the *transference to him as a person*. In addition, the transference interpretations he offered—having to do with the father complex, sibling rivalry, and psychic homosexuality—were in Freud's opinion sufficient to account for the affects aroused in Ferenczi and so to give him support.

The countertransference situation was further complicated by Freud's own personality and plans for Ferenczi, which, after the disappointment caused by Jung, included his desire to establish him as a spiritual son and heir to the psychoanalytic corpus. Faced with his disciple's pressing demands for an intimacy that went beyond friendship, however, Freud seems to have tried to free himself from a tie that he felt was marked by passion and liable to become overwhelming.

As time passed, the cumulative effect of these factors weighed heavily on the relationship. One of the consequences was the reinforcement in Ferenczi of an *eroticization of his request for analysis,* as Freud's support became more and more equivocal and his pleas remained unanswered. Another was the insidious emergence of a *transference depression,* which could be neither recognized nor analyzed.

Three decisive features of the relationship between Freud and Ferenczi can be discerned from the outset. The first is what Ferenczi in a letter of April 5, 1910, called his "unsatisfied need for support" (Brabant et al. 1992, 157). This phrase evokes the deprived child *inside* the analyst, who feels depressed, dejected, and exhausted. Ferenczi likewise told Freud during their September 1910 tour of Sicily that he was counting on him for everything, just as a depressed child has every reason to count on his parents, especially his mother. This is why Ferenczi demanded absolute veracity and reciprocity from Freud, who must have felt somewhat perplexed.

The second feature is the sentimental "affair" between Ferenczi and Elma Pálos, his analysand and the daughter of his intimate friend, Gizella.

He found himself drawn into a *period of turmoil and confusion,* which occupied his letters to Freud from the end of 1911 through 1912. This "acted-out" *transference love* had a deep impact on the relationship between Freud and Ferenczi; it occasioned a revival of Ferenczi's epistolary self-analysis and his urgent appeal for help and support.

The third feature, which I shall mention only in passing, is Ferenczi's *hypochondria* in his relationship with Freud. One would be justified, I think, in calling this a *transference hypochondria,* given that Ferenczi's symptoms, fluctuating along with the mood of the letters, were an obvious mediating object in the transference between the two men.

"My Unsatisfied Need for Support"

During the American tour with Jung in September 1909, the teacher-pupil relationship between Freud and Ferenczi ripened into friendship. In the months following their return, Ferenczi felt depressed and lonely, both because of his celibacy and because of his psychoanalytic work. Confessing his "unsatisfied need for support," he sought to alert Freud to his personal problems and to induce him to accept a kind of analysis by correspondence. Freud, apparently sympathetic, nevertheless strove to table the issue and urged that Ferenczi resign himself to his lot. There followed an exchange of letters in which Ferenczi's disappointment is obvious, as is his unspoken hostility at feeling so little understood.

This situation, comprised of latent resentment that neither man could interpret, formed the backdrop to their trip to Sicily at the end of August 1910. During this journey, what came to be known as the "Palermo incident" took place. For the next twenty years it remained a landmark; Freud and Ferenczi would recall it whenever matters between them turned difficult.

Ferenczi reported the incident in a letter to Groddeck dated Christmas 1921:

For years we travelled together every summer. I could not open myself to him completely freely; he had too much of that "aloofness"; he was too great for me, too much the father. The result was that in Palermo, where he wanted to do the famous study of paranoia (Schreber) together with me, on the very first evening of work, when he wanted to dictate something to me, in a sudden access of rebellion I sprang up and declared that it was not working together if he simply dictated to me. "Is that how you are?" he said in astonishment. "Obviously you want to take the whole thing?" he declared; and from then on worked alone every evening, leaving me only the editing. Bitterness seized me by the throat. (Of course, I now know what "working alone in the evening" and "a tight throat" mean. I just wanted to be loved by Freud.) (Ferenczi and Groddeck 1982, 36–37)

This event set the tone for their trip, which lasted more than three weeks. For both, it was a disappointment, as Freud's letter of September 24, 1910, to Jung bears witness:

My travelling companion is a dear fellow, but dreamy in a disturbing kind of way, and his attitude towards me is infantile. He never stops admiring me, which I don't like, and is probably sharply critical of me in his unconscious when I am taking it easy. He has been too passive and receptive, letting everything be done for him like a woman, and I really haven't got enough homosexuality in me to accept him as one. These trips arouse a great longing for a real woman. (McGuire 1974, 353)

On their return, Ferenczi, fearful that Freud might feel resentment toward him, made the first move. Replying on October 2, Freud suggested that Ferenczi's disappointments were a result of his unrealistically high expectations:

You will believe me when I say that I think back about your company on the trip only with warm and pleasant feelings, although I often felt sorry for you because of your disappointment, and I would like to have had you different in some respects. Disappointment because you certainly expected to wallow in constant intellectual stimulation, whereas nothing is more repugnant to me than posing, and I then often let myself go in the opposite direction. So I was probably mostly quite an ordinary old gentleman, and you, in astonishment, realized the distance from your fantasy ideal. On the other hand, I would have wished for you to tear yourself away from the infantile role and take your place next to me as a companion with equal rights, which you did not succeed in doing; and further, in practical perspective, I would have wished that you had carried out more reliably your part of the task, the orientation in space and temporality. But you were inhibited and dreamy. (Brabant et al. 1992, 215)

Ferenczi was unwilling to leave matters there and tried on October 3 to plead his case by appealing to "ψα. candor." He wrote of his desire to establish with Freud a relationship of unreserved trust, as should exist "between two men who tell each each other the truth *unrelentingly,* sacrificing all consideration. . . . *That* was the ideal I was looking for; I wanted to enjoy the man, not the scholar, in close friendship" (218). Ferenczi then reported a dream in which he saw Freud naked, interpreting it in terms of the combined effects of his homosexuality and his desire for "*absolute mutual openness.*" He tried to convince Freud that his "ideal of truth" conformed to Freudian teaching and recalled a remark the latter had made that analysis was a "science of facts" (219). Ferenczi agreed entirely and urged Freud to draw its full implications:

The final consequence of such insight—when it is present in two people—is that they *are not ashamed in front of each other, keep nothing secret, tell each other the truth without risk of insult or in the certain hope that within the truth there can be no lasting insult.* If you had scolded me thoroughly instead of being eloquently silent! . . . I would have owed you a very large debt of gratitude for it. (220)

Freud replied in his letter of October 6:

Why didn't I scold you and in so doing open the way to an understanding? . . . I couldn't do it, just as I can't do it with my three sons, because I like them and I feel sorry for them in the process.

Not only have you noticed that I *no longer* have any need for that full opening of my personality, but you have understood it and correctly returned to its traumatic cause. Why did you thus make a point of it? This need has been extinguished in me since Fliess's case, with the overcoming of which you just saw me occupied. A piece of homosexual investment has been withdrawn and used for the enlargement of my own ego. I have succeeded where the paranoiac fails. (221)

But on October 12 Ferenczi insisted:

I do not want to give up hope that you will let a part of your withdrawn homosexual libido be refloated and bring more sympathy to bear toward my "ideal of honesty." . . . It certainly has also a healthy core.—Not everything that is infantile should be abhorred; for example, the child's urge for truth. . . . I still hold firm to the conviction that it is not honesty but superfluous secrecy that is abnormal, although I do admit that the former can be overly emphasized by infantile influences. I am grateful to you for every word that you say or write about my behavior, no matter unpleasant it may be. (224)

Freud registered Ferenczi's plea, but his reply on October 17 was just as uncompromising: "You are still asserting your point of view, and, I concede, ardently and with good arguments. But there is nothing obligatory in that. . . . It occurs to me that a paralyzing influence emanated from you to the extent that you were always prepared to admire me" (227). On October 29, three weeks after it all began, the controversy ended with Ferenczi's remark: "Why didn't you mention the 'shy admiration and mute contradiction' in Italy? Everything could have turned out differently" (231).

This episode reveals the sources from which, twenty years later, Ferenczi developed his influential technical innovations and ideas on trauma. The child's desire for truth—the *language of tenderness*—comes up against what the adult falsifies or leaves unsaid—the *language of passion*. This dynamic is at the root of trauma. By the same token, the reciprocal trust between analyst and patient is intended to free them from the traumatic effect induced by the hypocrisy of the "classic" setting. This conviction lies behind Ferenczi's creation in 1930–33 of the technique of mutual analysis (Bokanowski 1992).

"Turmoil and Confusion": Ferenczi and Elma Pálos

In 1904, Ferenczi began an affair with a married woman, Gizella Pálos, who had two daughters, Elma and Magda (the latter later married Ferenczi's younger brother, Lajos). The affair was more or less clandestine, because the husband, Géza Pálos, refused to grant a divorce. Gizella was eight years older than Ferenczi and could no longer have children. Elma was a much-courted young woman, somewhat flighty and incapable of a long-term relationship with any man who might take an interest in her. When Gizella worried about her daughter's emotional instability, Ferenczi, in a reparatory frame of mind, offered to analyze Elma. When he informed Freud of this, Freud wrote back on July 20, 1911: "I . . . wish you much practical success in the new enterprise with Fräulein Elma, but, of course, I fear that it will go well up to a certain point and then not at all. While you're at it, don't *sacrifice* too many of your secrets out of an excess of kindness" (Brabant et al. 1992, 296).

Despite this warning, Freud could not have guessed how quickly events would overtake his fears. Scarcely half a year had elapsed before Ferenczi wrote, on December 3, of the collapse of his analytic neutrality with his young patient:

I still have no right to declare myself mature. . . . I was not able to maintain the cool detachment of the analyst with regard to Elma, and I laid myself bare, which then led to a kind of closeness which I can no longer put forth as the benevolence of the physician or of the fatherly friend. . . . Perhaps in the end my sight was clouded by passion. . . . Elma became especially dangerous to me at the moment when—after that young man's [a former suitor's] suicide—she badly needed someone to support her and to *help* her in her need. I did that only too well. (338)

Freud's uncompromising rejoinder came on December 5: "First break off treatment, come to Vienna for a few days . . . don't decide anything yet, and give my regards many times to Frau G" (318–19). Thoroughly confused and distressed—"Of course, I myself cannot continue the treatment" (324), he wrote on January 1, 1912—Ferenczi sought a way out of his self-imposed deadlock and asked Freud to analyze Elma. Freud was reluctant, but agreed the following day: "If you do not ask about my inclinations and expectations but rather *demand* of me that I undertake it, then I naturally have to assent" (325).

During the three months that Elma was in analysis with Freud—from January to the end of March 1912—he and Ferenczi were in constant communication about her treatment. Elma was obviously an issue between them, just as her mother would later become. Freud had from the outset championed Gizella, not disguising his preference for the mother over the daughter. In 1912 the friendship between the two men was seriously put to the test by Ferenczi's interminable hesitations between Gizella and Elma. They, too, vied with each other in love and devotion for Ferenczi, and their declarations of affection for each other and lack of self-interest exacerbated the imbroglio. In a letter to Freud on March 8, Ferenczi admitted that his amorous difficulties were directly related to his unconscious hostile impulses toward Freud: "You were right when, on my first trip to Vienna where I revealed to you my intention to marry, you called attention to the fact that you noticed the same defiant expression I had on in my face when I refused to work with you in Palermo" (353).

However, overwhelmed by contradictory feelings toward both Gizella and Elma, Ferenczi constantly asked Freud's advice. The latter remained cautious, trying to play for time, and could find no other solution than to maintain an appearance of neutrality at all costs. When Ferenczi realized that he would obtain nothing more than he had already been given, he told

Freud on April 23 of his decision to take Elma back into analysis. In proposing such a course, Ferenczi's conscious aim was to enable Elma to express her real feelings toward him and thus to make up her own mind in the name of freedom of thought and speech. Freud remained ostensibly unruffled, replying on April 28: "I am in great suspense as I devour your news about the course of your family affairs. . . . Of all your misgivings, one has made an impression on me: whether your daily schedule and life-style have room for a young woman who is in love with life and not deeply interested in your work" (371).

Ferenczi took Elma back into analysis from the end of April until August. What he was trying to prove to everyone concerned was his ability "to resist the urgings of the passions and to regain the coolness of the intellect" (374). In this way he hoped to succeed in correcting "the mistakes that [he] made in the first analysis" (397), but in the end he admitted that Elma "is subjecting herself to analysis against her will, solely because of her hoped-for and impatiently anticipated marriage." Under such circumstances, as Ferenczi reported to Freud, he himself told Elma that "analysis was pointless" (402).

As he reached the climax of this struggle against his own passionate nature, Ferenczi claimed during the summer of 1912 to have recovered his coolheadedness:

I must confirm that my cruelty and severity toward Frau G. could be infantile revenge against my mother. . . . Along with this infantile desire for revenge, however, my behavior may also in part influenced by the fact that in the last four years, since I have been testing myself analytically, I have actually been carrying on a continuing struggle for liberation against my maternal fixation. (383)

It was at this point, when he accepted Freud's interpretation concerning his "mother complex," that Ferenczi put an end to his relationship, both analytic and sentimental, with Elma, who soon afterwards married an American called Laurvik. But this did not resolve his procrastination with Gizella, whose age remained a problem for him and whom he did not marry until 1919. Their married life never got over this crisis; Gizella, disappointed, remained torn between her erotic and maternal roles. Ferenczi's acting out of *transference love* reveals his primary depression and need for primary love, projected on to Elma.

Transference Love

When certain patients regress during analysis, they relive the early environmental deprivations that are responsible for the distortions of their ego or
self. When maternal and autoerotic deprivations have had too severe an
impact on the child's development, pathological and excessively passionate
transference can arise. The eroticization of the transference then becomes a
defense against fears of collapse and the sudden return of primary depression. The plea for "love" is an appeal for "linking" in the sense of reor-
ganizing something that causes disruption. Such patients make the analyst
experience their despair and distress; they want the analyst to feel the
misery and helplessness they were unable to symbolize during childhood.

The excitement aroused in the analyst by the patient's transference
projections, and in particular by the eroticization of the transference, tests
the analyst's superego organization. More fundamentally, it tests his capacities for linking and symbolization, as well as the resolution of his own
depressive position and desires for reparation. Analysis of the personal
and "cultural" countertransference, which restricts the analyst's ability to
understand, is essential. Otherwise the situation no longer embodies the
patient's suffering, but that of the analyst. An analyst suffers; he is in despair;
he can no longer identify what he is up against; he is overly excited and
feels helpless. The analyst suffers because inside himself there is a depressed
infant, disheartened and in despair. In such a case, in contrast to dreams,
there is no possibility of representation of the trauma. What traumas are at
work? What kind of absence of symbolization are we up against?

Unlinking overwhelms the mind. Despair enters the analysis in the
form of *primary depression* with its concomitant deceit, confusion, loss of
idealization and of any reverential aura. The issue becomes one of seeking
completeness with a sufficiently loving and good-enough mother who
agrees to invest her "primary maternal preoccupation"; there is a quest for
"reparation." The primary conditions of depression, involving deficits in
symbolization, are repeated. The erotic demand in the transference is an
attempt at relinking for both protagonists, who are faced with the abyss of
failure in symbol formation.

It was precisely at the time of his *transference love* that Ferenczi went through a *transference depression*. Freud lacked the conceptual tools that would have enabled him to deal both theoretically and practically with Ferenczi's bouts of inadequate symbolization related to maternal depression. By the double mechanism of projective and introjective identification, Ferenczi displaced on to Elma his hopes that Freud would take care of him.

In the tumultuous episode involving Elma and Gizella, in which love for the mother opposed that for the daughter, Ferenczi probably experienced the repetition of an infantile trauma that aggravated his inherent primary depression. In the same way that Elma asked him for reparation after the loss of her friend by suicide, Ferenczi constantly demanded reparation from Freud. In the years to come he structured his psychoanalytic writings around the idea of *damage to* and *reparation of narcissism*. By projective identification, he took on the role of the "good mother" in the psychoanalytic movement to compensate for his inability to introject a loving, tender, soothing mother who could contain and repair him. One of the Ferenczi's childhood traumas doubtless had to do with the mourning of his mother Rosa, who lost her one-year-old daughter Vilma when Sándor was only four years of age.

It appears wholly justified to hypothesize in Ferenczi a traumatic primary depression, reactivated and crystallized by Elma, a young woman in mourning, who reawakened the memory of a mother who also had been mourning a loss.

Primary Depression and Advances in Theory

In treating "difficult" cases, Ferenczi encountered stalemate situations that he ascribed to flaws in the countertransference; hence his attempts to relate them to his own emotional problems. His need to extricate himself from his transference to Freud and to resolve his difficulties through sublimation led him to sketch out experimentally many new concepts that are today looked on as fundamental. Thanks to Ferenczi, the sources of trauma can be related to the economy of "excess" and "deprivation" in mental life; identification with the aggressor is seen to stem from a traumatic fantasy of seduction; and "passionate" transference can be ascribed to a narcissistic (psychotic) splitting, which is a consequence of primary trauma. The splitting of the ego induced by trauma takes myriad forms: "dead" zones, division between the soma and psyche, paralysis of thought and spontaneity, loss of affect, "as-if" personality, and objectless depression. Ferenczi likewise drew attention to the importance of primitive love and hatred and understood that hatred was a more powerful means of fixation than tenderness. He stressed the importance of the environment—that is, the mother and her mental functioning, her aptitude as container, etc.—and the emotional imprints left by early caretaking. He grasped the role of play in analysis and the need to take the countertransference into account as more than an obstacle that "counters" the transference. He looked upon it as a phenomenon created in one mind through its encounter with another mind and that reflects some aspects of the latter's unconscious functioning. In other words, he elevated the countertransference—and its accompanying affects—into a valuable instrument for the analyst and the treatment. It is for all these reasons that Ferenczi has had a fundamental impact on psychoanalytic thinking and doctrine.

The passion inherent in Ferenczi's transference to Freud and the psychoanalytic corpus reactivated his latent *primary depression*. Given the inadequacy of the theoretical tools of the time to respond to failures in symbolformation, his primary depression turned into a *transference depression*. When Freud did not analyze this, it drove Ferenczi into distress, bewilderment, and hatred. In order to extricate himself from the transference, he was spurred on to invent new concepts. To distress corresponds the "wise baby," to bewilderment the "confusion of tongues," and to hatred the "introjection of the adult's guilt" that produces the "terrorism of suffering," splitting, and fragmentation in the child.

NOTES

1. In this letter Freud uses the same arguments concerning Ferenczi's lack of a negative transference that he would later put forward in "Analysis Terminable and Interminable."

2. On March 17, 1932, Ferenczi wrote: "My own analysis could not be pursued deeply enough because my analyst (by his own admission, of a narcissistic nature), with his strong determination to be healthy and his antipathy toward any weakness or abnormalities, could not follow me down into those depths, and introduced the 'educational' stage too soon" (1985, 62).

3. There is no doubt that Ferenczi's encounter with psychoanalysis, through and with Freud, aroused deep emotional impulses in him. These perhaps reactivated an acute "maternal conflict" because of his hypochondriac ("oral-narcissistic dependent") personality, which led him to adopt technical innovations related to maternal identification. See Grünberger (1974).

4. I use "transference depression" in the sense defined by André Green (1983). See also Miller (1983) and Janin (1988).

REFERENCES

Bálint, M. 1967. *The Basic Fault: Therapeutic Aspects of Regression.* London: Tavistock.

Bokanowski, T. 1979. Présence de Ferenczi dans "Analyse terminée et analyse interminable." *Ét. freud.,* 15–16:83–100.

———. 1988. Entre Freud et Ferenczi: Le traumatisme. *Rev. franç. psychanal.,* 52:1285–1304.

———. 1992. Sándor Ferenczi: La passion, l'analyse et les limites. *Rev. franç. psychanal.,* 56:683–99.

Brabant, E., E. Falzeder, and P. Giampieri-Deutsch, eds. 1992. *The Correspondence of Sigmund Freud and Sándor Ferenczi. Volume 1, 1908–1914.* Supervised by A. Haynal. Trans. P. T. Hoffer. Cambridge, Mass.: Harvard University Press, 1993.

Cahn, R. 1983. Le procès du cadre ou la passion de Ferenczi. *Rev. franç. psychanal.,* 47:1107–33.

Dupont, J. 1985. Introduction to Ferenczi 1985.

Ferenczi, S. 1928. The Elasticity of Psycho-Analytic Technique. In Ferenczi 1955, pp. 87–101.

———. 1933. The Confusion of Tongues between Adults and the Child. The Language of Tenderness and Passion. In Ferenczi 1955, pp. 156–67.

———. 1955. *Final Contributions to the Problems and Methods of Psycho-Analysis.* Ed. M. Bálint. Trans. E. Mosbacher et al. New York: Brunner/Mazel, 1980.

———. 1985. *The Clinical Diary of Sándor Ferenczi.* Ed. J. Dupont. Trans. M. Bálint and N. Z. Jackson. Cambridge, Mass.: Harvard University Press.

Ferenczi, S. and G. Groddeck. 1982. *Briefwechsel 1921–1933.* Frankfurt am Main: Fischer, 1986.

Freud, S. 1933. Sándor Ferenczi. In *The Standard Edition of the Complete Psychological Works.* Ed. and trans. J. Strachey et al. 24 vols., 19:267–69 London: Hogarth Press, 1954–73.

———. 1937. Analysis Terminable and Interminable. *S.E.,* 23:211–53.

Green, A. 1983. The Dead Mother. Trans. K. Aubertin. In *On Private Madness,* pp. 142–73. London: Hogarth Press, 1986.

Grünberger, B. 1974. From the "Active Technique" to the "Confusion of Tongues": On Ferenczi's Deviation. In S. Lebovici and D. Widlöcher, eds., *Psychoanalysis in France,* pp. 127–52. New York: International Universities Press, 1980.

Janin, C. 1988. À propos du "Journal Clinique" de Ferenczi. *Bull. Groupe Lyonnais de Psychanal.,* 11:27–34.

McGuire, W., ed. 1974. *The Freud/Jung Letters.* Trans. R. Manheim and R. F. C. Hull. Princeton: Princeton Univ. Press.

Miller, J. 1983. Ferenczi, "Enfant terrible" de la psychanalyse: Un aspect du transfert négatif. *Rev. franç. psychanal.,* 47:1165–76.

Eight

The Tragic Encounter between Freud and Ferenczi and Its Impact on the History of Psychoanalysis

■

MARTIN S. BERGMANN

As both the recent volume edited by Lewis Aron and Adrienne Harris (1993) and a series of international conferences attest, a revival of interest in the work of Sándor Ferenczi is currently taking place. One reason for this phenomenon is the appearance of hitherto unavailable documents that afford new insights. These include Ferenczi's *Clinical Diary* (1985), Freud's *Phylogenetic Fantasy* (1985) — discovered by Ilse Grubrich-Simitis among Ferenczi's papers — and the ongoing publication of the full Freud-Ferenczi correspondence. Beyond the confines of psychoanalysis, there is in popular culture, particularly in the United States, an urgent concern with the sexual abuse of children by adults. Among psychoanalysts Ferenczi was prominent in differentiating between actual seduction and fantasies. His attempt to blur the distinction between analyst and analysand through mutual analysis likewise has a special appeal to postmodernists. The interpersonal school of psychoanalysis, furthermore, represented in New York by the William Alanson White Institute, which is still excluded from the International Psychoanalytic Association, has discovered Ferenczi as its ancestor and through him sought to gain a new legitimacy in the psychoanalytic movement.

This chapter was read in July 1993 at the meeting of the International Psychoanalytic Association in Amsterdam and at the Fourth International Conference of the Sándor Ferenczi Society in Budapest.

In an earlier paper (1993) I have argued that psychoanalysis is in dire need of a better understanding of its own history. A more objective perspective may help to protect psychoanalysis from a "confusion of tongues" between different schools. In that paper I suggested that we need to differentiate between three types of creative psychoanalysts—the *extenders, modifiers,* and *heretics.* During Freud's lifetime there were only the extenders or loyal disciples, and the heretics who left psychoanalysis to establish their own schools. Only after Freud's death, when Anna Freud in her controversial discussions with Melanie Klein and her followers (King and Steiner 1991) failed to establish the authority of the founder, did the modifier emerge as an acceptable member of the psychoanalytic community. The first self-conscious statement of a modifier was Melanie Klein's avowal: "I am a Freudian but not an Anna Freudian." However, from a broader standpoint, Ferenczi deserves to be seen as the first modifier in psychoanalytic history.

The present chapter moves on two levels—the level of the personal relationship between Freud and Ferenczi and the level of psychoanalytic theory and technique. The first appeals to our human interest. We see two outstanding men working closely together and stimulating each other to productive work; then the hostile component of Ferenczi's relationship to Freud gains the upper hand. The rift could have been mended had Freud not been so deeply injured. We need to acknowledge also that Ferenczi wrote his most original work while he was rebelling against Freud. But the personal story, moving though it is, is not at this temporal distance the most important dimension. The controversy between Freud and Ferenczi touches on key issues of psychoanalysis itself.

No other collaborator, not even Karl Abraham, was as close to Freud as Ferenczi. Freud's *Phylogenetic Fantasy,* which he sent to Ferenczi in 1915, and Ferenczi's *Thalassa,* published in 1924, are closely related. In a letter written on April 8, 1915, Freud explained to Ferenczi the mechanisms of scientific creativity as a "succession of daringly playful fantasy and relentlessly realistic criticism" (Grubrich-Simitis 1985, 83). If we take this to be an implicit self-description, we might imagine that of Ferenczi as "utmost fascination with clinical details supplying the raw material for daring speculations." Ferenczi's flights of fantasy must have liberated Freud from excessive self-criticism, particularly during periods when his correspondence shows a deepening depression. A shared commitment to Lamarckianism also played a role in cementing their relationship.

In a letter of July 12, 1915, Freud outlined for Ferenczi the main ideas of his *Phylogenetic Fantasy.* He hypothesized that human life originated in a state of tropical bliss, where nutritional needs were satisfied with little exertion. This early state reappears in the various myths of paradise, often projected onto early childhood. With the advent of the Ice Age, libido was transformed into anxiety, an observation in keeping with Freud's theory of anxiety prior to the shift introduced in 1926 with *Inhibitions, Symptoms and Anxiety.* "What are now neuroses were once phases in human conditions." Freud concluded by assuring Ferenczi, "Your priority in all this is evident" (Grubrich-Simitis 1985, 79).

In 1919 Ferenczi wrote a paper, "Technical Difficulties in the Analysis of a Case of Hysteria," which even today is a model in its dealing with technique. He presented the case of a woman whose symptoms improved while she was in treatment, only to relapse when she left. The patient could not be persuaded that her erotic wishes were based on transference. She refused to search for the unconscious object of her desires.[1] Ferenczi prohibited her from crossing her legs during the hour, thus uncovering what he called a "larval form of onanism" (1919, 191). Further inquiry showed that throughout the day she eroticized every activity by pressing her legs together. Eventually this patient reached the capacity for satisfaction in normal sexual intercourse. Ferenczi was not yet advocating what he would call "indulgence," but an active technique in which the analyst forbade all masturbatory equivalents.

Freud's "Lines of Advance in Psychoanalytic Therapy," read in 1918 at the Fifth Psychoanalytic Congress in Budapest, was a response to Ferenczi's active technique. Freud divided treatment into two distinct phases. First, the therapist uncovers the analysand's resistances and makes the unconscious conscious; then he exploits the patient's transference to convince him that regressive processes adopted in childhood are no longer expedient in adulthood and that it is impossible to conduct life on the pleasure principle:

Does the uncovering of these resistances guarantee that they will also be overcome? Certainly not always; but our hope is to achieve this by exploiting the patient's transference to the person of the physician, so as to induce him to adopt our conviction of the inexpediency of the repressive process established in childhood and the impossibility of conducting life on the pleasure principle. (1919, 159)

This is an important historical moment. In 1919 Freud believed that psychoanalytic cure comes about as a result of both insight and love expressed in the positive transference. It is evident from this quotation that Freud no longer assumed that merely making the unconscious conscious would bring about cure. Because the patient has to be induced to adopt a healthier attitude at this juncture, the power of suggestion cannot be denied. Both Freud and Ferenczi were convinced that the neurotic has constructed his life according to the pleasure principle. Like a child, the neurotic has refused to accept the reality principle. Neither was aware of the full complexity that a neurotic structure presents to both analysand and analyst.

Ferenczi's influence on Freud is evident in the following passage: "Developments in our therapy, therefore, will no doubt proceed along other lines; first and foremost, along the one which Ferenczi in his paper 'Technical Difficulties in an Analysis of Hysteria' (1919) has lately termed 'activity on the part of the analyst' " (Freud 1919, 161–62).

Clearly, in the realm of technique Freud was willing to follow Ferenczi's lead. There is no evidence of tension between them. Aware of the problem, raised by Ferenczi, that many analysands cling to their therapists, Freud advocated conducting treatment in a state of abstinence. Furthermore, aware that the good achieved in treatment can easily become the enemy of the better, and that many analysands simply substitute an unhappy marriage or a physical illness for the neurosis they were forced to give up, Freud demanded that no basic decisions be made during analysis. He encouraged analysts to be active in preventing such substitute formations. "Cruel though it may sound, we must see to it that the patient's suffering . . . does not come prematurely to an end" (165). Many direct intrusions by psychoanalysts into their analysands' lives were later rationalized under this heading.

In subsequent papers Ferenczi reported he employed other prohibitions, such as forbidding the patient to use the toilet during the analytic hour. On one occasion he forbade a patient to have sexual intercourse. In 1924 he published a short paper, "On Forced Phantasies," where he recommended that in certain cases the analyst demand that the analysand produce even against his will aggressive or sexual fantasies about the analyst. All these papers were motivated by a wish to achieve better and faster results than Freud's technique allowed. Together they represent the first modification of psychoanalytic technique, soon to be overshadowed by that of Wilhelm Reich, who extended the analyst's activity even further in his advocacy of character analysis (Bergmann and Hartman 1976).

In 1927 Ferenczi published the first psychoanalytic paper on termination. In retrospect, it is significant that Freud did not include a paper on termination among his early works on technique. Before "Analysis Terminable and Interminable" (1937), his main contribution to the subject followed Ferenczi's idea of "active technique," as in his insistence that the Wolf Man terminate at a given date. Ferenczi states: "A neurotic cannot be regarded as cured if he has not given up pleasure in unconscious fantasy, i.e., unconscious mendacity" (1927, 79). Ferenczi here equates fantasy with mendacity. He advocated leaving the decision to terminate in the hands of the analysand. "The proper ending of an analysis is when neither the physician nor the patient puts an end to it, but when it dies of exhaustion. . . . A truly cured patient frees himself from analysis slowly but surely; so long as he wishes to come to analysis he should continue to do so" (85).

Reading this paper today, it seems to be written chiefly from the point of view of an analysand unpressured by reality considerations and wishing to enjoy an unending analysis. Ferenczi did not foresee the danger of an analysis creating a new equilibrium of forces in which the analyst facilitates an adjustment that makes termination impossible. The paper neglects the point of view of the analyst, who must always take the reality principle into account, and evidently idealizes the analytic process.

Ten years later, Freud was in part motivated to write "Analysis Terminable and Interminable" by the need to reply to Ferenczi's accusations. Without mentioning him by name, Freud quoted Ferenczi's allegations that he (Freud) failed to detect Ferenczi's latent negative transference and to analyze hidden problems in their relationship. Freud maintained that such an analysis would have been needlessly painful, that in fact one cannot analyze problems prematurely. By contrast, Otto Fenichel, in a posthumously published paper (1974), pointed out that latent problems are always analyzed. It is the analysis itself that actualizes what has previously been only dormant (Bergmann 1993).

A historian of psychoanalysis should not deny that during the period where Ferenczi became critical of Freud he also wrote his most original papers. Ferenczi's paper, "The Unwelcome Child and His Death Instinct" (1929), marked a new departure. In it Ferenczi was the first to apply Freud's death instinct theory to a clinical situation. He anticipated the finding of René Spitz on hospitalism by fifteen years when he wrote, "Children who are received in a harsh and unloving way die easily and willingly" (105). The human infant, unlike most animals, needs love to overcome the death instinct. He laid the foundation for object relations theory by pointing out that it takes an immense expenditure of love, tenderness, and care for a child to forgive his parents for bringing him unasked into the world. For this reason the greatest obstacle to cure in all psychopathologies is the imbalance between libido and aggression. Elsewhere (1992) I have applied this insight to the history of religion.

Ferenczi's last paper, "The Confusion of Tongues between Adults and the Child" (1933), was also revolutionary. He postulated that seductions of children are far more prevalent than has been acknowledged. Incestuous seductions by adults occur when they "mistake the play of children for the desires of a sexually mature person" (161). Seduced children, he maintained, introject the aggressor and attempt to gratify the wishes of these adults, becoming oblivious to their own needs. A dreamlike state develops in which the child is no longer sure whether the seduction actually occurred. This gives way to a traumatic trance that eventually succumbs to the primary-process distortions. Ferenczi stressed that seduced children accept the seducer's denial of reality, adapting to it at the expense of the development of their own sense of reality.

Ferenczi raised another disturbing problem. He postulated a stage of "passive object-love or of tenderness" and reached the conclusion that "if *more love* or *love of a different kind from that which they need,* is forced upon the children in the stage of tenderness, it may lead to pathological consequences in the same way as the *frustration or withdrawal of love*" (163–64). As his *Clinical Diary* further attests, Ferenczi saw infantile sexuality in a new light:

A large part of children's sexuality is not spontaneous, but is artificially grafted on by adults, through overpassionate tenderness and seduction. It is only when this grafted-on element is reexperienced in analysis, and is thereby emotionally split up, that there develops *in the analysis,* initially in the transference relationship, that *untroubled* infantile sexuality from which in the final phase of analysis, the longed for normality will grow. (1985, 75)

In my experience, to let the untroubled infantile sexuality emerge and flourish in the transference is very difficult. It is always complicated by the paranoid suspicions that all analysands who were seduced as children bring into the transference. Nevertheless, Ferenczi's formulation of the analytic task is admirable.

Freud's initial great discovery was his recognition that traumatic events—primarily infantile seductions by adults—were not always facts but all too often fantasies, and that in the unconscious fact and fantasy cannot be distinguished. Ferenczi returned to a traumatic theory of neurosis. He believed that an early blissful phase of the infant is typically interrupted by traumatic events. The task of psychoanalysis is to uncover this early traumatic state and lead the patient back through regression to the prior pretraumatic phase. From this angle Ferenczi defined memory as "a collection of *scars of shocks* in the ego" (1985, 111). Analysis must go back before the original splitting occurred to a pretraumatic time when the patient was still one with himself (1933, 270–71). To put it in Bálint's (1968) terms, Ferenczi thought, as Winnicott did also, that psychoanalytic cure can take place only in a state of regression. The problem of regression is still with us as an important issue in psychoanalytic technique.

Is this new hypothesis of tender love in conflict with Freud's and Abraham's tables of psychosexual stages? Does it negate the centrality of the Oedipus complex? These are serious questions demanding dispassionate discussion, but Freud saw in Ferenczi's observations only a return to the old seduction theory he had relinquished with so much inner struggle.

On a theoretical level, Ferenczi raised an important problem. Is the aim of psychoanalysis the acquisition of insights, in the sense that the analysand learns to understand why he became the kind of person he is and why he developed the particular neurosis? Or does psychoanalysis, in the person of the analyst, give the analysand a second chance to rework childhood problems with a new and different loving parental figure? In clinical practice both processes operate simultaneously, but the weight assigned to each differs in the emphasis of different psychoanalytic schools. We are here confronted with another major debate in psychoanalytic technique. Is regression indispensable for psychoanalytic cure? When confronted with seriously depressed, suicidal, or paranoid patients, is it desirable, or even permissible, to let them enter such thoroughgoing regression?

On December 13, 1931, Freud sent Ferenczi the famous "kissing" letter, the best-known document in their exchange:

I see that the difference between us comes to a head in a technical detail which is well worth discussing. You have not made a secret of the fact that you kiss your patients and let them kiss you. . . . You have to choose between two ways: either you relate this or you conceal it. The latter, as you may well think, is dishonorable. What one does in one's technique one has to defend openly. . . . We have hitherto in our technique held to the conclusion that patients are to be refused erotic gratifications. You know too that where more extensive gratifications are not to be had, milder caresses very easily take over their role, in love affairs, on the stage, etc. (Jones 1957, 163–64)

Freud admonishes Ferenczi that where he allows kissing, a more radical therapist will proceed to genital relationships. Freud may well have been right, but in fairness to Ferenczi we must say that he advocated only the kind of intimacies that take place between parent and child.

According to Ernest Jones, Freud was greatly shocked by Ferenczi's last paper and did his best to keep Ferenczi from reading it at the 1932 Wiesbaden Congress. In attempting to understand this conflict, it may be helpful to examine Freud's obituary of Ferenczi, written in 1933. Freud first described their early close friendship, their travels in 1909 to the United States, where he delivered the Clark University lectures, and Ferenczi's proposal for the formation of the International Psychoanalytic Association. He then recalled how, in 1923, a special number of the *International Journal* was dedicated to Ferenczi, and he praised above all Ferenczi's *Thalassa*. Freud then concluded:

After this summit of achievement, it came about that our friend slowly drifted away from us. On his return from a period of work in America he seemed to withdraw more and more into solitary work, though he had previously taken the liveliest share in all that happened in analytic circles. We learnt that one single problem had monopolised his interest. The need to cure and to help had become paramount in him. He had probably set himself aims which, with our therapeutic means, are altogether out of reach today. From unexhausted springs of emotion the conviction was borne in upon him that one could effect far more with one's patients if one gave them enough of the love which they had longed for as children. (1933, 229)

Freud's sadness at Ferenczi's last stage of development is obvious, but so is his belief that Ferenczi's endeavors were essentially motivated by a neurosis, especially in the oblique reference to "unexhausted springs of emotion." Freud's analysis of Ferenczi may have been correct, but the history of psychoanalysis shows that all heretics and most modifiers were criticized as being imperfectly analyzed and their innovations ascribed to resistances. Freud believed that Ferenczi's innovations endangered psychoanalysis, and, like every creative person, his commitment to his creation went deeper than any object relationship.

Ferenczi's feelings about Freud can be gleaned from his *Diary,* though we should remember that these remarks were not intended for publication.

He [Freud] could . . . tolerate my being a son only until the moment when I contradicted him for the first time. . . . The advantages of following blindly were: (1) membership in a distinguished group guaranteed by the King, indeed with the rank of field marshal for myself (crown-prince fantasy). (2) One learned from him and from his kind of technique various things that made one's life and work more comfortable: the calm, unemotional reserve; the unruffled assurance that one knew better; and the theories, the seeking and finding of the causes of failure in the patient instead of partly in ourselves. The dishonesty of reserving the technique for one's own person; the advice not to let patients learn anything about the technique; and finally the pessimistic view, shared only with a trusted few, that neurotics are a rabble, good only to support us financially and allow us to learn from their cases: psychoanalysis as a therapy may be worthless. (1985, 185–86)

Ferenczi maintained that analysands scrutinized their analysts much more thoroughly than analysts assumed. But when they note the analyst's weaknesses, they identify with him rather than criticize him. Ferenczi emphasized the hypocrisy inherent in the analytic situation:

We greet the patient with politeness when he enters our room, ask him to start with his associations and promise him faithfully that we will listen attentively to him, give our undivided interest to his well-being and to the work needed for it. In reality, however, it may happen that we can only with difficulty tolerate certain external or internal features of the patient, or perhaps we feel unpleasantly disturbed in some professional or personal affair by the analytic session. (1933, 158–59)

In his *Diary* Ferenczi pursued the same idea with less restraint: "While the patient is going through agonies, one sits calmly in the armchair, smoking a cigar and making seemingly conventional and hackneyed remarks in a bored tone. . . . In one or another layer of his mind the patient is well aware of our real thoughts and feelings" (1985, 178). He advocated that in such a situation the analyst should be candid with his patient about his emotions. Eventually this approach led to mutual analysis. The dilemma whether or not the analyst should tell the patient how he feels about him personally is still an important problem that separates psychoanalytic schools.

Freud accused Ferenczi of *furor sanandi,* an excessive zeal to cure, and Ferenczi reciprocated by accusing Freud of educating rather than analyzing. This accusation would surface again in Melanie Klein's controversy with Anna Freud. As a former patient, Ferenczi was aware of the analysand's capacity accurately to discern the analyst's negative feelings expressed by boredom, irritation, or falling asleep when his complexes are stimulated. Reversing the stand he took in 1927, Ferenczi in his *Diary* accused psychoanalysts of prolonging analysis for financial gain and turning patients into "taxpayers for life" (1985, 199).

Freud stressed the principle of abstinence; Ferenczi, the principle of relaxation. Ferenczi felt that greater responsiveness on the part of the analyst could prevent a lifeless and drawn-out analysis. In his view, all patients who asked for psychoanalytic help should receive it. It is the analyst's task to discover the specific technique necessary for cure. Ferenczi disregarded Freud's differentiation between narcissistic and transference neuroses. He did not believe in any criteria of analyzability. The analogy with Moses, with whom Freud was so strongly identified, is appropriate here. Freud offered his analysands a form of secular salvation, provided they could live up to certain requirements: free associations, remembering and not reenacting, and willingness to analyze the transference. Ferenczi, by contrast, offered his analysands unconditional understanding and a right to find their own path to cure. In my view, it is hard enough to be a creative analyst on Freud's model; it is next to impossible to live up to Ferenczi's.

Ferenczi maintained that when the analyst ascribes his own shortcomings to transference reactions on the part of the patient, he damages the patient in three ways: (1) he injures the analysand's capacity to test reality; (2) he behaves like the rationalizing parent in the analysand's infancy; and (3) he demonstrates his lack of courage and reinforces the resistances of the analysand by demonstrating that free associations are not really possible, even within the analytic situation. Patients then surmise that the psychoanalytic relationship is no more based on truth than are other human relationships.

Reflections on the Controversy

I have included the word *tragic* in the title of this chapter because the break between Freud and Ferenczi was painful to both men. Neither could transcend the role allotted to him by history. For us, the heirs to their controversy, the results have also been tragic. Instead of fostering two complementary lines of research and therapy, in which the differences are permitted to emerge and become clarified, a rigid polarity of either/or set in. Observing the events from a distance, one can see that they mirror many of the later problems in the development of psychoanalysis.

Ferenczi was the first psychoanalyst who also experienced himself as an analysand and who suffered a premature interruption of his treatment. Like many patients in that position, he became hostile toward his former analyst. He yearned for greater mutuality in his analysis with Freud. Once, in 1926, he even offered to go to Vienna and analyze Freud, who at that time had developed psychosomatic symptoms and become depressed. Ferenczi's unmastered yearnings did not find sublimation, and the mutual analysis he could not achieve with Freud he later attempted with some of his patients. In Freud's defense, one can say that even had he been willing to continue analyzing Ferenczi, the intimate relationship between the two and the fact that Ferenczi had knowledge of Freud's personal traits would have made it impossible.

Earlier I alluded to recent biographical material about Freud's childhood. Josef Sajner (1968), Harry Hardin (1987, 1988) and Ilse Grubrich-Simitis (1991) have changed our view of Freud's early years. While Freud presented himself as the golden child, the firstborn to a young mother, these biographers have pointed out that his early years contained many traumatic events, including the deaths of his brother and uncle, both named Julius. These events must have affected Freud's mother significantly during a decisive period of his infantile development; his nanny's arrest for theft and the crowded living conditions in Freiberg, where the whole family shared one room, must have added to the emotional difficulties. It seems that Freud himself, in his self-analysis, could not penetrate back to these years. Instead he created what Ernst Kris (1956) has called a "personal myth." This defensive structure prevented Freud from returning to his own early years, as his analysis of Ferenczi, who likewise had many siblings and grew up in crowded conditions, demanded.[2]

It is beyond the scope of this chapter to trace the impact—direct and indirect—of Ferenczi on subsequent developments within psychoanalysis, but I wish to highlight a particular moment. In 1961 Leo Stone delivered a Freud Anniversary Lecture, "The Analytic Situation." By that time, the idea that love plays a role in the analytic process of cure was anathema within the orbit of the American Psychoanalytic Association. Stone attempted to redress the balance:

I do not believe that any patient can ever, except in a morbid sense, accept even the possibility (not to speak of the fact) that the analyst is not all interested in the course of his personal life or his illness. . . . Whereas purely technical or intellectual errors can, in most instances, be corrected, a failure in a critical juncture to show the reasonable human response which any person inevitably expects from another on whom he deeply depends, can invalidate years of patient and largely skillful work. (1961, 55)

Nevertheless, Stone took pains to disassociate himself from Ferenczi. He accused Ferenczi of disregarding the difference between the traumatized child and the adult undergoing psychoanalysis and assuming that the two were interchangeable (58). He also believed that Ferenczi's demand that the analyst show love was incompatible with an honest and emotionally healthy attitude. I believe that such disclaimers serve essentially to maintain group cohesion within a given psychoanalytic school. Similar reactions can be found when ego analysts find something useful in the work of Melanie Klein. A kernel of truth can be granted to a modifier, but it has to be followed by massive criticism.

What are the larger implications of this controversy for our understanding of psychoanalysis? Elsewhere (1993) I have suggested that, unlike the discoveries of Darwin and Copernicus, with whom Freud identified himself, there was nothing inevitable in the discovery of psychoanalysis. Had Freud not lived, quite different techniques of coping with hysterical patients and psychoneuroses would have been established. Ferenczi was one of Freud's first pupils to show that the technique Freud devised was not the only one that can be used in helping to ameliorate neurotic suffering.

Thus, Freud's discoveries and Freud's technique of healing are not identical. By stressing how the child is received and valued by the parent, Ferenczi originated the object relations school of psychoanalysis. We may assume that the history of psychoanalysis would have taken another course had Freud feared less for its future and been more open to other investigations. But history cannot be undone. Psychoanalytic technique is so complex that, with hindsight, we can see that both Freud and Ferenczi captured a part of the truth. In retrospect, we can sympathize with both and, I hope, narrow the gap between Freud's focus on intrapsychic conflict and Ferenczi's empathy with the child who did not obtain from his parents what he needed for a happy childhood and productive adulthood. Ferenczi emphasized reliving the past with an understanding and even loving parental substitute. The idea of the analyst as a substitute parent led Ferenczi to permit the usual intimacies that take place between parent and child. Not the sexual intimacies between two adults! Freud did not believe that this line of demarcation could be maintained.

Ferenczi's method demanded a deeper regression to bring about the acceptance of the analyst as a new primary parental figure. Freud's technique relied heavily on the ability of insight to bring about cure. Psychoanalytic experience has shown that, when it is skillfully done, the establishment of new connections between past and present will usually bring relief. There is, however, another aspect that I believe Freud did not fully appreciate. I became aware of its role in my work with Holocaust survivors (Bergmann and Jucovy 1982). Those who have suffered major trauma as children or adults cannot expect to be cured by insight alone. They have to mourn what was taken away from them and will never be replaced. We may paraphrase Freud by saying that, aided by their therapists, such patients must learn to transform depressive feelings and melancholia into ordinary mourning. Ferenczi's method tends to avoid the need to mourn.

Some psychoanalysts belong to Freud's camp, and others to Ferenczi's. Still others use a mixture of both approaches. I present these reflections on an early chapter in the history of psychoanalysis in the hope that they will help forestall orthodoxy and a premature closure of issues that should remain open until they can be discussed on less partisan lines.

NOTES

1. As I have argued elsewhere (1993), the dangers of eroticized transference haunted early psychoanalytic writings on technique.

2. For a different interpretation, which holds that Freud in his self-analysis did reach preoedipal problems, see Blum (1977).

REFERENCES

Aron, L., and A. Harris, eds. 1993. *The Legacy of Sándor Ferenczi.* Hillsdale, N.J.: Analytic Press.

Bálint, M. 1968. *The Basic Fault: Therapeutic Aspects of Regression.* London: Tavistock.

Bergmann, M. S. 1992. *In the Shadow of Moloch: The Sacrifice of Children and Its Impact on Western Religions.* New York: Columbia University Press.

———. 1993. Reflections on the History of Psychoanalysis. *J. Am. Psychoanal. Assn.,* 41:929–55.

Bergmann, M. S., and F. R. Hartman. 1976. *The Evolution of Psychoanalytic Technique.* New York: Columbia University Press, 1990.

Bergmann, M. S., and M. E. Jucovy. 1982. *Generations of the Holocaust.* New York: Columbia University Press, 1990.

Blum, H. P. 1977. The Prototype of Preoedipal Reconstruction. *J. Am. Psychoanal. Assn.,* 25:757–85.

Fenichel, O. 1974. A Review of Freud's "Analysis Terminable and Interminable." *Int. Rev. Psychoanal.,* 1:109–16.

Ferenczi, S. 1919. Technical Difficulties in the Analysis of a Case of Hysteria. In *Further Contributions to the Theory and Practice of Psycho-Analysis,* pp. 189–97. Ed. J. Rickman. Trans. J. I. Suttie et al. New York: Brunner/Mazel, 1980.

———. 1927. The Problem of Termination of the Analysis. In Ferenczi 1955, pp. 77–86.

———. 1929. The Unwelcome Child and His Death Instinct. In Ferenczi 1955, pp. 102–7.

———. 1933. Confusion of Tongues between Adults and the Child. In Ferenczi 1955, pp. 156–67.

———. 1955. *Final Contributions to the Problems and Methods of Psycho-Analysis.* Ed. M. Bálint. Trans. E. Mosbacher et al. New York: Brunner/Mazel, 1980.

———. 1985. *The Clinical Diary of Sándor Ferenczi.* Ed. J. Dupont. Trans. M. Bálint and N. Z. Jackson. Cambridge, Mass.: Harvard University Press, 1988.

Freud, S. 1919. Lines of Advance in Psychoanalytic Therapy. In *The Standard Edition of the Complete Psychological Works.* Ed. and trans. J. Strachey et al. 24 vols., 17:159–68. London: Hogarth Press, 1954–73.

———. 1933. Sándor Ferenczi. *S.E.,* 19:267–69.

———. 1985. *A Phylogenetic Phantasy: Overview of the Transference Neuroses.* Ed. I. Grubrich-Simitis. Trans. A. Hoffer and P. T. Hoffer. Cambridge, Mass.: Harvard University Press, 1987.

Grubrich-Simitis, I. 1985. Metapsychology and Metabiology. In Freud 1985, pp. 73–107.

———. 1991. *Freuds Moses-Studie als Tagtraum.* Munich: Verlag Internationale Psychoanalyse.

Hardin, H. T. 1987. On the Vicissitudes of Freud's Early Mothering: I. Early Environmental Loss. *Psychoanal. Q.,* 56:628–43.

———. 1988. On the Vicissitudes of Freud's Early Mothering: II. Alienation from His Biological Mother. *Psychoanal. Q.,* 57:72–86.

Jones, E. 1957. *The Life and Work of Sigmund Freud.* Vol. 3. New York: Basic Books.

King, P., and R. Steiner, eds. 1991. *The Freud-Klein Controversies 1941–45.* London: Tavistock.

Kris, E. 1956. The Personal Myth: A Problem in Psychoanalytic Technique. In *Selected Papers,* pp. 272–300. New Haven: Yale University Press, 1975.

Sajner, J. 1968. Sigmund Freuds Beziehungen zu seinem Geburtsort Freiberg. *Clio Medica,* 3:167–80.

Stone, L. 1961. *The Psychoanalytic Situation.* New York: International Universities Press.

Nine

Ferenczi's Mother Tongue

■

K A T H L E E N   K E L L E Y - L A I N É

> Words are magical in the way they affect the minds
> of those who use them. "A mere matter of words"
> we say contemptuously, forgetting that words have
> power to mould men's thinking, to canalize their
> feelings, to direct their willing and acting. Conduct
> and character are largely determined by the nature
> of the words we use to discuss ourselves and the
> world around us.
> —Aldous Huxley, *Words and Their Meanings*

We are all familiar with the wonderful image of a baby captured by its mother's words and gazing at her face with its mouth wide open. The baby is drinking the sounds and swallowing the words; it is ingesting the milk of the "mother tongue."

The nature and importance of these first words and their indelible effects on the human psyche are often forgotten in later years along with our preverbal experiences. The consolidation of linguistic skills tends to relegate the accumulated impressions of our earliest years to a realm of somatic and affective memory to which we can only gain access through moods and feeling states. We tend to accept these aspects of our individual being,

This chapter was presentd at the Fourth International Conference of the Sándor Ferenczi Society, Budapest, July 1993.

including the language we speak, as parts of our natural environment in the same way that we do the air we breathe.

Paradoxically, however, if the acquisition of one language causes us to take this state of affairs for granted, the learning of a second or third may help us to become conscious of the power not only of our mother tongue but also of the preverbal realm that underlies it. The experience of speaking a foreign language brings with it a sense of cultural distance that is invaluable in fostering an awareness that reality can be constructed in different ways.

The subject of this chapter is charged with personal meaning for me. As is true of many Hungarians who left their native land early in life, to me Hungarian has remained my true "mother tongue" in that it was not contaminated by the public experiences of school, social life, etc. Hungarian was the private and intimate language of the home, parent-child relationships, and my emotions. Growing up, the maturing ego, and sexual relationships all went on in another language.

This kind of "bilingual splitting" has significant effects on psychic development and the way that repression and defenses are organized. One could say that the "mother tongue" retains id-like qualities and the subsequent language takes on the valence of the superego. Christian Flavigny (1988) posits the existence of a "maternal pole" of language and analyzes the development of the echoing relationship between mother and child. He notes that the mother's first words are addressed to a "you" who is in fact herself and that little by little, through her desire to understand her child, she is led to realize that her baby is in fact an "alter ego" in the process of becoming a separate person. In a striking etymological analogue to this idea, the word for child in Hungarian is *gyerek,* which means literally "he or she who comes."

It is through these first interactions based on the mother's intentions (L. *intendere,* "to stretch out") and comprehension (L. *cum prehendere,* "to seize with") that the meaning of words and their symbolic significance are born. Symbolic meaning emerges gradually as the baby passes from simply echoing the sounds of the mother's voice to imitating her words and constructing his or her own. The combination of sounds, gestures, odor, and touch invest these first words with the feelings and emotions of "mother." The birth of the sense of "self" is intimately linked to the construction of symbolic meaning. According to André Green, "Our mother tongue creates roots within us that can never be destroyed, because they are the foundations of our very substance; they contain the memories that anchor us to the 'mother' through the pleasure of repetition" (1984, 119).

Freud states in his *Introductory Lectures* (1916–17, 207) that once the mother becomes a whole object for the child, the process of repression has already begun. No sooner does the child become aware of this first love than it is already lost; and like any lost paradise, it leaves behind a bittersweet nostalgic memory. The mother tongue becomes the indelible mark of this first love, which may be the reason why one can never be truly bilingual.

The urge to recapture this original maternal tenderness exerts an influence throughout adult life and is particularly strong at crucial moments of emotional development. Even when the mother is long gone, the style and structure imprinted by her way of handling the infant remain, and the quest for these memories must necessarily proceed through the words associated with them. But when exile or other traumatic events cause the original linguistic milieu to be lost and the mother tongue to become inaccessible, the consequences for the psyche can be disastrous.

Ralph Greenson (1950) presents the case of a bilingual patient to investigate the conscious and unconscious factors influencing attitudes toward language and speech. Following Freud, who links visual thinking to the primary process, Greenson holds that words, like images, originally have a hallucinatory quality and are believed by children to have the magical power of wish-fulfillment. During the maturational process with its attendant ego development, the child gradually learns to distinguish words from both images and thoughts and gains the capacity for abstract reasoning.

Children routinely treat words as though they were objects, and adults continue to do so in dreams. Greenson cites Ferenczi (1911) to argue that obscene words retain a close tie to visual imagery and the primary process. For purposes of communication, most words lose this hallucinatory component in order to facilitate their more efficient use.

The exception to this rule, according to Greenson, occurs when the images associated with words concern situations of conflict. These words then remain the living bearers of unresolved memories. A second language may then assume superego qualities and help to repress early conflicts and incestuous feelings. By thus keeping oedipal conflicts in check, however, the new language maintains the individual's unconscious fixation on the pregenital mother.

Ferenczi's mother tongue was Hungarian, but he communicated with his mentor, Freud, in German, the language of the Austrian overlords. During Ferenczi's childhood, moreover, Hungarian was not recognized as an official language in the Austro-Hungarian Empire, and all instruction and political communication took place in German.

In view of this political context, I surmise that Ferenczi was caught between two languages—Hungarian, his mother tongue, a non-Indo-European language spoken only by the indigenous people and regarded as vulgar; and German, the paternal tongue of the rulers and the intellectual elite of the time. Freud, of course, invented psychoanalysis in German. According to G. A. Goldschmidt (1988), German "oriented" Freud, and psychoanalysis would not have been the same conceptually in another language.

I wish to propose a hypothesis concerning the impact of this "bilingual splitting" on Ferenczi's psychoanalytic thinking. Elsewhere (1992) I have tried to link the Hungarian language with the prescient concern of the Hungarian psychoanalytic school with the primary relationship between mother and child. I believe that Hungarian remained for Ferenczi the mother tongue in his relationship to Freud, that is, the language encapsulating early childhood conflicts as well as the lost pregenital mother. The isolation and repression of these conflicts was enhanced in his initial encounters with Freud, who served as a father-figure and spoke German, the language of authority.

Ferenczi's early loss of his father when he himself was fifteen years old doubtless heightened his sensitivity to German as a *Vatersprache,* and the promise held out to him by analysis surely included the hope of strengthening an ego in danger of being taken over by an all-powerful *Urmutter.* For Ferenczi, as for Beckett (Casement 1982), the best way of separating from "mother" may have been to immerse himself in a foreign language. However, given Ferenczi's passionate desire for truth and the probing nature of his psychoanalytic thought, it was impossible for him to suppress the function of the mother tongue. It is in the "split-off" realm of the Hungarian language that Ferenczi made his original psychoanalytic discoveries and broke away from Freud's authority.

A compelling illustration of how Hungarian functioned as a psychic refuge for Ferenczi is provided by his letter of December 26, 1912, to Freud. After acknowledging his feelings of rivalry with Jung, Ferenczi tells Freud about a recent dream and reveals some intimate early memories about his mother: "As a small boy I had a colossal un . . . . rage against my mother, who was too strict with me; the fantasy of murder (which I don't remember with certainty) was immediately turned toward my own person" (Brabant et al. 1992, 452). The word that Ferenczi is unable to remember in German and can only express in Hungarian is *tehetetlen,* meaning "impotent" or "powerless." He continues: "But the German word still escapes me! Substitute words: without result, gagged, lost labour (?), Love's Labour's Lost." Ferenczi seems to imply that writing in German is a lost labor, as opposed to the profound unconscious mother tongue.

The phrase "lost labour" appears in English in Ferenczi's letter, and "Love's Labour's Lost" is of course an allusion to Shakespeare. In a recent article, Brigitte Galtier (1994) analyzes Ferenczi's *Clinical Diary* from the standpoint of his use of various languages, especially English. She cites (98) a July 19, 1932, passage in which Ferenczi writes: "In opposition to Freud I developed to an exceptional degree a capacity for *humility*," where "humility" appears in English, and suggests that "to relax for this analyst is achieved through relaxing his tongue by means of another language." Galtier, however, does not discuss the role of the mother tongue and its role in the repression of early conflicts; and, in my opinion, Ferenczi's use of English as a third language to express his "conscious" opposition to Freud does not involve the earlier intrapsychic processes affected by the traumas that lead to "bilingual splitting." This phenomenon is not just a matter of "relaxing his tongue," since the very structure of thought is at stake. But I do agree with Galtier that "it was thanks to his analysis in another language and to the polyglot writing of the *Diary* that the theoretical model of the two languages was born — that of tenderness and that of passion, that of the child and that of the adult" (98).

Could it be this private space of freedom afforded by the Hungarian language that enabled Ferenczi to remain the "wise baby" all his life, so uncannily sensitive to primary processes? Bálint observes in his obituary that Ferenczi played at being an adult, but was destined to remain a child: "Freud and Abraham were essentially mature adults. Ferenczi, in spite of his profound insight, of his many-sided talents, his unsurpassed qualities as a clinical observer, and his unbounded scientific fantasy, was essentially a child all his life" (Bálint 1949, 245).

A reading of Ferenczi's two major papers on language, "The Confusion of Tongues between Adults and the Child" (1933) and "On Obscene Words," sheds light on his unstinting quest for maternal tenderness and empathy and his deployment of this unconscious striving in the development of his own psychoanalytic insights and techniques. The split-off mother tongue helped him to maintain his sensitivity in an acute state and to put it to use in understanding his patients.

Obscene Words

"On Obscene Words" is indeed about the "mother tongue" in the sense that I have defined it in this paper. Ferenczi points out that "taboo words" give access to profound latent memories concerning sexual and excremental functions. Unlike medical terms that maintain the repression of these early conflicts — Ferenczi alludes to Freud's advocacy of the use of technical language in the Dora case — obscene words "possess the capacity of compelling the hearer to revive memory pictures in a regressive and hallucinatory manner" (1911, 116).

Ferenczi insists on the visual and auditory nature of these words — and hence their marked regressive tendency — and notes that at a primitive stage of development all words are believed to be of this "hallucinatory-motor" kind. Like Freud, he argues that all representational activity — including language — is motivated by the desire to overcome frustration by reviving former means of satisfaction. This lends support to the idea that the first words of the mother tongue function as replacements for the lost body of the mother. Melanie Klein (1923) draws attention to the magical nature of the word "mummy" and its frequently calming effects on the child.

Ferenczi adds that "only gradually, sharpened by bitter experiences of life," does the child learn to distinguish real satisfaction from hallucinations (1911, 117–18). (The subjective undertone of Ferenczi's melancholy account is noteworthy.) Words, that is, cannot really replace the mother. Grammatical, abstract thinking, according to Ferenczi, represents the culmination of this development; it enables subtler mental operations to take place since the sensuous memory traces of preverbal intercourse with the mother now give way to verbal cues that can be manipulated at a distance.

It is my thesis that acquiring a second language—as German was for Ferenczi—facilitates the repression of the mother tongue because it lacks any association with the tactile experiences of tenderness, comprehension, and intentionality of the mother. To adapt Freud's metapsychology in *Beyond the Pleasure Principle* (1920), the use of a second language promotes an ostensible "short cut" in development, which appears to renounce hallucinatory satisfaction, while actually preserving the mother tongue in a safely split-off area of the psyche.

Ferenczi underscores that the development of abstract thinking does not occur suddenly, but is rather a slow process with moments of regression to earlier states. In *Jokes and Their Relation to the Unconscious* (1905), Freud points out that children treat words as objects. (The same is true of psychotics.) The representation of things forms a "perceptual identity" with reality. Like jokes, dreams and obscene words revive the hallucinatory motor perceptions associated with the mother tongue. According to Ferenczi, the use of obscene words in analysis with neurotic patients can aid in opening the door to repressed material. He cites two cases to illustrate the intimate connection between obscene words—for example, that for flatus—and the parental complex.

The role of obscene words, furthermore, is important not only in the psychoanalytic treatment of neurotics but in the development of all children. According to Ferenczi, at about four or five years of age—"i.e., at a time when children are restricting their 'polymorphous-perverse' impulses" (1911, 122) and beginning to enter the latency period—they regularly revel in hearing, speaking, and writing profanity. In my experience, this phenomenon can again be observed at the onset of adolescence.

The successful repression of sexual desires and fantasies is a sign that the powerful instinctual drives will be diverted to higher cultural pursuits such as the desire for knowledge. In the case of neurotics, Ferenczi remarks that the repressed material is split off in the psyche like a "foreign body" and hence unable to contribute to the organic growth and development of the individual as a whole (123). I submit that "bilingual splitting" can function in a similar way to safeguard the primary aura of the mother tongue by using the second language for abstract, secondary processes. I believe that Ferenczi experienced a version of this split between Hungarian, his mother tongue, and German, the language of Freud, in the arena of psychoanalysis.

Confusion of Tongues

In Ferenczi's final paper, "The Confusion of Tongues between Adults and the Child: The Language of Tenderness and of Passion," presented in 1932 (less than a year before Ferenczi's death) at the twelfth conference of the International Psychoanalytic Association in Wiesbaden, the effects of the bilingual split in his mind and work reach their denouement.

Ferenczi was already seriously ill and his relationship with Freud had reached a crisis. Freud tried to discourage him from presenting his paper, but Ferenczi was determined to say what he thought publicly. In the paper he criticized Freud for not paying sufficient attention to the environmental factors in neurosis and for resorting to constitutional explanations too hastily.

I would argue that, at an unconscious level, Ferenczi was alluding to the confusion of tongues between Hungarian and German, between the mother tongue associated with his own access to "the almost hallucinatory repetitions of traumatic experience" and the language bound up with the *"professional hypocrisy"* of Freud, whom Ferenczi had come increasingly to regard as a cold, cruel, and insensitive analyst (1933, 156, 158).

Ferenczi warns that patients are capable of identifying with the secret desires, tendencies, and wishes of their analysts, while the latter remain unconscious of them. In so doing, the patients abandon their "mother tongues"—as did Ferenczi with Freud—to adapt to the language of the analyst. This means resistance, not simply on the part of the patient but also of the analyst. If the patient manifests certain external and internal characteristics that the analyst cannot bear, the only honest response, according to Ferenczi, is for the analyst to confess these hidden personal feelings. When he was able to avow his own insincerity, Ferenczi reports, his "frank discussion freed, so to speak, the tongue-tied patient" and gave access to repressed material (159).

Ferenczi adds that this open attitude of the analyst, which he calls a "maternal friendliness" (160), creates a favorable contrast between the present analytic situation and the unbearable, traumatic past. This contrast is indispensable if the patient is to recover the past in the form of an objective memory rather than a hallucinatory reproduction.

In the terms I am proposing here, Ferenczi urges that the analyst should take on the attitude of the mother of the "mother tongue," whose empathy and comprehension are sufficiently attuned to make it possible for the child to graduate from mere echoing—that is, hallucinatory reproduction—to the creation of symbolic meaning. This means that the analyst must accept the idiom of the patient's mother tongue, a language and style that may be radically different from his own.

Ferenczi spoke fluent German, but Freud never tried to learn Hungarian. Freud could not be, in Winnicott's phrase, the "good-enough mother" who realizes that her child is not a narcissistic extension of herself but a "thou" that is wholly "other." As long as Ferenczi confined himself to Freud's psychoanalytic discourse, all was well; but once he began to explore his mother tongue with its dangerously seductive lure, Freud became frightened.

" 'Help! Quick! Don't let me perish helplessly!' " exclaims one of Ferenczi's regressed patients (1933, 157). But Freud was unwilling and unable to save Ferenczi's life. The confusion of tongues had gone too far, and Ferenczi's lifeblood was spent in the quest for maternal tenderness.

REFERENCES

Bálint, M. 1949. Sándor Ferenczi. In *Problems of Human Pleasure and Behaviour*, pp. 243–50. London: Maresfield Library, 1957.

Brabant, E., E. Falzeder, and P. Giampieri-Deutsch, eds. 1992. *The Correspondence of Sigmund Freud and Sándor Ferenczi. Volume 1, 1908–1914.* Supervised by A. Haynal. Trans. P. T. Hoffer. Cambridge, Mass.: Harvard University Press, 1993.

Casement, P. J. 1982. Samuel Beckett's Relationship to His Mother-Tongue. In *Transitional Objects and Potential Spaces: Literary Uses of D. W. Winnicott,* pp. 229–45. Ed. P. L. Rudnytsky. New York: Columbia University Press, 1993.

Ferenczi, S. 1911. On Obscene Words. In *Sex in Psycho-Analysis.* Trans. E. Jones, pp. 112–30. New York: Dover, 1956.

———. 1933. Confusion of Tongues between Adults and the Child. In *Final Contributions to the Methods and Problems of Psycho-Analysis,* pp. 156–67. Ed. M. Bálint. Trans. E. Mosbacher et al. New York: Brunner/Mazel, 1980.

Flavigny, C. 1988. La langue maternelle. *Psychanalyse à l'Université,* 13:609–25.

Freud, S. 1916–17. *Introductory Lectures on Psycho-Analysis.* In *The Standard Edition of the Complete Psychological Works.* Ed. and trans. J. Strachey et al. 24 vols. Vols. 15 and 16. London: Hogarth Press, 1953–74.

Galtier, B. 1994. La seconde langue, moyen de restaurer le conflit: Genèse de "Confusion de langue entre les adultes et l'enfant" dans le *Journal* de Sándor Ferenczi. *Psychanalyse à l'Université,* 19:67–100.

Goldschmidt, G. A. 1988. *Quand Freud voit la Mer: Freud et la langue Allemande.* Paris: Buchet-Chastel.

Green, A. 1984. Le Langage dans la psychanalyse. In *Langages II. Recontres psychanalytiques d'Aix-en-Provence,* pp. 19–113. Paris: Les Belles Lettres.

Greenson, R. 1950. The Mother Tongue and the Mother. *Int. J. Psycho-Anal.,* 31:18–23.

Kelley-Lainé, K. 1992. Une mère, une terre, une langue. La place de la rélation mère/enfant dans la psychanalyse hongroise. *Le Coq-Héron,* 125:53–56.

Klein, M. 1923. Early Analysis. In *Love, Guilt and Reparation and Other Works,* pp. 77–105. New York: Delta, 1977.

Ten

Mutual Analysis: A Logical Outcome of Sándor Ferenczi's Experiments in Psychoanalysis

■

CHRISTOPHER FORTUNE

In the early days of analysis, people were very casual about things that we're very careful and nervous about today. In fact, they did things that we would consider crazy today. They didn't know what we know about the transference. They didn't know its dangers. They were like Marie Curie, who didn't know about the dangers of radiation, and who got leukemia from treating it casually.
—"Aaron Green," in Janet Malcolm,
Psychoanalysis: The Impossible Profession

All analyses end badly. Each "termination" leaves the participants with the taste of ashes in their mouths; each is absurd; each is a small, pointless death. Psychoanalysis cannot tolerate happy endings. . . . Throughout its history, attempts have been made to change the tragic character of psychoanalysis, and all have failed.
—Janet Malcolm, *Psychoanalysis:
The Impossible Profession*

Preparation of this chapter was supported by the Social Sciences and Humanities Research Council of Canada.

Psychoanalysis has a history of advancing through artful failures. For example, the fact that a number of Freud's case histories, notably Dora and the Wolf Man, are literary successes but therapeutic failures has not reduced their importance to psychoanalysis.

Sándor Ferenczi's recently revealed experiment in mutual analysis (Ferenczi 1985), in which he agreed to be analyzed by one of his patients, is generally viewed as a psychoanalytic misadventure—a rash and radical act by an overzealous and undisciplined "wild analyst." As Arnold Modell writes: "Today this experiment now strikes us as naive and imprudent" (1990, 143).

What possessed Ferenczi, this talented pioneer of psychoanalysis, Freud's closest friend for twenty-five years, to consider such a "crazy" experiment in the early 1930s? Didn't he know that such an analytic relationship was impossible?

With the help of new historical research and present-day psychoanalytic theory and practice, I will attempt to answer these questions and show that in the best spirit of early psychoanalysis, Ferenczi's experiment in mutual analysis was an inspired—albeit, therapeutically flawed—act of following, and learning from, the patient. In mutual analysis, Ferenczi left the protection and safety of classical analytic "neutrality" and confronted himself in the therapeutic relationship. Ultimately unworkable, the experiment was, however, consistent with the thrust of Ferenczi's evolving explorations of analytic technique—extreme, but an inherently logical outcome.

An imaginative technical leap, mutual analysis generated rich analytic results, such as insights into transference, the subjectivity of the analyst, and a revaluation of the trauma theory. Through it, Ferenczi tested the limits of and defined a "two-person" analytic process. In challenging the classical Freudian blank-screen, one-way, or "one-person" analytic process, mutual analysis, along with Ferenczi's other pivotal technical experiments, helped to prepare the ground for contemporary relational theories, including British object relations, American interpersonal theory, self-psychology, and the current notion of intersubjectivity.

Psychoanalysis is only now beginning to assess the historical significance of mutual analysis as part of a resurgence of interest in the complete Ferenczi oeuvre, and of the Hungarian school generally—now recognized as a primary source for today's relational theories (Aron 1990; Bowlby 1988; Eagle 1984).

Throughout the 1920s, Ferenczi experimented with psychoanalytic technique. His wide-ranging "revolutionary technical innovations" included activity, passivity, elasticity, and relaxation. Mutual analysis, his last experiment, was the most dramatic and notorious of these therapeutic explorations.

Mutual Analysis: The Patient, the Analyst, an Impasse, and the Therapeutic Moment

Ferenczi's 1932 *Clinical Diary* (1985) introduced a number of his last patients, most notably "R.N.," a critically important yet virtually unknown woman whose analytic treatment dominated his final years (Fortune 1993). "R.N." was Ferenczi's code name for Elizabeth Severn, an early American "psychotherapist" whose chronic symptoms and desperate mental state led her to seek the help of the famous Hungarian analyst. Severn's case—as R.N. (in this chapter, I shall use Ferenczi's case name)—fills the diary's pages and establishes her profound influence on Ferenczi and her role in his final radical challenge to classical psychoanalysis and to Freud himself.

R.N. was not only Ferenczi's patient but his pupil, a colleague and a therapist in her own right. His "principal patient," R.N. was in analysis with Ferenczi in Budapest for eight years—from 1924 until just before his death in 1933. It was during this period that Ferenczi marshalled his most intense critique of classical Freudian theory and therapy. R.N.'s case and her analytic relationship with Ferenczi are an important paradigm, a pivotal point in the history and development of psychoanalysis in the tradition of Anna O. and Dora. Through her initiation of mutual analysis, R.N. was the catalyst for Ferenczi's recognition of the clinical significance of counter-transference (Wolstein 1989). She was also a critical agent in his early understanding of the dynamics of childhood sexual trauma, including his own. This understanding led Ferenczi to reconsider the pathogenic importance of early external trauma, and in doing so, to challenge Freud and to question the emphasis of psychoanalysis on unconscious fantasy. In fact, R.N. may have been the first sexually abused analysand whose actual childhood trauma was the focus of psychoanalytic treatment since Freud abandoned his "seduction theory" in the late 1890s (Fortune 1989, 1993).

When she began treatment with Ferenczi, R.N. reported having no memory of her life before she was twelve years old. Throughout her life she had been chronically fatigued and suicidal and had experienced multiple personalities. Prior to Ferenczi, R.N. had seen a number of early psychiatrist-analysts in the United States who had little success in treating her difficult pathology. Designated a hopeless case, R.N., in her mid-forties, inevitably found her way to the analyst of last resort—Sándor Ferenczi.

In 1932, near the end of R.N.'s eight-year analysis, Ferenczi (1985) recorded her extreme and challenging case—a "case of schizophrenia progressiva"—in his diary. At first, Ferenczi wrote, he had found R.N. disagreeable. In his diary he admitted to being apprehensive and in awe of her. On May 5, 1932, recollecting his earliest impressions, he wrote, "[She had] excessive independence and self-assurance, immensely strong willpower" (97). Admittedly threatened and defensive, Ferenczi assumed a "conscious professional pose, partly adopted as a defensive measure against anxiety" (97).

Even though Ferenczi wrote that he felt challenged in his masculinity, the analysis had a promising start. For the next few years R.N. divided her time between Budapest and New York, where she maintained a small psychotherapy practice. Several of her devoted and financially well-off American patients even followed her to Budapest to continue therapy with her.

In 1926, after a few years of intensive analysis, R.N.'s treatment stalled. For the next two years, her case showed little progress. In response, Ferenczi (1928) experimented with his indulgence and elasticity techniques and openly overcompensated. He recalled: "I redoubled my efforts . . . gradually I gave in to more and more of the patient's wishes" (1985, 97).

In 1928 a breakthrough came. Utilizing relaxation and regression techniques, including trance states, R.N. and Ferenczi lifted the veil of early amnesia and began to reconstruct the events of her "traumatic infantile history"—a severe case of early abuse. Their reconstruction suggested that R.N.'s father had physically, emotionally, and sexually abused her from the age of one-and-a-half.

As horrendous childhood "memories" flooded her consciousness, R.N.'s condition became acute. Already his most demanding and difficult patient, her case occupied much of Ferenczi's attention. Driven by what Freud called his *furor sanandi* (rage to cure), Ferenczi regularly saw R.N. four to five hours each day, as well as weekends; at her home and at night, if necessary. He even continued her analysis during vacations abroad. (This may sound extreme, but at that time it was not uncommon for analysts to see patients during their vacations.)

Not surprisingly, Ferenczi's attentions convinced R.N. that she had found her "perfect lover." Faced with this development, Ferenczi retreated and began to "limit [his] medical superperformances" (1985, 98). As he did so, he interpreted for R.N. that she now ought to hate him. However, R.N. countered with her own interpretations—that Ferenczi harbored hidden feelings of anger and hate toward her, and that these feelings blocked her analysis. Until *she* analyzed those feelings in *him,* she said, the analysis would remain at an impasse. Even though he conceded that R.N.'s interpretations were justified, Ferenczi resisted her demand. Finally, after a year, he reluctantly submitted to her analysis of him (99).

On the couch, Ferenczi confessed "I did hate the patient in spite of the friendliness I displayed" (99). Expecting the worst, he was surprised by R.N.'s reaction. He wrote: "The first torrent of the patient's affects (desire to die, notions of suicide, flight) is succeeded, quite remarkably, by relative composure and progress in the work: attention becomes freer of exaggerated fantasies. . . . Curiously this had a tranquilizing effect on the patient, who felt vindicated" (11, 99).

Ferenczi felt afraid, humiliated, and exposed by his self-disclosures, yet he was intrigued by what they produced: "Once I had openly admitted the limitations of my capacity, she even began to reduce her demands on me. . . . I really find her less disagreeable now. . . . My interest in the details of the analytical material and my ability to deal with them—which previously seemed paralyzed—improved significantly" (99). As a patient, Ferenczi had the valuable experience of being subjected to his own analytic technique (surely, at some point, every analysand's revenge fantasy), aspects of which he didn't like. "The mechanical egocentric interpretation of things by the analyst [R.N.] touched me in a highly disagreeable way. . . . However, this is the method this patient has learned from me" (96).

In summary, through mutual analysis, Ferenczi found that honesty, even admitting his dislike for R.N., increased her trust, deepened the therapy, and made him a better analyst for all his patients. He was less sleepy during sessions and made "sincerely sensitive" interventions. Ferenczi concluded that the "real" relationship between analyst and analysand can be therapeutic and strengthen the therapeutic alliance. "Who should get credit for this success?" (99–100), he asked. His answer? Himself, for risking the experiment, but "foremost, of course, the patient, who . . . never ceased fighting for her rights" (101).

Although mutual analysis brought analytic progress and yielded significant clinical insights, Ferenczi decided there was some risk in putting himself "into the hands of a not undangerous patient" (100). As well, he recognized that the central concern of the analysis might be jeopardized; that by analyzing the analyst, the patient could deflect attention from herself. Needless to say, there were other practical difficulties. Ferenczi concluded that mutual analysis could only be a last resort. "Proper analysis by a stranger, without any obligation, would be better," he cautioned (xxii).

Toward the end, Ferenczi tried to return to a traditional analytic relationship with R.N. It proved to be impossible. On October 2, 1932, in his final diary entry headed "Mutuality—sine qua non," discouraged and exhausted (he was to die of pernicious anemia within the year), Ferenczi recorded these fragments: "An attempt to continue analyzing unilaterally. Emotionality disappeared; analysis insipid. Relationship—distant. Once mutuality has been attempted, one-sided analysis then is no longer possible—not productive" (213). Finally, anticipating future interest in the analytic relationship, Ferenczi asked: "Now the question: must every case be mutual?—and to what extent?" (213).

Mutual Analysis: A Present-Day Theoretical-Clinical Aside

Theoretically and clinically, how might R.N.'s demand that Ferenczi not only disclose himself but also submit to her analysis, and her ensuing response to this eventuality, be understood today? To pick only one of a number of possible theoretical perspectives, R.N.'s challenge could be understood as an early example—albeit extreme and seemingly conscious—of the Mt. Zion group's Control-Mastery theory (Weiss and

Sampson 1986) of the *"test"* of an analyst.[1] Interpreted within this frame-work, Ferenczi passed R.N.'s test by being honest and admitting his thera-peutic failure. As Weiss and Sampson would have predicted, once Ferenczi passed her test, R.N. not only produced new analytic material, but this was accompanied by a decrease in her anxiety. In addition, it does not seem far-fetched to suggest that in confronting what she perceived as Ferenczi's unexpressed hostile feelings toward her, R.N. attempted to establish what Weiss and Sampson identify as "conditions of safety."

The outcome of mutual analysis confirmed Ferenczi's early belief in the inherent therapeutic value of the analytic relationship, a notion with much clinical support today. Morris Eagle affirms aspects of the Mt. Zion per-spective: "Passing tests and establishing conditions of safety . . . facilitate insight and awareness (i.e., the emergence of warded-off contents) *and* constitute direct relationship factors which may be anxiety-reducing and thereby ameliorate symptoms" (1984, 105). Echoing an idea contained in Ferenczi's clinical diary and last papers—later defined as "corrective emo-tional experience" by Alexander and French (1946)—Eagle notes: "The establishment of conditions of safety can itself be seen as an implicit inter-pretation to the effect that the patient is not in the original traumatic situation and that the therapist is different, in important respects, from traumatic figures of the past" (105).

Eagle links the Mt. Zion work with G. S. Klein's (1976) idea of "reversal of voice"—from passive to active—as a prime factor in the therapeutic process. This notion can be used to interpret R.N.'s (and Ferenczi's) ulti-mate analytic "role reversal"—mutual analysis. While it may stretch the original idea of "reversal of voice," it is difficult to dispute that by turning her analyst into her patient, R.N. exerted an incredible degree of active mastery in therapy. Again to some extent mirroring Ferenczi's diary, Eagle writes: "The patient's active role in presenting tests, in determining whether or not conditions of safety exist, and in deciding whether or not to bring forth traumatic material all can be seen as instances of attempts to reverse passively endured traumatic experiences into active attempts at mastery" (105).

Ferenczi's readiness to establish the analytic conditions whereby R.N. could shift from a passive to an active therapeutic role was the result of a complex number of critical factors in Ferenczi's personal and professional background.

Mutual Analysis: Ferenczi's Logic

Whatever his motivations—therapeutic chutzpah, desire to heal, personal pathology, or their mix—there is little doubt that Ferenczi's success with difficult patients was due in part to his "psychotherapeutic personality" (Federn 1990).[2] Ferenczi had an indomitable therapeutic zeal. As he wrote in "Child Analysis in the Analyses of Adults":

I have had a kind of fanatical belief in the efficacy of depth-psychology, and this has led me to attribute occasional failures not so much to the patient's "incurability" as to our own lack of skill—a supposition which necessarily led me to try altering the usual technique in severe cases with which it had proved unable to cope successfully. (1931, 128)

Ferenczi's shift of the burden of responsibility for analytic failure from the intractable patient to the analyst's "lack of skill," including countertransference weaknesses and blindspots, marks a turning point in analytic therapy, and is still clinically relevant today. For example, extending the implications of the Mt. Zion view, and again echoing Ferenczi (1933, 1985), Eagle suggests that "therapist failures of tests put forth by patients—perhaps frequently because of the therapist's own countertransference reactions and difficulties—may be the most frequent reason for therapeutic failures" (1984, 184).

Ferenczi challenged Freud's limiting of psychoanalysis to healthy neurotics. In his diary entry of August 4, 1932, he criticized Freud because he "sacrifices the interests of women [and] . . . makes deprecating remarks about psychotics, perverts and everything in general that is 'too abnormal' " (1985, 187). Galvanized by what he saw as Freud's disparaging attitude and constricted view of the patient population, Ferenczi set out to expand the bounds of psychoanalysis and to prove Freud wrong. Throughout the 1920s he experimented with analytic technique, at times as though impelled by a missionary calling. Ferenczi wrote:

It is only with the utmost reluctance that I ever bring myself to give up even the most obstinate case, and I have come to be a specialist in peculiarly difficult cases, with which I go on for very many years. I have refused to accept such verdicts as that a patient's resistance was unconquerable, or that his narcissism prevented our penetrating any further, or the sheer fatalistic acquiescence in the so-called "drying-up" of a case. I have told myself that as long as a patient continues to come at all, the last thread of hope has not snapped. (1931, 128)

As Janet Malcolm has paraphrased: "[Ferenczi] simply refused to give up when the key didn't fit and, if necessary, kicked down the door" (1981, 132).

Ferenczi's "all-comers" therapeutic approach led to a caseload weighted with seemingly untreatable patients. Other analysts were only too happy to send him their "hopeless incurables." In contrast to most analysts of the time, Ferenczi treated severe cases of hysteria, obsessional neurosis, border-lines, and multiple personality.

However well intentioned he was, the relentless demands of his severely needy patients inevitably exhausted Ferenczi, physically and emotionally. In letters to his good friend, doctor, and fellow "wild analyst" Georg Grod-deck, Ferenczi wrote: "I am afraid that the patients . . . are literally trying to overwhelm me. . . . Analysis, the way I practice it, requires a lot more self-sacrifice than what we were used to up until now" (Ferenczi and Groddeck 1982, 81, 83).

What was Ferenczi trying to prove? What drove him to such extremes—including mutual analysis? Ferenczi's revelations in his clinical diary, and the Freud-Ferenczi correspondence, provide insights into these questions.

As these sources reveal, in light of his complicated relationship with Freud, Ferenczi's motivation to risk mutual analysis was also personal. He blamed Freud, his analyst, for failing to love him enough and analyze him completely—specifically his negative transference. Years after his brief analysis—consisting of a total of five to six weeks of treatment in 1914 and 1916 and a subsequent correspondence—an intense transference to Freud, common among early (as well as more recent) analysts, was still active. Mutual analysis was, in part, Ferenczi's response to his own unresolved transference-countertransference issues with Freud.

Ferenczi's patchy analysis with Freud was typical of the training of the day—"rapid, fitful analyses, often undertaken abroad, in a foreign language, during walks or travels together or visits to the home of analyst or patient"

(Dupont 1985, xxii). Ferenczi suggested that these inadequate training analyses "may lead to an impossible situation, namely, that our patients gradually become better analyzed than ourselves" (1933, 158).

To some degree, mutual analysis helped to convince Ferenczi that the best protection from countertransference problems was an analyst's own thorough analysis. In his last paper, "Confusion of Tongues between Adults and the Child," he insisted that "above all, we ourselves must have been really well analysed, right down to 'rock bottom' " (1933, 158). Clearly drawing on his coanalysis with R.N., he added: "We must have learnt to recognize all our unpleasant external and internal character traits in order that we may be really prepared to face all those forms of hidden hatred and contempt that can be so cunningly disguised in our patients' associations" (158). In his ongoing critique of analysts, analytic training, and therapy, Ferenczi extended this idea of the analytically experienced patient. "The best analyst is a patient who has been cured," he noted in his diary (1985, xxii).

Ferenczi's passionate therapeutic rhetoric, aspects of which he self-critically confessed were exaggerations, can, in part, be seen as barbs directed at Freud. Ferenczi was determined to shift psychoanalysts' attention to a deeper, more subjective and relational experience of the patient—an experience he himself was immersed in at that moment. It was not lost on Ferenczi that Freud, as the original analyst, was unanalyzed beyond his "self-analysis." Freud was never a patient, cured or otherwise. For Ferenczi, who saw analysis as an inherently social act, a thorough "self-analysis" was an impossibility. In his diary, he does not mince words as to what he sees as the result: "[Freud] is the only one who does not have to be analyzed" (188). "He only analyzes others but not himself. Projection" (92).

Mutual analysis was a part of Ferenczi's personal and professional struggle to clarify his enmeshed and ambivalent relationship to Freud. His observations and criticisms of Freud in the diary, frequently charged with the hostility of accumulated grievances, yet laced with startlingly accurate insights garnered over many intimate years, should not be used to devalue the objective validity of Ferenczi's clinical insights.

Mutual analysis was not mentioned in any of Ferenczi's last published papers, only in his clinical diary; in fact, he seems to have tried to keep it a secret (Fortune 1993). Ferenczi knew that he was pushing the therapeutic edge, at times beyond the possible, and certainly beyond the classically acceptable. He knew he needed room to experiment without having prematurely to defend his methods. Though he was aware that Freud resolutely disapproved of his clinical and theoretical directions, in his letters Ferenczi continued to plead his case to him, often clouded in a vague, metaphorical language. In September 1931, Ferenczi wrote to Freud:

[I am] immersed in extremely difficult "clarification work"—internal and external, as well as scientific—which has not yet produced anything definitive; and one cannot come forward with something that is only half completed. . . . In my usual manner, I do not shy away from drawing out their conclusions to the furthest extent possible—often to the point where I lead myself "ad absurdum." But this doesn't discourage me. I seek advances by new routes, often radically opposed. (Quoted in Dupont 1985, xiv)

In a May 1932 letter, in the middle of the mutual analysis, Ferenczi hinted to Freud: "[I am] immersing myself in a kind of scientific 'poetry and truth.' " In his reply, Freud reproached him for isolating himself on an "island of dreams which you inhabit with your fantasy children [probably Ferenczi's patients]" (xvi).

In September 1932, when Ferenczi read to Freud his aptly titled "Confusion of Tongues" paper, Freud noted that Ferenczi was silent on the technique with which he had gathered his clinical material supporting the reality of patients' early traumas (Gay 1988, 584). Had Freud read Ferenczi's diary, he would have seen that not only did Ferenczi believe his patients' "memories," but that coanalysis with R.N., one of his most deeply disturbed patients, had, in part, led him to reconsider the pathogenic role of external trauma in mental disturbance. As Ferenczi noted in his January 31, 1932, diary entry: "The first real advances toward the patient's gaining conviction [of the external reality of the childhood trauma] occurred in conjunction with some genuinely emotionally colored fragments of the . . . analysis of the analyst" (1985, 26).

Following the presentation of his paper at the 1932 Wiesbaden Congress, Ferenczi's estrangement from Freud and the wider psychoanalytic community increased. Possibly for the first time in his psychoanalytic career,

Ferenczi was alone (outside of his intimate Hungarian circle) with his difficult clinical and theoretical explorations. Also, it was no longer a supportive and encouraging Freud, but the specter of a stern, disapproving father, that hovered in the wings. Since the more moderate avenue of sounding out his clinical directions through discourse with Freud was closing, Ferenczi may have been driven to radical alternatives, such as mutual analysis, to satisfy his desire to explore legitimate clinical questions—particularly aspects of the analytic relationship (Eagle 1991).

On October 10, 1931, after an exchange of letters in which he tried unsuccessfully to gain Freud's understanding of his work, Ferenczi wrote to Freud affirming his path and throwing in his lot with his patients: "I am, above all, an empiricist. . . . Ideas are always closely linked with the vicissitudes in the treatment of patients, and by these are either repudiated or confirmed" (quoted in Dupont 1985, xv).

The Experienced Patient and the Desire to Complete an Analysis

What was it about R.N. and her analysis that convinced Ferenczi to risk mutual analysis with her? In his diary, Ferenczi wrote of the underlying clinical conditions that led up to mutual analysis. After years of treatment, R.N.'s analysis had been at an impasse for at least two years. It is clear from his diary that Ferenczi undertook mutual analysis as an experiment in this specific context (1985, 97–98). Opinions differ as to the number of patients with whom Ferenczi engaged in mutual analysis. While the diary seems to indicate that he attempted mutual analysis with at least one other patient, "Dm" (15), Judith Dupont suggests that, besides R.N., there was also the patient named in the diary as "S. I." (1993, 153). In any event, Ferenczi did not advocate mutual analysis as a standard practice.

For Ferenczi, R.N. was an unusual analysand, one whom Bálint describes as a " 'worth-while' patient" (1968, 112).[3] In *The Basic Fault,* Bálint characterized Ferenczi's intense work with an unnamed female patient—whom I identify as R.N.—as a "grand experiment" (112). Although Ferenczi was ambivalent about her exceedingly strong will and demanding nature, Ferenczi admired R.N. and respected her as a therapist in her own right. As she was his pupil and colleague, R.N.'s analysis was also a training analysis during which she and Ferenczi discussed their work together and its broader implications.

R.N. seems to have embodied Ferenczi's ideal of the experienced patient. Prior to the years with Ferenczi, R.N. had been treated by a number of early analysts. Given the immense amount of time Ferenczi devoted to her—it is hard to imagine how he had time for other patients—R.N. may have been the most extensively analyzed patient-analyst of her day. Ferenczi must have recognized that, as a patient, R.N. had a breadth of therapeutic experience lacked by most analysts—including Freud. In R.N., Ferenczi may have cultivated his notion of the ideal analyst as "cured" patient. In December 1930, an unduly optimistic Ferenczi wrote to Groddeck that through his work with R.N., he would "soon, or in the not too distant future, finally be able to say what it means to complete an analysis" (Ferenczi and Groddeck 1982, 83). Did Ferenczi wish to "complete" R.N.'s analysis to prove to Freud and the psychoanalytic community the efficacy of his clinical techniques, and to convince them that early actual trauma was a critical factor in the etiology of mental illness?

Mutual Analysis: Historical Perspectives

R.N.'s intensive, long-term, experience as both patient and therapist, coupled with her personal strength, allowed her to perceive and confront Ferenczi's countertransference and their "real" therapeutic relationship. Benjamin Wolstein argues that Ferenczi's willingness to take seriously his part in R.N.'s analytic impasse, and their subsequent mutual analysis, marks the birth of the recognition of the clinical importance of countertransference (1989, 676).

The experiment in mutual analysis has other historical implications for psychoanalysis. Through all his cases, but particularly his work with R.N., Ferenczi stepped outside Freud's influence and gained new perspectives, many of which are now receiving the most lively attention of psychoanalysts. For example, Ferenczi grasped the critical importance of the analytic relationship and its potential to promote therapeutic change. He expanded the range of psychoanalytic therapy to include countertransference disclosures and interpretations. Although this experiment in mutual analysis was extreme, Ferenczi anticipated the current emphasis on the role of the analyst's subjectivity and the value and risk of the analyst's self-disclosure. Ferenczi addressed the significance of the analyst's personality, particularly with respect to stalemates in treatment. As a result, he highlighted the idea that a patient's resistance could itself be a function of the analyst's countertransference.

In today's psychoanalytic literature there is considerable controversy concerning the significance of Ferenczi's late work, which, albeit tacitly, inextricably includes mutual analysis. Ferenczi's influence can be heard in many of the new psychoanalytic voices of the past sixty years. Some acknowledge their debt to Ferenczi, while others do not. Through his *Clinical Diary*, many in psychoanalysis are only now becoming aware of Ferenczi's final radical ideas. Lewis Aron writes:

Contemporary relational psychologies may rightfully be traced back to the technical experiments of the Hungarian psychoanalyst, Sándor Ferenczi. . . . Bálint, Ferenczi's student, elaborated on Ferenczi's work in his notion of "two-body psychology," and this played an important role in the development of British object relations theory . . . American interpersonal theory, self-psychology, and currents within contemporary Freudian theory. (1990, 477)

Completing the quotation given at the outset of this paper, Modell pays tribute to Ferenczi on a number of specific issues: "Although this experiment [mutual analysis] now strikes us as naive and imprudent, Ferenczi was struggling with therapeutic dilemmas that are still very much with us. . . . The matter of equality between analyst and analysand is still a current therapeutic issue" (1990, 143). Modell notes two present-day examples whose lineage clearly goes back to Ferenczi's mutual analysis: "Echoes of Ferenczi's egalitarian concerns can be heard in Kohut's advice that the analyst acknowledge his own empathic failures, and Gill's objection to the concept that transference distorts, which assumes that it is the *analyst* who is the judge of what is real" (143).

Links between Ferenczi's mutual analysis and a wide range of nonpsychoanalytic approaches, while not direct, are also apparent. For example, the therapeutic attitude embodied in mutual analysis reminds one of Carl Rogers's (1951) client-centered therapy. Rogers's egalitarian approach, particularly as reflected in his "leaderless" encounter group and its values of "immediate expression of interpersonal feelings, confrontation, . . . and receiving feedback—even negative" (1970, 7), evokes Ferenczi's encounter with R.N.

Conclusion

As the most brilliant therapist of the early circle of analysts, acknowledged by Freud as a "master of analysis," Ferenczi knew the bounds of classical psychoanalytic therapy—both what it had accomplished and its limits. In fact, since meeting Freud in 1908, he had been one of its prime architects. Ferenczi's unquenchable therapeutic optimism, and his willingness to treat extremely disturbed patients, converged to draw him to the analytic edge. Courageously, and as circumspectly as his nature would allow, he expanded the horizons of psychoanalysis. Like a poet or an artist, he adapted himself to his materials, his patients—at times even following his "not undangerous" ones (1985, 100). They and their pathology became his teachers. In allowing his patients to shape aspects of his therapeutic approach, Ferenczi was, in spirit, an empirical (and alchemical?) researcher, no longer dependable as a loyal soldier of the Freudian army. He was determined to engage his patients, to descend with them into his own psyche to see what emerged in the analytic encounter. What he discovered has enriched all of psychoanalysis. However, it was both a hero's and a fool's journey. Sándor Ferenczi caught therapeutic fire, and tragically it ultimately consumed him.

Given his passionately held views that the best analyst was a thoroughly analyzed patient, and his growing awareness of the gaps in his own personal analysis, Ferenczi's decision to submit to mutual analysis with R.N., while highly unusual, was not only inherently logical but, in light of his professional isolation from Freud, pragmatic. Although it uncovered rich personal and clinical insights, it also proved to be impossible.

NOTES

1. Morris Eagle summarizes the Mt. Zion view: "A patient comes to therapy, not to gratify unconscious instinctual impulses, but to *master* certain conflicts,

wishes, irrational beliefs, and anxieties originating from childhood traumas and experiences. With mastery as his basic goal, the patient presents *tests* to the therapists. The passing of tests constitutes *conditions of safety* which then make it safe for the patient to lift repression and *bring forth warded-off contents*" (1984, 100).

2. In writing of his father, Ernst Federn attributed Paul Federn's success in treating psychotic patients to his "psychotherapeutic personality" (1990, 125–40). Like Ferenczi, Paul Federn (1952), in contrast to Freud's pessimism, was optimistic about the potential of psychoanalysis to treat psychotics.

3. Bálint does not define what he means by this term. He seems to imply an analyst's subjective view of a highly regarded patient.

REFERENCES

Alexander, F., and T. French. 1946. *Psychoanalytic Therapy: Principles and Application.* New York: Ronald Press.

Aron, L. 1990. One Person and Two Person Psychologies and the Method of Psychoanalysis. *Psychoanal. Psychol.,* 7:475–85.

Aron, L., and A. Harris, eds. 1993. *The Legacy of Sándor Ferenczi.* Hillsdale, N.J.: Analytic Press.

Bálint, M. 1968. *The Basic Fault: Therapeutic Aspects of Regression.* London: Tavistock.

Bowlby, J. 1988. Foreword to I. Suttie, *The Origins of Love and Hate,* pp. xv–xviii. London: Free Association.

Dupont, J. 1985. Introduction to Ferenczi 1985, pp. xi–xxvii.

———. 1993. Michael Bálint: Analysand, Pupil, Friend, and Successor to Sándor Ferenczi. In Aron and Harris 1993, pp. 145–57.

Eagle, M. 1984. *Recent Developments in Psychoanalysis: A Critical Evaluation.* New York: McGraw-Hill.

———. 1991. Personal communication.

Federn, E. 1990. *Witnessing Psychoanalysis.* London: Karnac.

Federn, P. 1952. *Ego Psychology and the Psychoses.* London: Imago.

Ferenczi, S. 1928. The Elasticity of Psychoanalytic Technique. In Ferenczi 1955, pp. 87–101.

———. 1931. Child Analysis in the Analyses of Adults. In Ferenczi 1955, pp. 126–42.

———. 1933. Confusion of Tongues between Adults and the Child. In Ferenczi 1955, pp. 156–67.

———. 1955. *Final Contributions to the Problems and Methods of Psycho-Analysis.* Ed. M. Bálint. Trans. E. Mosbacher. London: Karnac, 1980.

———. 1985. *The Clinical Diary of Sándor Ferenczi.* Ed. J. Dupont. Trans. M. Bálint and N. Z. Jackson. Cambridge, Mass.: Harvard University Press, 1988.

Ferenczi, S., and G. Groddeck. 1982. *Briefwechsel 1921–1933.* Frankfurt am Main: Fischer, 1986.

Fortune, C. 1989. Review of *The Clinical Diary of Sándor Ferenczi*. *The Village Voice,* February 21, pp. 60–62.

———. 1993. The case of "RN": Sándor Ferenczi's Radical Experiment in Psychoanalysis. In Aron and Harris 1993, pp. 101–20.

Gay, P. 1988. *Freud: A Life for Our Time.* New York: Norton.

Klein, G. S. 1976. *Psychoanalytic Theory: An Exploration of Essentials.* New York: International Universities Press.

Malcolm, J. 1981. *Psychoanalysis: The Impossible Profession.* New York: Knopf.

Modell, A. 1990. *Other Times, Other Realities.* Cambridge, Mass.: Harvard University Press.

Rogers, C. 1951. *Client-Centered Therapy.* Boston: Houghton Mifflin.

———. 1970. *Carl Rogers on Encounter Groups.* New York: Harper and Row.

Weiss, J., H. Sampson, and the Mount Zion Psychotherapy Research Group. 1986. *The Psychoanalytic Process: Theory, Clinical Observation and Empirical Research.* New York: Guilford.

Wolstein, B. 1989. Ferenczi, Freud and the Origins of American Interpersonal Relations. *Contemp. Psychoanal.,* 25:672–85.

PART III

Theory and Technique

Eleven

Hermann's Concept of Clinging in Light of Modern Drive Theory

■

WOLFGANG BERNER

(Translated by Lindsay Adshead)

Variations on Drive Theory from Hermann to Kernberg

Born in Budapest in 1889, Imre Hermann became a member of the Hungarian Psychoanalytic Association in 1919 and was one of the founders of the "Budapest School." As one of the few analysts who remained in Budapest during the totalitarian regime, he was a pillar of the Hungarian psychoanalytic movement until his death in 1984. He published over 150 works in several languages, many of which have provided a valuable impetus to other studies. Among other subjects, his writings dealt with the theory of clinging, latent and manifest thought processes, the analyses of artistically gifted people and philosophers, and psychoanalytic methodology.

At an international conference held in Budapest on November 11–12, 1989, to commemorate the 100th anniversary of his birth, it was asked why, considering Hermann's anticipations of much modern psychoanalytic thought, he is relatively seldom quoted. The reason is probably not only because of his isolation in Budapest, but also because his style of writing was not always very systematic. I shall be looking more deeply into his clinging theory as it seems to me not only to be characteristic of Hermann's original way of thinking, but also to provide a major stimulus for contemporary psychoanalysis. I shall do this by way of John Bowlby, who held clinging to be one of the five drive patterns forming so-called attachment.

I consider Hermann's clinging theory still superior to Bowlby's attachment theory in some respects, although Bowlby's theory derives in part from Hermann's. My work with pedophiles has proved the usefulness of clinging as a concept, which has often been used by Hungarian psychoanalysts, especially in the interpretation of psychosomatic illnesses and depressive conditions (Veress 1989; Lukacs 1989; Nemes 1990).

According to Livia Nemes (1990), Hermann concentrated on this theme beginning in the early 1920s (1923, 1926, 1931, 1933), before finally identifying (1936a) a new pair of (component) instincts—clinging/searching—with the intention of investigating their connection with sadomasochism. In "Clinging, Fire, Feelings of Shame" (1941) and "Man's Basic Drives" (1943), he elaborated on these thoughts. In brief, Hermann saw a connection between the need of small children to cling to their mothers and the biological instinct universally observed among young primates to cling to their mothers. At the same time, however, he defined this need as a component instinct analogous to the partial drives—especially sadism/masochism and voyeurism/exhibitionism—described by Freud in "Instincts and Their Vicissitudes" (1915). He postulated the variability of the drive object, with the possible permutations being reversal into the opposite, the subject's turning against himself, repression, and sublimation. In the case of the clinging drive, reversal into the opposite leads to "searching," but is also reflected in hiding and the resistance to enforced separation as possible drive vicissitudes.[1]

It was partly the variability of the drive pattern that led Freud to postulate the existence of a basic psychic energy (libido), which can be invested in the representations linked with the drive patterns (especially the objects) in various and alternating ways. Unlike Bowlby later, Hermann did not reject this concept of psychic energy, but his acceptance of it was equivocal. He held that the pair of opposite drives, clinging and searching, derived originally from the ego instincts (i.e., those serving self-preservation), but then became effective through anaclisis (1941, 257). He believed that aggression too was closely connected with the clinging drive (which may be compared to the oral phase in its time of onset and cathexis). This means that clinging can express itself on the one hand in physical tenderness and on the other in "aggressive grasping."

It remains unclear whether the partial drive of clinging as described by Hermann is a result of libido and aggression, or whether the latter secondarily invest in this partial drive, which is in fact an innate instinctual pattern, a neuronal automatism, that only becomes linked with mental representations as a result of psychological development. This confusion has a historical basis, as the concept of instinct as understood by Konrad Lorenz or Bowlby had at that time still not been worked out. In any case, Hermann, like Ferenczi (1913, 1924), spotlights the biologically important relationship between mother and child. He designates the primal trauma to be the separation from the mother and the fact that clinging becomes forbidden. The fear of separation is innate and independent of maternal traumatization. It represents the primal model of the trauma, so that even the fear of castration becomes merely a reflection and recollection of this early object loss (1936b, 445). In this sense Hermann may be considered one of the forerunners of object relations theorists. He also makes reference to Melanie Klein, but criticizes her theory for its neglect of clinging as a generally observable phenomenon. He links Klein's *Beraubungswunsch* (desire to rob) with a frustrated wish, i.e., the nonappearance of drive-related clinging behavior in the child. This gives the child the feeling—or should one say the fantasy?—from the very beginning that something, or rather someone, has been taken away from him. The later *Gegenraub* (counterrobbing) tendency is only a reaction to this anxiety-invested representation (1941, 269).

In 1943 Hermann almost totally dismissed the idea of primary aggression (Hermann 1943; Vikár 1989) and advanced the idea that aggression derives from a frustration of clinging and therefore supports the "aggression-frustration hypothesis" and not the hypothesis of the primary death drive (Thanatos), as claimed by Klein. Hermann interestingly describes the vicissitudes of this primary clinging drive, which are obviously linked with affects and ideas. A paradigmatic experience is that of feeling warmth (like warm milk) flowing from the mother's body into the child's. The gestures of raised hands to be found in many representations of Egyptian deities and in hieroglyphics are interpreted by Hermann as unconscious symbolizations of clinging.[2]

One vicissitude of the clinging drive is the grooming (delousing) behavior among young apes. Initially this was wrongly considered to be solely a hygienic procedure in which they removed parasites from each other. In fact, as more recent studies by researchers into primates have shown (Goodall 1988), it is a gesture of tenderness that plays a major role in the social life of higher apes. In humans this clinging drive (easily observable in babies) is massively frustrated, as the female body has lost its hair (to which a baby can cling) and babies are carried around much less than in the case of primates, especially in the more developed cultures. Reactions to frustrations of this need can include hair and skin disorders (alopecia, eczema), destructive behavior with the hands or feet, and self-inflicted wounds, or a total reversal into extreme "searching," flight tendencies, etc. Hermann also describes how the experience of the dual union in clinging has a direct influence on the structure of thinking.

With his hypothesis that frustration can be converted more or less directly into affects and ideas, Hermann's outlook shows similarities in methodology with that of Klein and her followers, many of whom came from the Budapest School. At the same time, however, it demonstrates a certain distancing from Freud's point of view regarding instinctual drive economy. Like the Kleinian School, rather than referring to abstract sources of drives, Hermann tends to refer to primal fantasies, which generate new fantasies when frustrated.

Reviewing Hermann's work, Dénes Lukács (1989) tried to determine why so few subsequent psychoanalytic authors discussed his theory or cited it only in passing. For example, the ego psychologist Heinz Hartmann (1953) did not consider the opposites "clinging" and "searching" to be a partial drive. He saw them as an aspect of object relations, as for him drive and object were opposed as concepts. René Spitz (1965), Willi Hoffer (1947), Edith Jacobson (1964), and Margaret Mahler et al. (1975) all mentioned clinging, but none of them could decide if Hermann's observation derived from the sphere of drives or rather from the sphere of the instinctually "automatic" (reflex).

In 1959 Michael Bálint constructed the typology "ocnophile" and "philobat," which is similar to the pair of opposites "clinging" and "searching," and referred to Hermann's work. Nemes (1989) emphasizes that the relationship between Hermann's ideas and the pair of opposites ocnophile-philobat goes much farther than Bálint would admit. Sometimes Bálint even used the same words as Hermann to describe the ocnophilic (clinging) and philobatic (searching) types. Bálint believed, however, that the child's need to cling was not primary, but a reaction to separation anxiety. The philobat has been separated from a labile, unreliable object and thus avoids ties, sometimes in a paranoid way. Bálint is referring here to Ferenczi (1913, 1924), with his metaphor of the boundlessness of the intrauterine condition and the feeling of omnipotence associated with it. This was for Ferenczi the basis of "primary love." But Bálint and Hermann both believed in the idea of a deeply innate need for attachment.

John Bowlby is the psychoanalyst who has tried most consistently to work out a change of paradigm, away from Freudian drive theory and toward the instinct theories commonly found in ethology, such as those of Lorenz and Tinbergen (1938). In *Attachment* (1969), Bowlby radically reformulates the bond between mother and child, though he leaves uncontested the importance of the child's early attachment to its mother. Bowlby distances himself from the "secondary drive" theory, which plays a central role in both psychoanalysis and learning theory. According to this theory, the mother assumes an importance for the child only as a result of fulfilling its vital needs. But Bowlby also distances himself from the assumption of a primary need to return to the womb (as claimed by Ferenczi in his attempt to formulate a genital theory in 1924). He provides a new framework for the observation that there is a primary need for an object expressed in sucking and clinging to it.

In accordance with the "control theory" and the "instinct theory" propounded by Lorenz and Tinbergen, he assumes there are preformed motor behavioral programs in the brain, automatic reflexes which are set in motion by certain stimuli from the environment (signals) and brought to an end by other stimuli. Automatisms of this kind have been proved to be behind the "egg-rolling movement" seen in the greylag goose and in many other movement sequences unique to given species. It is assumed that the "following behavior" observed in young animals is due to the phenomenon of imprinting, which is responsible for adaptation to the surroundings in general. Instinct patterns are compared to a fragmentary (i.e., incomplete) computer program. The gaps in the program are closed up only through experience with the surroundings the first time the program is run through. (Chicks are imprinted by the clucking of the mother hen.) But this metaphor from modern technology merely provides another mechanistic model to explain instinctual drives, in the same way that Freud used the hydrodynamic metaphor. The attachment behavior described by Bowlby has the biological task of creating an attachment between the baby and its mother.

According to Bowlby's control theory (1958), this attachment is established and secured primarily by five instinctual motor patterns. These are sucking, clinging, crying, laughing, and following. The stimulus ending these patterns of attachment is the sound of the mother's voice, her appearance, or her touch. Bowlby later elaborated on his theory and adopted a large number of other instinctual patterns, some of which compete with each other and which may likewise bring about attachment. The classic signs of attachment appear in the human baby later than in primates and can be observed between the first and fifth years. They then disappear at least superficially, on the one hand due to the fact that there is greater variation in the objects of attachment, and on the other because the growing capacity for symbolization removes the attachment pattern from the physical sphere, bringing it into the sphere of mental representations and feelings.

This radical reformulation seems to make it unnecessary to refer to drive economy, to displaced libido and aggression, and to cathexes and anticathexes (making theory a kind of pseudophysics). Just as when using a computer one does not need to think about how much energy is required to change its program—its flexibility is only a question of its storage capacity and software—in Bowlby's control theory one does not need to fall back on Freud's conceptualization of drives as the constantly effective energy from the soma to explain the searching for an object. It is much more a question of finding out which interfering factors in everyday experiences render the attained level of symbolized attachment insufficient, and make it necessary to create attachments anew in the most direct form possible, perhaps even a physical one. But many psychoanalysts have rejected this, claiming that it sounds just as mechanistic as Freud's original drive model.

Bowlby's model is in fact inadequate, especially with regard to the changeability of drive-needs, described so clearly by Freud in "Instincts and Their Vicissitudes" (1915). Consider that the passive role can be just as satisfying as the active role under certain circumstances. (In children's games it can be as much fun to play the child as to play the mother, to play the hunted animal as to play the lion hunter.) Consider too that objects are to a great extent interchangeable, that symbolizations are so variable that a wide range of activities (from reading a novel to going to the opera, from running a race to waging an election campaign) could in theory correspond to similar drive needs. Hermann's model describes in a more comprehensible way than Bowlby's the mutability of these models of component instincts. This can also be seen in Hermann's originality regarding the vicissitudes possible in the case of the clinging drive, i.e., the attitude toward fire and prudishness on the one hand, and laws of black-and-white, dualistic logic on the other. Bowlby, however, mentions Hermann's works merely in passing (1969, 435; 1973, 425, 447). He regrets above all that Hermann did not consider clinging to be an object relation.

I believe that difficulties experienced by Hermann in bringing the phenomena surrounding instinctive clinging within a theoretical framework can be overcome by applying theoretical models that go one step farther than Bowlby's. For example, according to Heinz Lichtenstein (1961), the instinct patterns clearly delimited by ethologists can hardly be observed any longer in man. A large number of gestures, facial expressions, impulsive movements, and so forth, do show their affinity with these instinct patterns. But he believes that, in the primary relationship, the mother helps the child to choose from among a large number of impulses, many of which are totally contradictory and not adapted to reality, those which lead to satisfying communication. As a consequence, this guarantees an individual form of adaptation to reality, partly by identification with the mother. This "identity theme" resulting from communication with the mother represents a totally individual selection from the stock of preexisting instinctual patterns and controls later motivation, mainly unconsciously. Like Bowlby, however, Lichtenstein rejects the Eros-Thanatos polarity as the effective energy behind the unconscious.

The current state of the controversy over drive theory cannot be reviewed in detail here, but the most accommodating synthesis would seem to be that formulated by Otto Kernberg in *Object Relations Theory and Clinical Psychoanalysis* (1976). Kernberg takes into consideration not only the most divergent needs but also the most up-to-date knowledge. He too presupposes that there are innate instinctual patterns and basic affects that, when activated, initially form memory traces that combine perceptions of part of the self, part of the object, and affect into a kind of "affective memory." His explanation for psychological splitting is based on the hypothesis that these seeds are initially stored in the memory only according to the criteria of "good" and "bad," and can only be recalled in connection with the appropriate affect. Later, once constancy of the self and object have been achieved and objects can not only be perceived but also experienced as a whole, simple, automatic, physical instinctual patterns will hardly be observable. These will give way to more integrated drives that have grown out of experience with objects, and only then can one reasonably refer to memory-linked motivation as "libido" and "aggression." Libido and aggression thus become secondarily integrated products of primitive affects (such as arousal and anger) that are the "building blocks" of drives and of biological instinctual patterns like "clinging" or "fight and flight" (Kernberg 1990). If Hermann had used this model, he would probably have found it easier to see clinging as an instinctual pattern in the ethological sense and yet to chart its fate according to the development of libidinal and aggressive impulses.

I should like to try to clarify Hermann's "clinging concept" by showing how drive-related behavior patterns seen in primates are directly observable in some people and by showing with what fantasies (ideas and affects) they may be linked. I shall take as an example only certain aspects of pedophilia and refer the reader to other publications (Berner 1985, 1993) for further discussion of the phenomenon of pedophilia. The importance to pedophiles of the complex and intense relationship with the mother, combined with the frequent absence or inadequacy of contact with the father, was observed initially by Freud in *Leonardo da Vinci and a Memory of His Childhood* (1910). Otto Fenichel (1931) believes the psychic mechanism leading to pedophilia to be the same as the one generally underlying male homosexuality, i.e., identification with the mother and the subsequent narcissistic object-choice. This is also true in the case of heterosexual pedophiles. They tend to be rather effeminate men who in their childhood and puberty often fantasized that they were girls. "They fall in love with little girls, whom they see as an embodiment of themselves, and to whom they want to give everything which their own mother denied them" (21). In this chapter the role of the objects will not assume primary importance. Instead I shall focus attention on the kind of attachment need, the drive-related feelings of attraction, and the "clinging" element, i.e., the desire to grasp hold, exhibited in pedophilia.

The Phenomenology of Pedophilia

Many pedophiles see themselves as extremely tender and caring, even in their sexualized behavior toward children; holding close, stroking, and touching are the main erotically charged actions. They also feel that they are merging into one with the object of their desire, and they overlook the dominance and the suggestive pressure they are exerting. In psychotherapy it very soon becomes clear that the theme of dominance—the contrast between big and small, powerful and powerless—plays a major role in their erotic feelings. There is an erotically charged relationship between a totally dependent, small partner, who still needs looking after and teaching, and a dominant partner, who in his fantasy takes on the role of the caring teacher. It also becomes clear that elements from the pedophile's relation with his mother are repeatedly acted out in his erotic fantasies, although no solution to the aggressive conflicts behind them can be found.

Patient G was a thirty-four-year-old man who came voluntarily to psychotherapy following a prison sentence. He had married very early (at eighteen years old), and the marriage had been a disaster for both partners. When his wife threatened him with divorce after four years of marriage, he responded by threatening to commit suicide; but this did not prevent his wife from divorcing him. Two years later he was found guilty on eight counts of committing sexual acts with under-age girls. Following this first conviction, the patient married his first wife again and lived with her for another six years. The marriage became increasingly difficult, however, as his wife began to drink and had extramarital relationships. At this point the patient turned to his daughter, then aged twelve, and began abusing her.

This led to a second and final divorce and eventually to psychotherapy on release from prison after a conviction on that charge.

The patient had never known his father, who had died in the war. He had grown up with his mother and his sister, who was two years older than he. When he was twelve he was sent to a welfare institution for frequently running away from home. There he had his first homosexual relationships with boys of the same age. His future wife, the sister of a social worker in the children's home, was much more sexually experienced than he. In therapy it soon became clear that small hands had a particular erotic importance for the patient (a common phenomenon with pedophiles). In the tram he could not resist grabbing hold of the hand of a foreign-looking child and holding it tight for several stops. In addition to his obviously dominant position, it was the delicate little hand that created an important precondition for his sexual striving and the impulse to act it out. In the course of therapy the patient got to know a much younger woman. Here too he found that his intellectual superiority played a sexually stimulating role. The strangely split relationship with this partner became clear in a scenario in which he would go for a walk with her in the park and sense a deep, pleasurable feeling of security on holding her hand and feeling its pressure. This can be compared with the feeling of being held. At the same time, he sought to avoid being seen with this woman, whom he despised both for her unfortunate taste in clothes and also for her silliness. He feared being despised by others for being her partner.

The importance of holding hands and stroking plays a role not only for this patient. Another of my patients was caught by the police only because he could not resist ostentatiously walking hand-in-hand with a child he had seduced. A third patient described his main sexual fantasy as the idea of touching girls' delicate hairless genitals with his fingers. As he spoke of this, he continually uttered the word "delicate" in an emotional way. Another relatively young pedophilic patient recorded his fantasies in the form of children's comics that he drew himself. He was fixated on children's hands and lower arms; here fluffy hair and protruding veins were major elements of his arousal. But it was not only the hands and arms that figured prominently in his fantasy, but the acts of clinging and holding on. This is further demonstrated in the following example.

Patient K was a young man who had not only had numerous contacts with male prostitutes, but had sometimes even actively seduced little boys. He stressed that the children were "totally in agreement" and prided himself on the extreme tenderness and understanding that allegedly characterized his seductive behavior. He was never able to accept that his physical superiority played a role, although this was the very aspect determining his erotic strivings toward the children. A dream from the initial phase of therapy throws light on the specifically pedophilic type of relationship, where the borderlines between self and object have ceased to exist.

The dream: The patient is a small boy and does not want to play with the other children in the field as they seem to him to be too rough and wild. The other children fight and hit each other. He runs away across a field to a wood. A man follows him and opens his arms to pick him up. He runs into the man's arms, is picked up, and looks into his face, only to see that he himself is this man.

A second dream related by this patient demonstrates the theme of dominance from another angle. He grew up more or less without a male role model and was frequently forced to change foster mothers due to an unusual home situation. This dream shows how frighteningly superior and sexually aggressive women appeared to him to be, and how delicate little boys served to calm his fears.

Second dream: He was playing an organ surrounded by a boys' choir. A woman teacher, a friend of his, pushed her way through the group of boys and destroyed the wonderful musical harmony with her shrill, powerful soprano voice. The boys smiled condescendingly; the woman was embarrassed and ran away. He felt sorry for her.

According to Hermann, the fantasies of harmony and merging are aspects of clinging. But let us focus on this instinctual clinging drive, rather than on the character of the object, as is customary in modern psychoanalysis. Since it is mainly aspects of very early maternal object relations that are repeated here, the corresponding patterns of drive-determined relations also appear in their original form, which is to a certain extent animal-like and closely related to the reflex instinctual pattern. In Hermann's view, running away (hiding) and being found are both related to clinging and form a diametrically opposed drive pair. Bowlby regards running away as separate from clinging in the proper sense and as one of the five instinctual patterns that form attachment. However, running away, hiding, searching, and clinging are all so dynamically and dialectically intertwined that to have them stand as independent "instinctual patterns" ignores important issues. Running away can serve to ward off the desire to cling, but on the other hand, it can also serve to intensify emotional excitement, making clinging even more pleasurable.

Clinging and Pubic Hair

Pubic hair can take on a strongly phobic character among pedophiles. This is usually interpreted on the oedipal level, but can also be understood within the framework of the dynamics of clinging. The hair initially represents the dominance of the adult. As a remnant of the fur of our ancestors, hair is also the passive organ of clinging. Hermann realized that children have a primal attraction to fur/hair, e.g., to furry toys and to animals that can be stroked. This fur initially has the character of a transitional object and does not attain a secondary—or dangerously phallic—character until later. Fear of hair can also express a deep ambivalence toward the pregenital mother, and in certain circumstances can hide a fear of the mother's mouth.

Many pedophiles consciously avoid sexual intercourse. Sexual fear is focused on fear of penetration. The erection vanishes as soon as the penis enters the feared vagina. In fantasies that are initially only preconscious, the vagina becomes the dangerous, all-devouring mouth, which swallows everything up. The representation of the powerful maternal object leads to a fear that the mother's animal greed would destroy the penis. The preference for small, delicate openings, however, also means the preference for an object to which the pedophile is superior. He can identify with this inferiority to such an extent that he himself no longer needs to be afraid.

The idea of the powerful, superior woman leads pedophiles to perceive their penis by contrast as acutely small and absolutely insufficient. Here the fear felt by many men of being sexually inadequate is exaggerated and cannot be overcome. The background is not so much unconscious rivalry with other men and (conscious) feelings of envy, but the frightening idea of being swallowed up or laughed at by the powerful mother.

Patient K, for example, reported the traumatic experience of his sexual attempts in puberty, where girls of his age had made fun of him for his small penis. *Patient G,* on the other hand, still slept with his mother in one bed at the time of therapy. He often dreamed that he was lying on top of somebody whom he could smother, or that someone was lying on top and smothering him. Sometimes this was accompanied by the fear of being buried alive. Then he would wake up bathed in sweat. In association with these dreams he remembered the war, and it occurred to him that, as they were walking across a field in the war, his mother had in fact thrown herself on top of him, and he had heard the sound of planes and shooting in the distance. (If we try to understand this memory in the psychoanalytic tradition as a "primal scene fantasy," although the patient had no associations confirming this, we might stress the overwhelming closeness of the mother and the abstract distance of the father who was in the war and who was here represented only in the form of threatening sounds.)

It is often noticeable that pedophiles use their hands and fingers as more or less the only penis substitute with which they try to penetrate the dangerous female openings. This substitute formation could be a regressive step toward the clinging pattern. In young primates, when the clinging need is frustrated, a number of activities with the hands can be observed as surrogates, ranging from "grooming" (delousing) themselves and others, to mutual touching of the hands, and tickling with the index finger. This kind of exploratory approach using the index finger can also often be observed in young adult primates (Goodall 1988). Older and sexually exhausted male animals often react to genital presentations by females with tender grooming behavior instead of sexual activity. Here, too, male animals show clearly that when sexual stimulation is obstructed, it is replaced by caring behavior.

But what triggers off this regression into the early clinging pattern? Perhaps early traumatizations caused by a mother figure perceived as overly powerful and not counterbalanced by a father cause pedophiles to attribute the castration threat to the mother. Indications of conscious and unconscious fear of castration can in fact be found among pedophiles much more often and more clearly than fully developed oedipal conflict constellations (Berner 1993).

Consequences of a Frustration of the Clinging Need

Hermann described the hand as an erogenous zone in the act of clinging. He believed that

clinging to the mother's body is not merely directed behavior leading to a particular end (just as sucking and coitus do not merely fulfill biological needs). It is the first manifestation of the libido and of the love for the mother, and the instruments of this love are hands and feet. The hands of the human baby are frustrated in this libido satisfaction and so look for replacement satisfaction. They try to find the replacement satisfaction either independently or in connection with replacement satisfaction from the oral zone (finger-sucking). If the baby sucks its finger it obviously does not become aware only of the function of the mouth, but also of that of the hand. In the language of libido theory, this satisfies not only the mouth zone but also the hand zone. The fact that the satisfaction of the hand zone is dependent on the need for satisfaction of the mouth zone leads us to another group of observations. Let us look at what happens to the hands during the sucking or feeding. . . . As the food reaches the mouth the child opens its hand. . . . At a certain age the baby expresses its strength by means of its hands; its fingers are stretched out wide or pressed tightly together. If we assume that this power behind sucking has erogenous origins we must also accept that the strength in the hands observable during sucking also has the same origins. . . . Both mouth and hand are related parts of one system. (1941, 253)

According to Hermann, this "expression of strength" is a reflection not only of libido, but also of aggression. The clinging drive can become either gentler, leading to tender stroking, or more brutal, leading to aggressive grasping. In the erotic sensations of pedophile patients, this close connection between oral stimulation and stimulation of the fingers and hands does in fact play an important role. But this connection must be seen in the context of the patients' strangely ambiguous approach to tenderness. Tenderness is highly idealized. The nontender, coarse elements of the pedophile's sexual stimulation and their effect on the child are usually totally overlooked. During therapy, patients only seldom become aware of this discrepancy. Then they recall with pain the "lack of oneness" with the child at the moment of greatest arousal. Other patients, who are from the start more conscious of the discord between their own experience and that of the child, exhibit another form of splitting. They try to hide their own arousal from the child, to restrict the actual experience with the child, and to fulfill their erotic wishes only in fantasy and when they are alone.

The combined hand/mouth eroticism is linked for the most part with yearning fantasies of total merging and self-dissolution in the mutual embrace. This is easier to see in pedophiles than in cases described by Hermann and his followers. There these tendencies appeared as neurotic symptoms following a defensive process and could only be interpreted in the course of therapy. (According to Freud [1905], perversion resulting from regression to an infantile satisfaction pattern is—by analogy with photography—the "positive" picture. Neurosis stems from a defense against this same pattern, and is thus the "negative.")

Both the foregoing survey of the literature and my own clinical experiences show that for pedophiles the focus of traumatic experience in childhood lies mainly in an early conflict constellation with the mother, who is from the very beginning experienced as aggressive, moody, changeable, and lacking in tenderness. Father figures leave no memory traces for a long time. Sometimes two women (mother and grandmother) compete for the child. To understand how these constellations affect inner representations, it is important to see how bodily needs are dealt with. It has become clear to me that the frustration of the clinging drive as described by Hermann (hairlessness of the woman's body, clothes preventing skin-to-skin contact between mother and baby) plays a major role in pedophilia. A mother who is often overactive and nervous makes it difficult for the child to have longer phases of body contact and a "flowing of warmth" from body to body. I believe, however, that overindulgence of the child's needs for merging—by constantly carrying the child around, sleeping with the child, etc.—can also lead to a fixation in the form of an increased clinging need.

The frustration or fixation of the clinging need may lead to an increased psychic representation of the hand and mouth as erogenous zones. Only a few authors have so far studied the psychological meaning of these representations. D. W. Winnicott (1945) investigated the importance of the hand and the thumb, their relationship to the transitional object, and thus also to the sense of reality and to the sense of separation of subject and object. Willi Hoffer (1947) similarly described the importance of the hand in relation to orality and to initial ego-integration. He argued that the differentiation of the ego from the common matrix of ego and id shows itself on the surface of the child's body, when finger-sucking causes two sensations at the same time, one oral and one tactile. This satisfies the oral partial drive and results in autoerotic pleasure. Around the twelfth week, when the hand is capable of voluntary and not just reflex movements, the baby puts it in its mouth to reduce the oral tension. In the case of very small babies, the hand competes so much with the nipple that the hand has to be held away from the mouth so that the baby will suck at the breast. From the twelfth week the baby can be observed to bite other objects, but not its own fingers and hand, so these are not the victims of oral aggression. It is possible here to postulate the first experiences of separation between self and not-self. (It is unnecessary to rehearse these ideas anew in the light of the recent findings of developmental psychology [Stern 1985].)

In any case, the hand seems to represent an important center of self-experience for the baby. René Spitz (1962) observed babies who very early showed the tendency to put one of their hands into their mother's mouth in a sort of exchange for putting the mother's nipple into their mouth. Egle Laufer (1982, 103) studied the strange phenomenon that many women avoid masturbating with their hand and formed the hypothesis that the little girl unconsciously identifies her hand with that of her mother and that the form of relationship with the mother strongly influences girls' attitudes toward masturbation in various stages of development. The hand can thus become the source of fear, and the unconsciously aggressive fantasies against the mother can play a major role in the chronic wrist-slitting syndrome.

Self-Representation and Object-Representation

If one tries to imagine the picture that the pedophilic patient has of himself and of his mother, the hypothesis of drive-related clinging alone is insufficient. The structure of the object relations and their origins is worthy of study, both for its role in the concept of clinging and for its own sake. In a speech in honor of Hermann's eightieth birthday, Robert Bak (1972) attempted to trace the development of clinging from the oral to the phallic position. By means of examples, he demonstrated the link between sadism and traumas in the oral-sadistic phase. A reactive increase in the clinging need always plays a role here as a consequence of frustration by the mother (Bak 1968). This is also connected with the fantasy of the huge mother.

Bak sought to show that perversion is a question not only of drive needs, but also of the activation of differentiated object- and self-representations. It is beyond the framework of this chapter to try to pursue the important role played in pedophilia by object-representations and self-representations on the one hand and narcissism on the other. I have already mentioned several times that partial object representations of the mother can have a very cruel, sadistic character; images of the father role are usually abstract and distant but often just as sadistic (Berner 1993). The hostility expected from most objects contributes to the restriction and inhibition of many needs, and leads to the superficial inhibition of aggression (and corresponding unconscious hate) and to gestures revealing childish, anxious submissiveness and its underlying needs.

Conclusion

Hermann's understanding of clinging as a drive-pattern can be very useful in understanding the specific character of erotic desires and behavior in pedophiles. The clinging metaphor has great flexibility: it has links with Bowlby's instinctual patterns, but is less rigidly mechanistic and biologically preprogrammed. It has similarities with Freud's concept of partial drives and is compatible with the idea of secondary integration into libidinal and aggressive motivational systems. The many symbolizations of this primary physical clinging pattern have been described by Hermann and his followers. The formation of perversion in pedophilia offers an opportunity to study an erotic clinging pattern *in statu nascendi* (as a positive picture to the negative of neurosis). For the treatment of pedophilia it is important to be aware that the vicissitudes of self- and object-representations are closely bound up with the erotic drive. The narcissistic character structure behind paraphilic dynamics is crucial to therapy and has been more often described in the last few years than the erotic drive. The aim of this chapter has not been to discuss the complicated story of object-representations and character structures emphasized in modern psychoanalytic theory. I have sought rather to show how too few attempts have been made since Freud to work out a concept of drive and its links with instinctual patterns in animals. Hermann was a pioneer in this field. Phylogenetically old instinctual patterns found among primates are still observable among humans, although the form of these patterns is now no more than fragmentary. Despite their enormous theoretical importance, these have been given too little consideration by psychoanalysts since Hermann.

NOTES

1. For the German *Trieb* I will use the word "drive" as far as humans are concerned.

2. And today we know that even the oldest cave paintings, dating back some 30,000 years, have hands (both with and without fingers) as a theme (Nougier 1984, 101).

REFERENCES

Bak, R. 1968. The Phallic Woman: The Ubiquitous Fantasy in Perversions. *Psychoanal. Study Child*, 23:15–36.
———. 1972. Testimonial to Imre Hermann on His Eightieth Birthday. Unpublished manuscript.
Bálint, M. 1959. *Thrills and Regression*. London: Hogarth Press.
Berner, W. 1985. Das Selbstvertauschungsagieren Pädophiler. *Psychother. med. Psychol.*, 35:17–23.
———. 1993. Das Kastrationsthema und die Pädophilie. *Z. psychoanal. Theor. u. Prax.*, 8:361–73.
Bowlby, J. 1958. The Nature of the Child's Tie to His Mother. *Int. J. Psychoanal.*, 39:350–73.
———. 1969. *Attachment*. London: Hogarth Press.
———. 1973. *Separation: Anxiety and Anger*. London: Hogarth Press.
Fenichel, O. 1931. *Perversionen, Psychosen, Charakterstörungen*. Darmstadt: Wissenschaftliche Buchgesellschaft.
Ferenczi, S. 1913. Stages in the Development of the Sense of Reality. In *Sex in Psychoanalysis*, pp. 181–203. Trans. E. Jones. New York: Dover, 1956.
———. 1924. *Thalassa: A Theory of Genitality*. Trans. H. A. Bunker. New York: Norton, 1968.
Freud, S. 1905. *Three Essays on the Theory of Sexuality*. In *The Standard Edition of the Complete Psychological Works*. Ed. and trans. J. Strachey et al. 24 vols. 7:125–245. London: Hogarth Press, 1953–74.
Goodall, J. 1988. *In the Shadow of Man*. Rev. ed. London: Weidenfeld and Nicolson.
Hartmann, H. 1953. Contribution to the Metapsychology of Schizophrenia. *Psychoanal. Study Child*, 8:177–98.
Hermann, I. 1923. Zur Psychologie der Schimpansen. *Int. Z. Psychoanal.*, 9:81–87

————. 1926. Modelle zu den Oedipus- und Kastrationskomplexen bei Affen. *Imago*, 12:59–69.

————. 1931. Zur Psychologie eines Gorillakindes. *Psychoanal. Bewegung*, 3:38–40.

————. 1933. Zum Triebleben der Primaten. Bemerkungen zu S. Zuckermann. *Imago*, 19:113–25.

————. 1936a. Sich Anklammern-Auf die Suche gehen. *Int. Z. Psychoanal.*, 22:349–70.

————. 1936b. Neue Beiträge zur vergleichenden Psychologie der Primaten. *Imago*, 22:442–56.

————. 1941. Anklammerung, Feuer, Schamgefühl. *Int. Z. Psychoanal.*, 26:252–74.

————. 1943. *Az ember ösi östonei (Man's Basic Drives)*. Budapest: Pantheon.

Hoffer, W. 1947. Mouth, Hand and Ego Integration. *Psychoanal. Study Child*, 3/4:49–56

Jacobson, E. 1964. *The Self and the Object World*. New York: International Universities Press.

Kernberg, O. 1976. *Object Relations Theory and Clinical Psychoanalysis*. New York: Jason Aronson.

————. 1990. New Perspectives in Psychoanalytic Affect Theory. In H. Kellerman and R. Plutchik, eds., *Emotion: Theory, Research and Experience*, pp. 115–31. New York: Academic Press.

Laufer, E. 1982. Female Masturbation in Adolescence and the Development of the Relationship to the Body. *Int. J. Psychoanal.*, 63:295–302.

Lichtenstein, H. 1961. Identity and Sexuality: A Study of Their Interrelationship in Man. *J. Am. Psychoanal. Assn.*, 9:179–259.

Lorenz, K. and N. Tinbergen. 1938. Taxis und Instinkthandlungen in der Eirollbewegung der Graugans. *Z. Tierpsychol.*, 2–1:1–29.

Lukács, D. 1989. Clinging and the Object-Relations Theories. In Varga 1989, pp. 91–97.

Mahler, M., F. Pine, and A. Bergman, 1975. *The Psychological Birth of the Human Infant*. New York: Basic Books.

Nemes, L. 1989. The Psychology of Loss According to the Theories of Imre Hermann and Michael Bálint. In Varga 1989, pp. 105–12.

————. 1990. Die klinische Bedeutung der Anklammerungs theorie von I. Hermann. *Z. psychoanal. Theor. u. Prax.* 5:112–21.

Nougier, L. R. 1984. *Die Welt der Höhlenmenschen*. Hamburg: Reinbeck, 1992.

Spitz, R. 1962. Autoerotism Reexamined: The Role of Early Sexual Behavior Patterns in Personality Formation. *Psychoanal. Study Child*, 18:283–315.

————. 1965. *The First Year of Life*. New York: International Universities Press.

Stern, D. N. 1985. *The Interpersonal World of the Infant*. New York: Basic Books.

Varga, E., ed. 1989. *Memorial Conference on the Centennial of Imre Hermann's Birth*. Budapest: Sokszorosító.

Veress, K. 1989. Die Beziehung der Anklammerung mit psychosomatischen Hautkrankheiten. In Varga 1989, pp. 118–26.

Vikár, G. 1989. The Ideas of Imre Hermann and the Budapest School concerning the Problem of Aggression. In Varga 1989, pp. 127–133.

Winnicott, D. W. 1945. Primitive Emotional Development. *Int. J. Psychoanal.*, 26:137–43.

Twelve

Castration and Narcissism in Ferenczi

■

MICHÈLE BERTRAND

Ferenczi occupies an increasingly important place in contemporary psycho-analytic thought and clinical work. His writings shed light on numerous current pathologies, including borderline conditions, somatizations, and narcissistic frailties. Indeed, Ferenczi is the grand theorist of narcissism. He not only developed Freud's views on the subject, but made his own original contribution.

The notion of narcissism becomes pivotal to Ferenczi's writings during the decade from 1917 to 1927. It therefore seems worthwhile to investigate his understanding of the relationship between the castration complex and narcissism.[1] We know that for Freud the castration complex provides a structure in much the same way as does the Oedipus complex, with which it is closely allied: in men the castration complex marks the decline of the Oedipus complex, the withdrawal of investment from the objects of infan-tile love; in women, by contrast, the castration complex introduces the oedipal problematic. Freud later recognized the narcissistic element in the castration complex. The latter is a wound inflicted on the ego, symbolized by the loss (or absence) of the penis, but also, as Freud argues in *Inhibitions, Symptoms and Anxiety* (1926), by the loss of love, the loss of the object, separation, and death.

Hence, there are several levels of the castration complex, insofar as the ego instincts may or may not support erotic drives, and also depending on

A French version of this chapter, "La douleur d'être: Castration et narcissisme chez Ferenczi," appears in Michèle Bertrand et al., *Ferenczi, patient et psychanalyste* (Paris: Harmattan, 1994), pp. 83–102.

which of them are involved. Self-preservation is a reaction to a direct threat to life; autoerotism is an erotic self-investment in parts of one's body; narcissism refers to a specular image of oneself as a whole. These functions are quite distinct. Given this complexity, the lost or lacking penis could be considered as a metaphor for a lack of some part of the self, and sometimes of the whole self. Every lost object implies such an experience of lack projected into the external world.

Concerning some archaic structures of the mind, the key point is not with which body image the ego may be identified, but rather whether a person can love himself or herself sufficiently to live and share anything with fellow human beings. Ferenczi's works throw a new light on this problem.

In his earlier papers, Ferenczi adheres to a classical Freudian line of thinking. He accepts the idea of castration as meaning a loss of the penis or, more precisely, the phallic symbol and all that it represents. But he still gives much greater emphasis than Freud to the notion of a narcissistic wound. He also demonstrates that not only in certain mental disturbances but also in the very constitution of the subject this wound has a structural character, which one could call fundamental.

Ferenczi's early writings—those from 1908 to 1917—make no mention of the notion of narcissism. (Freud himself did not accord it its full value until "On Narcissism" in 1914.)[2] Nonetheless, certain elements of his discussion of the castration complex bring to mind a narcissistic wound. Such a wound appears mainly in two forms: in the memory of humiliating experience, and in the memory of pain following a bodily attack.

In "The Analytic Interpretation and Treatment of Psychosexual Impotence" (1908), Ferenczi discusses a boy who feels humiliated by the habit of masturbation. In addition, the external pressure felt by the child in his daily surroundings is accompanied by threats not strictly of castration, but rather of bodily attacks and illness. In this paper Ferenczi thus associates the castration complex with the memory of bodily pain. Already a minor difference from Freud is apparent. Freud emphasizes the image of the body; for him, the fear produced by the threat of castration is connected to the boy's vision of the female body lacking a penis. For Ferenczi this fear is connected primarily to the memory of a real injury to the body, which is not necessarily to the genital organs. To put it simply, to the extent that the threat of castration highlights humiliation, a wound to self-esteem, or the memory of a bodily attack, one can say that for Ferenczi it refers proleptically to narcissism.

The term "narcissism" first appears in 1913, both in Freud's *Totem and Taboo* as well as in Ferenczi's "Stages in the Development of the Sense of Reality." Ferenczi recurrently presents castration in a way that stresses the more general loss of a part of the self rather than the specific loss of the penis. "The Psychic Consequences of a 'Castration' in Childhood" (1916–17) does not discuss a castration in the strict sense, but a circumcision. " 'Nonum Prematur in Annum' " (1915) concerns the loss of bodily or intellectual products, and attributes the difficulty some people have in separating themselves from them to a "derivative from abnormal narcissism" (419). This separation is also equated with that between mother and child, which, according to Ferenczi, takes place not with the severing of the umbilical cord, but with the gradual withdrawal of maternal libido.

With Freud we are used to reading these representations as so many symbolic equivalents of the loss of the penis. What is at issue is a difference in emphasis. Whereas for Freud all these mutilations or losses are symbolic of the loss of the penis, for Ferenczi the loss of the penis is but one mutilation among many, one loss among others. There is the same chain of substitutions, but the universal role that Freud allots to the loss of the penis seems to be absent in Ferenczi. According to Freud, the fear aroused by traumas endangering the subject's life or physical and psychic integrity bear upon the representation of the self through its identifications and specular image; according to Ferenczi, the threat of castration draws its force less from a representation (the body without penis) than from a mnemic mark left by pain already suffered.

Another point of no small importance is the age at which this first traumatic experience takes place. In "The Psychic Consequences of a 'Castration' in Childhood," Ferenczi affirms that the critical age for narcissism is three. It therefore seems that if the circumcision had been performed earlier (or later), its effects on the child would not have been so pathological. This observation is tied to a genetic conception of psychic development, which Freud too held at this time. But it is noteworthy that many cultures practice ritual circumcision, and the rite is generally carried out at an age other than the one designated by Ferenczi as critical for narcissism. Jews circumcise on the eighth day after birth, Muslims during the sixth year of life, and certain African populations at puberty. The question arises whether circumcision is less harmful because it is practiced outside the critical phase of the fourth year of life, or simply because it is ritualized, part of a set of rules that are the same for everyone, a rite of social integration.

Freud's genetic conception includes the development of the Oedipus complex and its identifications, which even in Ferenczi's early period were not among his main concerns. One significant turning point occurs from 1916 to 1918, when he published several studies of war neuroses. From a certain point of view, these papers are consistent with Freudian theory, but they also explore new paths and themes that are unique to Ferenczi.

In "Two Types of War Neuroses" (1916–17b) Ferenczi analyzes the symptoms that follow a psychological shock caused by the terror induced by a shell explosion. He notes that they sometimes appear immediately, but at other times only after a second incident, which is insignificant in itself. This temporal model of deferred action recalls the original Freudian theory of trauma.

The symptoms of psychological shock include motor disturbances (tremors, spasms, ataxia, difficulty in walking, astasia-abasia), sensory disturbances (hyperesthesia, hyperacousia, photophobia), difficulties in sleeping and breathing, irregular heartbeat, anxiety, and, often, impotence and the loss of sexual desire. Many of these symptoms recall those of hysteria, and the idea of trauma is central to both. The question, then, becomes whether or not war neuroses are related to hysteria. The answer depends on whether one explains war neuroses in terms of a sexual or a narcissistic etiology. Ferenczi seems to waver between the two. His loyalty to Freud compels him to defend the master's theories of sexual etiology against criticisms from the medical establishment, whose preferred ground of attack was war neuroses. But he hesitates: "It is therefore not impossible that ordinary shocks may lead to the neuroses by way of a *sexual disturbance*" (1916–17b, 141).

A sexual etiology is in no way excluded, but neither is it proven. In fact, the cases Ferenczi cites seem to lead down other paths. What he shows above all is that the neurotic regression in war neuroses is primarily connected to a narcissistic loss, a breakdown in self-confidence going back to infantile megalomania: "For us psycho-analysts the assumption serves, as a preliminary explanation, we are dealing in these traumata with an *ego-injury, an injury to self-love, to narcissism,* the natural result of which is the retraction of the range of the 'object cathexis of the libido,' that is the cessation of the capacity to love anyone else than oneself" (141).

It is useful here to recall the specificity of narcissism, as distinguished from autoerotism. As I have already noted, Freud holds that in autoerotism the body itself is invested, but only by partial impulses, whereas in narcissism the ego is invested as a total object, which becomes unified through a self-image. But Ferenczi seems to favor a functionalist theory of narcissism tied to a partial impulse exchange, rather than a theory of the union of the self-image through identifications. In "Disease- or Patho-Neuroses" (1916–17a), Ferenczi shows that if one part of the body is libidinally invested, it is less because of the part itself than because it represents the entire ego. This is especially true for the face, since "the identification of the whole ego with parts of the face is common to all mankind" (85). Similarly, in the example of "The Psychic Consequences of a 'Castration' in Childhood," it appears that the actual wound has a specific role, in that it is not just an instigating factor, but undermines the entire self-image. For Ferenczi the distinction between primary and secondary narcissism is not clearly established.

Nevertheless, the major role played by narcissism in Ferenczi's thinking leads him to oppose hysterical neurosis and narcissistic neurosis. In the former, the subject defends himself against local libidinal increases through repression, so that the invested part of the body represents, by displacement, the sexual organs. In the latter, the subject identifies completely with himself, whether because of a narcissistic neurosis or because of the simple affliction of narcissism.

In his Introduction to *Psycho-Analysis and the War Neuroses* (1919), Freud distinguishes between several different kinds of neuroses: (1) transference neuroses, caused by "frustration in love" or the unsatisfied demands of the libido, where there is danger of a psychic conflict; (2) pure traumatic neuroses, where the danger is external; and (3) war neuroses, situated between the two, which Freud conceives as traumatic neuroses made possible or facilitated by an ego conflict or narcissistic injury, where the sexual element is unclear. However, Freud holds, the libido theory can be extended even to narcissistic (and traumatic) neuroses by positing the existence of narcissistic libido or "an amount of sexual energy attached to the ego itself" (209). Freud concludes that the problem is solved, once the relation between terror, anxiety, and narcissistic libido has been demonstrated. I would add that the representation of a "castration" must also be factored into the equation, but this fourth notion will show up only in *Inhibitions, Symptoms and Anxiety.*

It is clear that at this time Freud's and Ferenczi's concepts are not in absolute agreement. Ferenczi places traumatic neurosis and war neurosis on the side of narcissistic neuroses, while Freud contrasts traumatic and narcissistic neuroses and concludes that war neuroses are an intermediary form between the transference and traumatic neuroses. Ferenczi develops his theory of narcissism more amply from 1921 to 1927, distinguishing between the symptoms of transference neuroses and narcissistic disorders. The latter are manifested by tics, epilepsy, and the psychoneuroses accompanying menopause.

In "Psycho-Analytical Observations on Tic" (1921), Ferenczi identifies tics (which he does not essentially distinguish from stereotyped behavior) as "signs of narcissistic disorder that are at the most attached to the symptoms of transference neurosis, but are not capable of fusing with them" (144). He cites the case of a young man who is constantly coughing, touching his mustache, or fidgeting with his collar, and thus paying unconscious attention to his body or clothing. In this hyperesthesia Ferenczi detects the inability to tolerate the slightest physical stimulation without a defensive reaction.

At first comparing it to onanism, for which it substitutes, Ferenczi places the tic at the borderline between the psychic and the somatic, which indicates that the mnemic mark left on the body and "narcissistic disease" (145) are dominant here. He notes that the tic often follows a bodily affliction; for example, spasms of the eyelid often appear after a case of conjunctivitis or blepharitis. He goes on to specify three possible conditions that give rise to narcissistic disorders and the fixation of the libido on a given part of the body. These are the danger of death, injury to a libidinally invested part of the body (erogenous zone), and a constitutional narcissism that causes a wound to even the smallest part of the body to affect the entire ego. This last possibility, which marks narcissistic pathologies, seems to characterize subjects with tics.

Narcissism thus involves the integrity simultaneously of the body itself and of an image of the body. Yet this image remains unconscious, inscribed in the body and symbolized in the sense in which Freud uses the term in *Studies on Hysteria* (1895). That is to say, it is an image revealed by stereotypes rather than a specular image of the self as others see it and an awareness that they see it. Freud's "organic" hypothesis of narcissism thus seems verified, even though, according to Ferenczi, one cannot know whether the libido is connected to the organ itself or to its psychological representative.

The way to recovery from tics, then, seems to be through the transformation of this unconscious image into a conscious one, by making the stereotyped image specular. Here Ferenczi recalls the exercises that patients with tics are often made to perform in front of a mirror. Contrary to those who view the mirror as a simple means of control, Ferenczi considers its role to be of primary importance. The mirror shows the subject the deforming effect of the tic on his face and body. An elaboration of the specular image brings about recovery. The narcissistic dimension of tics is confirmed by the character traits of pride and an extreme sensitivity to praise and criticism that authors such as Henry Meije and E. Feindel (whose work is approvingly cited by Ferenczi) find in subjects with tics. These individuals cannot stand the idea of being mocked or appearing ridiculous.

Tics differ from hysterical conversion in that in the latter the libidinal relationship with the object is repressed and shows up as the symptom of an autoerotic symbolization of the body. In tics it is the memory of the organic trauma and not the object relationship that has a pathogenic effect. The symptomatology is reversed. In both hysterical conversion and tics there is a displacement of sexual libido onto the body itself and hence a sexualization of the body—the psychic leap into the somatic. But the most important factor in tics caused by constitutional narcissism is the traumatic memory of the ego. Ferenczi maintains that this is an autoerotism that takes on genital qualities. He continues that the tic is a hysteria of the ego and proposes to add to Freudian theory by hypothesizing a mnemic system of the ego, whose job it would be to register the psychic or somatic processes of the subject herself or himself. This system would be particularly well developed in constitutional narcissism, so that a powerful trauma could provoke, as with tics and traumatic neuroses, an excessive mnemic fixation of the expression worn by the body when the trauma struck. The fixation would be strong enough to cause a permanent or paroxysmal reproduction of this expression. There would thus be a residue of unreleased impulses of stimulation satisfied through motility. A tic is "a new instinct" (158). In order to explain the formation of the symbol in the tic, one must suppose that a conflict exists between the nucleus of the ego—perhaps the result of identifications—and narcissism, and that a process analogous to repression exists with tics as well.

This theoretical outline develops certain new points. The process of somatic symbolization offers an analogue to repression, but it differs from hysterical conversion in that it leaves out the sexual libido. Whereas in war neuroses the conflict is played out between the ego and the sexual libido (with the ego's narcissistic folding in on itself accomplished at the expense of the libido), here there is a different conflict between the nucleus of the ego and narcissism. Or, should we say, between identifications (and introjections) and primary narcissism?

This is indeed what Ferenczi intends by the therapeutic role of the mirror and the fact that various kinds of tics are at once substitutes for autoerotism (in the sense of partial impulses) and defense mechanisms against stimulation, with an element of turning against the self—for example, when scratching extends to the point of self-mutilation (comparable to autotomy in inferior animal species). The tendency to scratch and mutilate oneself is symbolic; what is at issue is not resisting actual stimulation but rather stimulating impulses, which are detached from the ego's mnemic system.

Considered in the preceding context, castration comes to be represented less by the loss of the penis as a symbol of power than by narcissistic losses of bodily integrity or of the ego. Although the word "castration" does not appear expressly in "The Symbolism of the Bridge" (1921), this paper demands such an interpretation. For Ferenczi the bridge recalls the virile member connecting the two parents. But it also extends over a vast and dangerous stretch of water, from whence all life springs; the bridge thus evokes the act of giving birth as well and the appearance and disappearance of the child's body. This coming and going, the conjunction between what is and is not yet—or no longer—living, underlies the anxiety and phobia concerning bridges.

Ferenczi's theory of castration thus shifts from an oedipal context to a more archaic organization of the ego, where the object relationship immediately draws on impulses of self-preservation. This is the opposite of anaclisis, where the sexual instinct is held to lean on survival needs. Ferenczi elaborates these ideas more fully in "On Epileptic Fits" (c. 1921) and "A Contribution to the Understanding of the Psychoneuroses of the Age of Involution" (c. 1921–22).

Like tics, epilepsy falls into an intermediate area between transference and narcissistic neuroses. Epileptic seizures, which Ferenczi observed in a hospital for incurables in Budapest, are "a regression to an extremely primitive level of infantile ego-organization in which wishes were still expressed by uncoordinated movements," such as one also finds in infants (c. 1921, 197–98). By blocking his patients' respiratory passages for a short period of time, Ferenczi was able to interrupt their seizures artificially and awaken them. For him the epileptic seizure constitutes a kind of turning against the self, a withdrawal of libidinal investment from the organism, which is then treated like something foreign and hostile to the ego. Since acute pain can strengthen the desire for absolute peace, the peace of death, the epileptic seizure is a suicide attempt by means of suffocation. Such an affliction threatens those with especially strong and violent impulses, against the explosions of which they seek to protect themselves by a severe repression of their impulses and by reaction formations, such as religiosity or submission. Yet periodically these individuals must let themselves rage, at times against their own persons, which have become foreign and hostile.

In the neuroses of menopause, which can occur in men as well as women, one finds the same narcissistic retreat. Ferenczi holds that people, as they grow older, tend to transfer their libido from objects back into the ego. Old people revert to the narcissism of infancy. They often lose their social interests and ability to sublimate. Their libido regresses to pregenital stages and partial impulses: anal and urethral eroticism, homosexuality, voyeurism, exhibitionism. They become mean and stingy, like the Struld-brugs of *Gulliver's Travels,* old men and women condemned to immortality. The Struldbrugs lose all these vices, says Swift, after they turn eighty, but in the process they become senile. Senile dementia thus compounds the loss of libido with that of intelligence. A meager consolation!

Strangely enough, however, neurotics of both sexes who go through this critical stage of menopause do not give any of the psychological signs of old age. They are generous, modest, and helpful to their families whenever the occasion arises. Yet they suffer from depression and a feeling of degener-ation. They attempt to protect themselves through various means of de-fense—by becoming religious or falling madly in love. But this amorous turmoil, says Ferenczi, is "comparable with the roll of drums used at executions to drown the shrieks of the victim, which in this case is object-libido" (c. 1921–22, 206). In reality, the libido has already been withdrawn from objects, and only the ego obliges the individual to maintain his old affective ties and conceal his present regression through these excessive demonstrations. The depression itself is an expression of the displeasure, the repugnance a highly civilized conscience feels toward incompatible desires. Ferenczi interprets the amorous compulsion that seizes certain people at the critical age as an offshoot of the narcissistic anxiety of castration.

This narcissistic component explains the depression (or manic overcom-pensation) that marks a double conflict—between the object libido and narcissism, but also, within narcissism, between various autoerotisms, to the extent that only one erogenous zone is used. This libidinal degeneration, which indicates a narcissistic loss, characterizes melancholy, neurasthenia, and senile dementia. The same holds true for the transitory depression following coitus; this corresponds (in men) to a temporary loss of the libido and bodily substance. The double narcissistic loss also explains the symbolic displacements of the aged onto money, and the resulting avarice. In "Psy-cho-Analysis and the Mental Disorders of General Paralysis of the Insane" (1922), Ferenczi adds that one finds the same features in the depressive symptoms of general paralysis—the "end of the world" feeling that expresses the unconscious grief at the loss of an ideal with which the ego has identified completely, and the wound the ego suffers because of its compromised value (362).

We have seen that throughout his writings Ferenczi postulates various equivalents of castration, along a narcissistic fault line: the loss of bodily integrity; the loss of bodily substance (sperm) or of one part of the self as a representative of the whole; the loss of object libido; the loss of the self in the face of death or the possibility of extinction; even the loss of a part of the ego and its identifications, in particular its social ideals and ego ideal; and last, the loss of the libidinal investment in the organism itself and a turning against the self, as in epilepsy or melancholy. In the final analysis, suicide would be the ultimate way to hold onto a residue of narcissism, since inflicting death on oneself is less painful than being subjected to it involuntarily. Ferenczi's speculative masterwork *Thalassa* (1924) provides the theoretical underpinning to his meditations on castration and narcissism, by articulating these equivalencies in a symbolic chain and finding a universal equivalent for them in the fantasy of the return to the womb.

Thalassa introduces the essential notion of *amphimixis,* the fusion of eroticisms or partial impulses into a higher union. Such a fusion implies a quantitative and qualitative displacement of the libido. In its progression toward genitality, amphimixis is the obverse of hysterical conversion, which constitutes a regressive genitalization of other parts of the body. The progress that makes up the primacy of the genital lies in the desexualizing of partial erogenous zones, thus leaving each organ free to accomplish its own functions. Behind this idea of amphimixis lie biological theories according to which the "organic division of labor" proceeds toward increased specialization and greater functionality, as one rises through the hierarchy of animal species.

In this functionalist perspective, coitus appears as the amphimictic process par excellence because it achieves a triple identification: of one partner with the other, of the organism with the genital organ, and of the (male) ego with the semen.[3] This triple identification is, in effect, the union of the part with the whole, of the partial impulse with the total object impulse, and of the ego libido with the object libido. All this, says Ferenczi, takes place in order "to return to the mother's womb" (1924, 18). The oedipal desire is thus "the psychological expression of an extremely general biological tendency which lures the organism to a return to the state of rest enjoyed before birth" (19).

We can thus discern the unconscious teleology of all these identifications—to bring about the primary merger or integration into an undifferentiated whole. The biological tendency of every living being, according to Ferenczi, is to return to its inorganic state, which is also a mystical or oceanic tendency on the part of life itself to fuse with the great Whole. It is not a coincidence that Ferenczi expounds these ideas in a work entitled *Thalassa.*

This tendency toward dissolution is unconscious and it is the ultimate aim of sexuality at each of its stages: orally, through incorporation into or penetration of the mother's body; anally, through the infant's identification with his feces, so that the container retains control of the content; autoerotically, through the symbolic equation between infant and penis, and between penis and clitoris, which enables every child to enact with its own body the double role of itself and mother; and genitally, through the realization of maternal regression in coitus. Although the return to the womb holds the key to every stage of sexual development for Ferenczi, it is also a symbolic castration. Thalassic regression ultimately means the loss of oneself in another, the annihilation of one's own identity.

Especially for the male, the emission of sperm in the sexual act is a kind of self-castration. The animal kingdom offers many examples of actual self-castration in coitus. As I have noted, this leads Ferenczi to consider autotomy as a biological model of coitus; erection is likewise the incomplete result of a tendency to detach the genital organ, filled with sensations of unpleasure, from the body. Erection can be seen as a by-product of repression, a battle between rejection and preservation of the endangered organ.

In contrast to Freud, who considers death a psychological representation of castration, Ferenczi deems castration to be a psychological representation of the annihilation or loss of self. This explains the anxiety caused by coitus. The sexual act not only brings pleasure, but also replays the first experience of anxiety—that is, birth—and the passing from nonbeing into being.

Coitus therefore entails the compulsion to repeat and has the qualities of a traumatic neurosis.

From ontogeny Ferenczi proceeds to the vaster perspective of phylogeny. The individual catastrophe of birth duplicates the collective catastrophe of the drying up of the oceans, which finds reverse expression in the flood accounts of many cultures. In biblical and other cosmic narratives, the earth separates from the primitive ocean, of which the mother is the symbol and substitute. Ferenczi remarks that the amniotic liquid exists only for terrestrial species.

Thus, the acts of coitus and insemination conflate not only the primal catastrophes of the individual and the species, but all the other catastrophes that have occurred since life began. And orgasm is the expression not just of intrauterine peace, but of the peace of inorganic existence that preceded the appearance of life. Ferenczi concludes that heredity is but the transmission to our descendants of the difficult task of eliminating the traumas that have left their marks on our bodies, no longer mnemic marks, but "engrams," a literal bodily memory. In this way sexuality, like sleep, accomplishes the return to a blissful edenic state without struggle, a primary narcissism of the womb or the inorganic. The death of the little mermaid, dissolved in the great ocean.

With all due respect to Ferenczi, however, one cannot help but feel a certain skepticism in reading *Thalassa*. For me there is no doubt that his personal equation and mystical search affects the way he resolves the castration complex on the theoretical plane. It is no small paradox to say that castration means access to a state of paradise that is, in fact, the negation of castration. Castration, in the sense that I use it, is a recognition of the fact that one is not the accomplished, completed, reconciled person that the specular image gives one the illusion of being. The human subject remains inescapably separate from himself, foreign to himself, at least in part.

There is nonetheless some truth to Ferenczi's paradisiacal representation, if one considers that this (fantasmatic) perspective supports the entire dynamics of human development. It is true that the recognition of castration gives access to desire and love. But it is also true, as Ferenczi elaborates in "Psycho-Analysis of Sexual Habits" (1925), that the unconscious representation of endless bliss—the negation of castration—allows one to cope with the anxiety that pleasure arouses.

He observes that many neurotics turn out to be hyperanxious subjects who forbid themselves the pleasure of anal and urethral eroticism for fear of the inevitable pain associated with it. He proposes that the courage to confront pregenital eroticism is a necessary factor without which there can be no secure genital eroticism. In other words, at every stage of sexual development the human being must meet—and overcome—castration anxiety. The inability to face castration anxiety causes the displacement of its threats through neurotic avoidance. Some rituals, on the contrary, as Ferenczi recognizes in "Contra-Indications to the 'Active' Psycho-Analytical Technique" (1925)—for example, the practice of circumcision by certain groups with the apparent aim of hardening the penis and preparing it for sexual pleasure—help to overcome castration anxiety.

We can only love objects at the price of our own narcissism. In "Gulliver Fantasies" (1926b), Ferenczi argues that anxiety in fact represents the fear of castration, associated with coitus. The threat of castration thus becomes over time the greatest trauma, erasing even the trauma of birth. It is perhaps ultimately the sole trauma, if one takes all its equivalents—oral (the threat of being devoured or swallowed), anal (the threat of separation), and phallic (the threat of mutilation)—as symbolic avatars. Although the mother in practice often holds "the word" and disciplinary power, it ultimately falls on the father and his paternal role to accompany and give identity to the child in a way that will allow him to confront this anxiety. Citing the case of Swift, whose father died when he was a child—and probably thinking of himself as well, since he was fifteen when his father died—Ferenczi writes: "Our psycho-analytical experience teaches us that sons who grow up without a father are seldom normal in their sexual life; most of them become neurotic or homosexual. The fixation to the mother is in these cases by no means the result of any birth-trauma, but must be attributed to the lack of a father, with whom a boy has to fight out the Oedipus conflict and whose presence helps to resolve the castration anxiety through the process of identification" (58). The Father, bearer of the Law, the Name of the Father, as Lacan would say, has the function of permitting separation, relieving mortal beings of their hallucinations of omnipotence. To the myth of perfect bliss, castration opposes the reality of human limits, and thereby grants access to the possibilities of life and love.

NOTES

1. I define "castration" as the limits involved in the human condition: people must die, they cannot be both male and female, simultaneously realize contradictory wishes, etc.

2. As André Haynal points out in his chapter of this volume, however, Otto Rank did write a paper on narcissism as early as 1911.

3. From this identification is derived the expression "to give oneself" in sexual intercourse.

REFERENCES

Ferenczi, S. 1915. "Nonum Prematur in Annum." In Ferenczi 1926a, pp. 419–21.

———. 1916–17a. Disease- or Patho-Neuroses. In Ferenczi 1926a, pp. 78–89.

———. 1916–17b. Two Types of War Neuroses. In Ferenczi 1926a, pp. 124–41.

———. c. 1921. On Epileptic Fits. Observations and Reflections. In Ferenczi 1955, pp. 197–204.

———. 1921. Psycho-Analytical Observations on Tic. In Ferenczi 1926a, pp. 142–73.

———. c. 1921–22. A Contribution to the Understanding of the Psycho-Neuroses of the Age of Involution. In Ferenczi 1955, pp. 205–12.

———. 1922. Psycho-Analysis and the Mental Disorders of General Paralysis of the Insane. In Ferenczi 1955, pp. 351–70.

———. 1924. Thalassa: A Theory of Genitality. Trans. H. A. Bunker. New York: Norton, 1968.

———. 1926a. Further Contributions to the Theory and Technique of Psycho-Analysis. Ed. J. Rickman. Trans. J. Suttie et al. New York: Brunner/Mazel, 1980.

———. 1926b. Gulliver Fantasies. In Ferenczi 1955, pp. 41–60.

———. 1955. Final Contributions to the Problems and Methods of Psycho-Analysis. Ed. M. Bálint. Trans. E. Mosbacher et al. New York: Brunner/Mazel, 1980.

Freud, S. 1919. Introduction to Psycho-Analysis and the War Neuroses. In The Standard Edition of the Complete Psychological Works, ed. and trans. J. Strachey et al. 24 vols. 17:207–10. London: Hogarth Press, 1953–74.

Thirteen

The Influence of Ferenczi's Ideas on Contemporary Standard Technique

PATRIZIA GIAMPIERI-DEUTSCH
(*Translated by Peter L. Rudnytsky*)

Not only in the scientific literature but also in the "common sense" of psychoanalysis are Freud and Ferenczi often polarized, in that their views on technique are set in opposition, and their standpoints are played off against each other.

Experience versus Insight

An alternative is frequently postulated in the analytic situation between the therapeutic effectiveness of *insight,* which arises in the patient through recollection, interpretation, and reconstruction, and *experience,* which is made possible by the patient's emotional participation in the analytic relationship. In a milder form, which can be traced back to Ferenczi and Rank's *Development of Psycho-Analysis* (1923), this formulation presupposes that a combination of affective and cognitive processes is indispensable for psychic transformation, a point of view that is by now no longer controversial (Thomä and Kächele 1985, 271–74).

Anyone who wishes to elevate this contrast into an absolute dichotomy can summon supporting evidence, especially since Freud and Ferenczi themselves on occasion depicted memory and experience as antithetical explanatory models of analytic effectiveness. Before the publication of *The Development of Psycho-Analysis,* Freud expressed reservations that Ferenczi and Rank "gave too much weight to the experiential factor—and too little to remembering" (quoted in Grubrich-Simitis 1980, 266). After its publication Freud criticized the book because " 'experience' is used like a catchword, its resolution not stressed enough"; in the same letter, on the other hand, Freud conceded that he was impressed by the work as an antidote to his "caution about 'acting out' " (267). In similar words, but no longer critically, Freud defended the work of Ferenczi and Rank in a circular letter of February 2, 1924:

> I value the joint book as a corrective of my view of the role of repetition or acting out in analysis. I used to be apprehensive of it, and regarded these incidents, or experiences as you now call them, as undesirable failures. Rank and Ferenczi now draw attention to the inevitability of these experiences and the possibility of taking useful advantage of them. (Freud and Abraham 1965, 345)

In *The Development of Psycho-Analysis*, Ferenczi advocates "attributing *the chief role in analytic technique to repetition instead of to remembering*," in order to achieve the *"transformation of the reproduced material into actual remembering"* (Ferenczi and Rank 1923, 4). The crucial factor is "the repetition of the Oedipus relation in the analytic situation," and subsequently the interpretation of the transference (54). Only thereby can one arrive at effective recollection:

> Thus the psycho-analytic method of treatment as we understand it today developed into a method which has as its purpose the full re-living of the Oedipus situation in the relation of the patient to the analyst, in order to bring it, with the help of the patient's insight, to a new and more fortunate conclusion.
> This relation develops of its own accord under the conditions of the analysis; the analyst then has the task of noticing its development from slight indications and of bringing the patient to a complete reproduction of the relation in the analytic experience. At times he must bring mere traces of the relationship to development by appropriate measures (activity). (54–55)

Although the discourse here focuses on the analytic situation as a relationship, it is the relationship of the patient to the analyst that is at issue. The emotional experience pertains exclusively to the patient, while the relationship of the analyst to the patient is not adequately contemplated. Therefore recent readings regard Ferenczi and Rank's book as an outmoded conception of the psychoanalytic process, because (at least explicitly) the analyst is still depicted as the observer or active helper—insofar as he or she modifies the analytic setting—of the psychoanalytic process of and in the patient (Fogel 1993).

Father versus Mother

The polarity between Freud as father and Ferenczi as mother is likewise not arbitrary and rests on the fact that they occasionally depicted themselves in diametrically opposed fashion—as when Freud defines the analyst as surgeon or as mirror (1912b, 115, 118), and Ferenczi defines the analyst as a tender mother (1931, 137). But without further elaboration this polarity risks becoming a caricature. Ferenczi, who participated from the beginning in the construction of the theory of transference and whose study, "Introjection and Transference" (1909), was published three years before Freud's "The Dynamics of Transference" (1912a), was well aware that the patient's emotional needs determined whether the analyst would assume the role of the father or mother—or, as a rule, both. In the second phase of his reflections on transference Ferenczi remarked:

For in every correct analysis the analyst plays all possible roles for the unconscious of the patient; it only depends upon him always to recognize this at the proper time and under certain circumstances to consciously make use of it. Particularly important is the role of the two parental images—father and mother—in which the analyst actually constantly alternates. (Ferenczi and Rank 1923, 41).

The dimension—above and beyond the transference—in which the analyst also always brings "real" aspects into the psychoanalytic process is that of the therapeutic alliance. Only in this arena can Freud's self-understanding as father and Ferenczi's as mother become meaningful. Ferenczi's insistence on sincerity, humility (which does not mean the inflicting of countertransferences), and symmetry in the relationship between patient and analyst can be appropriately understood as part of the therapeutic alliance, as contemporary practitioners have recognized (Etchegoyen 1991, 257).

Research and Theory versus Healing and Therapy

In addition to the aforementioned alternatives of insight/experience and father/mother, the polarities between Freud as theorist and Ferenczi as therapist, as well as between Freud's love of research and Ferenczi's mania for healing, are likewise widespread and not without support in their works and correspondence, so that scraps of evidence and anecdotes at any rate are easy to find. But in this connection it must be stressed that there exists a gap between Freud's instructions concerning method and their realization in his actual practice, as anyone can readily see through a parallel reading of Freud's technical writings and case histories (Haynal 1987, 1–18). That is not surprising, since Freud explicitly spoke out against a "mechanization of technique" (1913a, 123) and compiled his technical writings in the form of recommendations to readers of the *Zentralblatt für Psychoanalyse,* some of whom had heard him discuss these matters in person at the Vienna Psychoanalytic Society. It would be profitable to regard Freud's case histories as an amplification of his meager technical instructions.

The Periodization of Ferenczi's Technical Contributions

Should one acquiesce in the received view of Freud and Ferenczi as polar opposites and take sides in favor of one or the other? Or should one reconcile them? If Ferenczi's texts are investigated in a historical context, other formulations of the question emerge. In spite of all tendentious misinterpretations, Ferenczi is not always perfectly consistent. Ferenczi is often quoted and invoked without a precise chronological sense of his contributions, although the multifaceted nature of his technical writings was recognized from the beginning. As Alice Bálint records: "At the Wiesbaden Congress he said himself in the circle of his pupils that it often distressed and alarmed him to think of the various directions in which he had gone in the course of his life and to imagine that perhaps now, scattered throughout the world, there were some of his pupils who still remained true to one or another of his already abandoned methods" (1936, 47).

In each phase of his reflections on psychoanalytic technique, Ferenczi distanced himself from any regulative ideal that could be defined as "standard technique": "In the course of my practical analytic work, which extended over many years, I constantly found myself infringing one or another of Freud's injunctions in his 'Recommendations on Technique' " (1930, 114). Ferenczi's major innovations concern the psychoanalytic setting and are, in chronological sequence, the "active technique," based on the principle of renunciation; the "relaxation technique," based on the principle of permission; and "mutual analysis." As is well known, the active technique was tried by Freud in the case of the Wolf-Man and advocated in his 1918 lecture to the Budapest Congress (1919). If the normally immutable setting, the "nonnegotiable" aspect of the analytic situation, is changed, it itself becomes process (Etchegoyen 1991, 519); thus modifications of the setting influence the elements of the psychoanalytic process (transference, countertransference, therapeutic alliance).

Ferenczi's Experiments

Contemporary interest has been accorded especially to Ferenczi's brilliant technical experiments. This experimentation was grounded, among other factors, on the practical need to treat a broader spectrum of patients and appealed not least to what, in a letter to Freud of April 17, 1910, Ferenczi termed Freud's "newest principle (which, by the way, is becoming more and more clear to me)—that technique has to direct itself according to the uniqueness of each case" (Brabant et al. 1992, 163). This principle remained valid for Ferenczi as late as 1931, when he asserted that the analyst should introduce variations into the setting that facilitate the analysis especially "in severe cases with which [the usual technique] proved unable to cope successfully" (1931, 128). What is more, Freud too allowed for the possibility of technical modifications when psychoanalysis was used to treat institutionalized patients: "In practice, it is true, there is nothing to be said against a psychotherapist combining a certain amount of analysis with some suggestive influence in order to achieve a perceptible result in a shorter time—as is necessary, for instance, in institutions" (1912b, 118). Or in a more famous formulation: "It is very probable, too, that the large-scale application of our therapy will compel us to alloy the pure gold of analysis freely with the copper of direct suggestion" (1919, 167–68).

On Standard Technique

This contemporary interest in Ferenczi's technical variations should not conceal the degree to which he also made fundamental contributions to the elaboration of standard technique. Despite the Ferenczi renaissance, this aspect of his contribution remains insufficiently appreciated, so that a foray in this direction is warranted.

The term "standard technique" is preferable to "classical technique." The predicate "classical" encourages idealizations that might in turn lead to the devaluation of antithetical positions in the research process, and above all it makes no allowance for progress in psychoanalytic research. The term "classical technique," incidentally, as Freud reminded the members of the Committee in a circular letter on February 15, 1924, was coined by Ferenczi himself (Freud and Abraham 1965, 346; see Jones 1957, 63–64). The standard technique draws together rules of treatment, derived from Freud's recommendations, from which can be extrapolated "a procedure for the physician which is effective on the average" (Freud 1913a, 123). Beyond this, the term "standard technique" points to the international nature of psychoanalysis as a movement and to its status as a scientific discipline. It thus calls attention to the potential translatability of its laws as well as to the possibility of their cumulative development, without overlooking local tendencies and styles or, for that matter, internal and external controversies—for example, with philosophers of science—over its scientific legitimacy. By standard technique is meant something that is continually evolving along with the progress of research in the psychoanalytic community.

Two short tributes by Freud to Ferenczi are frequently quoted but perhaps not completely understood. After the dialogue between them was interrupted by Ferenczi's death, Freud wrote a sincere obituary in which he did not refrain from distancing himself from Ferenczi's recent experiments and yet openly proclaimed: "For many successive years we spent the autumn holidays together in Italy, and a number of papers that appeared later in the literature under his or my name took their first shape in our talks there" (1933, 227–28). Freud thereby communicated unmistakably to the psychoanalytic public the degree to which the exchanges with Ferenczi had influenced his own technical recommendations, and vice versa. Freud went on to add that Ferenczi a decade earlier "had already published most of the works which have made all analysts into his pupils" (228). Freud was obviously referring to those works which Ferenczi had published by 1923 and was acknowledging his role as the cocreator and mediator of the standard technique of that time.

Ferenczi's Importance for Contemporary Standard Technique

In reading Ferenczi's writings one gains the impression of encountering something familiar; one discovers that many concepts and rules in use today derive from Ferenczi, without one's having been aware of it. But certain overlooked features of Ferenczi's thought are particularly prominent. In particular, his investigation of the analytic situation can be seen as a precursor of contemporary standard technique.

Several of Ferenczi's previously mentioned efforts to modify the analytic setting seem to make his work indistinguishable from psychotherapy. These experiments, from which arose Ferenczi's earlier notoriety, have recently been thoroughly investigated. But since elements such as the renunciation of the active technique and the encouragement of relaxation have long been integrated into the fundamental rules of analysis, Ferenczi's experiments can be more profitably regarded as empirical reports on research into the boundaries of the standard setting.[1]

Ferenczi's initial premise was that the analytic process takes place in the patient. The analyst was thought to observe the patient and interpret his transferences on to the analyst. But in *The Development of Psycho-Analysis* Ferenczi took a step forward. The analytic process continued to be located in the patient, but the issue became one of a relationship in the analytic setting. That was an important breakthrough, but as I have already indicated, Ferenczi still spoke only about the *patient's* relationship to the analyst and the *patient's* emotional experience, while the relationship of the analyst to the patient was not taken adequately into account.

Finally, however, Ferenczi proposed an innovation that is especially relevant for contemporary standard technique. He defined the analytic process as taking place *between* patient and analyst and encouraged the analyst to interpret the transferences of the patient with the help of his own countertransference. The analyst and his psychic processes, as well as his theoretical allegiances or metapsychology, became legitimate objects of research in the psychoanalytic process.

What takes place between analyst and patient? What does the analyst contribute to the analytic relationship? This unique relationship consists of three elements: the transference of the patient, the countertransference of the analyst as a response to the transference of the patient, and the therapeutic alliance between patient and analyst. How does the analyst move from listening to associations and from feeling countertransferential affects to interpretation? Johannes Cremerius proposes that Ferenczi's "understanding of the analyst-patient relationship allows the analyst to become the central instrument of the treatment" (1983, 1001). But he simultaneously maintains that it is mandatory to read Ferenczi "through the lens of Bálint" (991).

Ferenczi and Drive Theory

Bálint and object relations psychology have, as is well known, been influenced by Ferenczi, even though its representatives have only rarely invoked him. Thus, one can freely invert the sequence and return to Ferenczi through his effects on Bálint and object relations psychology.

On the other hand, this is not the only possible way to read Ferenczi, so that the question arises: how much of Ferenczi's work—a many-sided opus divided into several periods—is lost in this perspective? To single out only one point, it is frequently contended that Ferenczi renounced drive theory. In "Confusion of Tongues between Adults and the Child," Ferenczi indeed proposes a qualification of drive theory: "I am certain—if all this proves true—that we shall have to revise certain chapters of the theory of sexuality and genitality. . . . Also my theory of genitality neglected this difference between the phases of tenderness and passion" (1933, 166). At the same time, Ferenczi does not give up the concept of phase-specific fantasies: "Thus almost without exception we find the hidden play of taking the place of the parent of the same sex in order to be married to the other parent" (163). Far from abandoning drive theory, even in the *Clinical Diary* (1985), where he vehemently attacks it, Ferenczi undertakes its continual revision. An appreciation of these aspects of his thought is long overdue.

On Transference

At least four phases can be demarcated in Ferenczi's theory of transference. In the first, Ferenczi investigates some important aspects of transference: its universality in neurosis, its relation to suggestion and hypnosis, and its role in differential diagnosis. All three of these aspects will be taken up again by Freud in later studies, so that the standpoints of both men are in accord. The correspondence between Freud and Ferenczi from late November 1908 through early February 1909 testifies to their common interest in technique and to the genesis of Ferenczi's "Introjection and Transference" (1909), as well as to Freud's effort to place this paper in a journal. In this initial phase both Ferenczi and Freud differentiate between transference and the reality elements of the therapeutic alliance in the analytic process.

Subsequently, at the time of his book with Rank, Ferenczi underscores "the repetition of the Oedipus relation in the analytic situation (transference)" (Ferenczi and Rank 1923, 54), and thereby places repetition at the heart of his own reflections. Repetition is a facet of transference that had been discovered and emphasized by Freud from the beginning. In his third phase, Ferenczi contends that all expressions of the patient should be understood as transferences on to the analyst. He thereby articulates an expanded conception of transference that foreshadows the Kleinian school. In his final reflections Ferenczi rejects the concept of transference altogether. Inasmuch as Ferenczi seeks to dispense with transference as a feature of the analytic process, he reduces the analytic relationship to an everyday relationship, in which only the therapeutic alliance remains intact.

The Universality of Transference in Neurosis

Ferenczi highlights the universality of transference in neurosis. He observes "that the psychoneurotic's inclination to transference expresses itself not only in the special case of a psycho-analytic treatment, and not only in regard to the physician, but that *transference is a psychical mechanism that is characteristic of the neurosis altogether, one that is evidenced in all situations of life, and which underlies most of the pathological manifestations*" (1909, 31). Three years later Freud writes similarly in "The Dynamics of Transference": "It is not a fact that transference emerges with greater intensity and lack of restraint during psycho-analysis than outside it. . . . These characteristics of transference are therefore to be attributed not to psycho-analysis but to transference itself" (1912a, 101).

The psychoanalytic cure therefore does not give rise to the transference, but simply provokes and discloses it as a *"catalysis"* (Ferenczi 1909, 39). As early as 1909 Ferenczi notes that the unsatisfied libido directs itself onto the analyst, as it can also direct itself onto other people. According to Ferenczi, the transference is "a special case of the neurotic's inclination to displacement" (1909, 33), and the analyst—like any physician—is predestined to become its object. In several cases Ferenczi found that "the relaxation of the ethical censor in the physician's consulting room was partly determined by the lessened feeling of responsibility on the patient's part" (1909, 37). The transference manifests itself in either a positive or a negative form, as Freud likewise maintains: "We must make up our minds to distinguish a 'positive' transference from a 'negative' one, and to treat the two sorts of transference to the doctor separately" (1912a, 105). In his final reflections in the *Clinical Diary* Ferenczi adopts a completely different view: "The analytic technique creates transference" (1985, 210). The immutability of the analytic setting brings about the formation of the transference neurosis.

Hypnosis and Suggestion

Hypnosis and suggestion are held to arise from transferences founded on sexual wishes toward parental figures. Out of his love or anxiety for his parents the patient transfers his wishes on to the hypnotist. In the first case the patient will be credulous; in the second, obedient: *"The capacity to be hypnotised and influenced by suggestion depends on the possibility of transference taking place, or more openly expressed, on the positive, although unconscious, sexual attitude that the person being hypnotised adopts in regard to the hypnotist; the transference, however, like every 'object love,' has its deepest roots in the repressed parental complexes"* (Ferenczi 1909, 57).

The Significance of Transference for Differential Diagnosis

Ferenczi furthermore draws attention to the importance of transference for differential diagnosis. Since all neurotics are inclined to transference, the presence of transference as a common trait allows the neuroses to be differentiated from other psychic disturbances, specifically dementia praecox and paranoia (1909, 40). The demented individual detaches his interest from the external world and becomes autoerotic; the paranoiac projects his unwanted libidinal excitations on to the external world. The neurotic, unlike either of these, seeks objects in the external world, cathects them with fantasies, takes them up into the "ego"—or what would be rendered in contemporary terminology as self-representations—and transfers his feelings on to them: "I described introjection as an extension to the external world of the original autoerotic interests, by including its objects in the ego" (1912, 316). Ferenczi attempts a summary formulation: "The psychoneurotic suffers from a widening, the paranoiac from a shrinking of his ego" (1909, 41).

This initial theory of transference held by Ferenczi condenses elements that appear scattered in various places throughout Freud's works. A comparison between Ferenczi's essay and Freud's "Dynamics of Transference" is fruitful. The latter belongs to the series of papers in the *Zentralblatt* that did not seek to introduce any new views, but simply didactically to impart the standard technique of the time.

Ferenczi's early reflections continued to influence clinical practice the 1960s. Ralph Greenson, for example, took over, among other ideas, Ferenczi's conception of transference as displacement: "Displacement refers to the shift of feelings, fantasies, etc. from an *object* or *object representation* in the past to an object or object representation in the present" (1967, 175). On the other hand, in contrast to Ferenczi, it seemed vital to Greenson to separate the concept of transference from that of introjection. He criticized the Kleinian conception of transference as projection and introjection, and thereby indirectly pointed to a contradiction in Ferenczi's first conceptions. Projection refers to the shifting of one part of the self-representation onto an external object or onto an object-representation, whereas introjection "is the incorporation of something from an external object into the self-representation" (175). Therefore, for Greenson introjection and projection do not coincide with transference understood as the displacement of something from the patient's past into the current analytic situation.

Ferenczi's Later Concepts of Transference

In his second phase, which culminates in *The Development of Psycho-Analysis,* Ferenczi elaborates an aspect of transference that is mentioned but not worked out in "Introjection and Transference." Transference is mainly seen at this time as a repetition of the oedipal relation in the analytic situation. But whereas in the first and second periods the real aspects of the analyst are preserved alongside the transference as the nucleus of the therapeutic alliance, in the third phase every relation of the patient to the analyst is seen by Ferenczi as a transference phenomenon: "I can only repeat here that for me and my analysis it is an advance that I take Rank's suggestion regarding the relation of patient to analyst as the cardinal point of the analytic material and regard *every* dream, *every* gesture, *every* parapraxis, *every* aggravation or improvement in the condition of the patient as above all an expression of transference or resistance" (1925, 225). Ferenczi admits that priority in this technical standpoint actually belongs to Georg Groddeck, "who when the condition of one of his patients is aggravated always comes forward with the stereotyped question, 'What have you against me, what have I done to you'?" (225). This concept was resuscitated and further extended by Melanie Klein, who began her career as Ferenczi's pupil.

In the *Clinical Diary*, finally, as I have indicated, Ferenczi attempts at least provisionally to abandon the distinction between analytic and everyday relationships: "Through the henceforth consciously directed unmasking of the so-called transference and countertransference as the hiding places of the most significant obstacles to the completion of *all* analyses, one comes to be almost convinced that no analysis can succeed as long as the false and alleged differences between the 'analytical situation' and ordinary life are not overcome" (1985, 129).

On Countertransference

The term "countertransference" first surfaces in Freud's correspondence with Jung in a letter of July 7, 1909, and then appears in print in "The Future Prospects of Psycho-Analytic Therapy" (1910). Freud avows his own paternal countertransference toward Ferenczi in a letter to Ferenczi of October 6, 1910, after the latter had lamented the misunderstandings on their shared Sicilian journey. Countertransference is understood by Freud, following a metaphor of Stekel's, as a "blind spot" (1912b, 116).

Long before Paula Heimann (1950) in London and Heinrich Racker (1948) in Buenos Aires, among others, recognized the countertransference to be not simply an interference but an important tool of the treatment, Ferenczi led the way in this direction with "The Control of the Counter-Transference," a section in his paper, "On the Technique of Psycho-Analysis" (1919).

In this work Ferenczi regards the countertransference first of all as a dangerous independent phenomenon: "The enthusiastic doctor who wants to 'sweep away' his patient in his zeal to cure and elucidate the case does not observe the little and big indications of fixation to the patient, male or female, but they are only too well aware of it, and interpret the underlying tendency quite correctly without guessing that the doctor himself was ignorant of it." Ferenczi warns that "insufficient consideration of the counter-transference puts the patient himself into a condition that cannot be altered and which he uses as a motive for breaking off the treatment" (1919, 188). These passages could be construed to foreshadow the idea of Lacan (1951)—or, in an entirely different theoretical framework, of Robert Fliess (1953, 273)—that the transference is a reaction of the patient to the analyst's countertransference. But Ferenczi did not adopt this radical concept of countertransference; it is understood by him above all as a neurotic remnant of the analyst's transference, a blind spot, and not yet as a response to the patient's transference. In the radical view of the reciprocal transferences between patient and analyst, the uniqueness of the analytic relationship is renounced, and the rules of communication of ordinary life, including symmetry and mutuality, prevail.[2] But "the course the analyst must pursue is neither of these; it is one for which there is no model in real life" (Freud 1915, 166).

In their reproaches, Ferenczi writes, "the patients are simply unmasking the doctor's unconscious. . . . In such arraignments, therefore, both the opposing parties, remarkably enough, are right. The doctor can swear that he—consciously—intended nothing but the patient's cure, but the patient is also right, for the doctor has unconsciously made himself his patient's patron or knight and allowed this to be remarked by various indications" (1919, 188). Only if this unconscious attitude of the analyst were to arise as a reaction to the transference of the patient could it be regarded as a "complementary attitude" (Deutsch 1926, 423) or a "complementary identification" (Racker 1948, 124–25; 1953, 134–35).

In a February 7, 1911, letter to Freud, Ferenczi described the counter-transference as a response to an induction process stimulated by the patient:

"L'autre danger" that the psychoanalyst is subject to . . . is that, in lovingly going into the determinants of a neurosis, one finds them, so to speak, *justified*. One is actually right in doing so: everything that exists is *eo ipso*—from a philosophical point of view—justified in existing. The only thing is that this all too forgiving understanding can make one too inclined to take a position in favor of the patient (i.e., in favor of fantasy) and against those close to him (i.e., reality).

Besides monitoring the countertransference, one must therefore also pay heed to this "being induced" by the patients. (Perhaps it is only a question here of a form of countertransference.) (Brabant et al. 1992, 253)

Later authors, who do not differentiate between complementary and concordant identification, have regarded the countertransference as a "creation of the patient" and a piece of his personality (Heimann 1950, 83). Racker has attempted a clarification by introducing the concept of a complementary identification on the part of the analyst as a reaction to the projective identification of the patient (1958, 66). Léon Grinberg has further attempted to distinguish between complementary identification and projective counteridentification. Although the former arises as a reaction, it is founded on neurotic remnants in the analyst. Projective counteridentification is the response to the projective identification of the patient, which is held to be independent of the analyst's conflicts (1979, 176–77).[3]

In "The Control of the Counter-Transference" Ferenczi depicts the emergence of the countertransference. First the analyst succeeds in controlling his attitude toward the patient, then he finds himself in a state of resistance to the countertransference, and finally the analyst can succeed in managing the transference:

If the psycho-analyst has learnt painfully to appreciate the counter-transference symptoms and achieved the control of everything in his actions and speech, and also in his feelings, that might give occasion for any complications, he is threatened with the danger of falling into the other extreme and of becoming too abrupt and repellent towards the patient; this would retard the appearance of the transference, the precondition of every successful psycho-analysis, or make it altogether impossible. This second phase could be characterized as the phase of resistance against the counter-transference. (1919, 188)

Ferenczi thereby justifies the countertransference, which arises as a response to the transference of the patient, as an instrument, provided that the analyst is aware of it. For this reason he speaks out in favor of the necessity of a training analysis, which has the aim of enabling the analyst to master the "blind spots" of countertransference. Thence ensued the introduction of the second "fundamental rule" (the first being that of free association), namely, the duty of every analyst to undergo a training analysis. Ferenczi concludes:

> Only when this has been achieved, when one is therefore certain that the guard set for the purpose signals immediately whenever one's feelings towards the patient tend to overstep the right limits in either a positive or a negative sense, only then can the doctor "let himself go" during the treatment as psycho-analysis requires of him. (1919, 189)

This letting-go characterizes the countertransference of the analyst as a response to the transference of the patient:

> In time one learns to interrupt the letting oneself go on certain signals from the preconscious, and to put the critical attitude in its place. This constant oscillation between free play of phantasy and critical scrutiny presupposes a freedom and uninhibited motility of psychic excitation on the doctor's part. (189)

Evenly Hovering Attention

The concept of evenly hovering attention defines the analytic mode of listening (Greenson 1967, 100; Thomä and Kächele 1985, 248). Such oscillation allows the analyst to adopt at once a detached and an engaged standpoint. Ferenczi describes the capacity of the analyst to shuttle back and forth between the positions of observer and participant and pleads for an equipoise between feeling and thinking. He says that technique requires the analyst to engage in "the free play of association and phantasy, the full indulgence of *his own unconscious;* we know from Freud that only in this way is it possible to grasp intuitively the expressions of the patient's unconscious that are concealed in the manifest manner of speech and behavior" (1919, 189). Ferenczi relies here on Freud's notion that analysis involves communication from unconscious to unconscious. Freud writes that the analyst

> must turn his own unconscious like a receptive organ towards the transmitting unconscious of the patient. He must adjust himself to the patient as a telephone receiver is adjusted to the transmitting microphone. Just as the receiver converts back into sound waves, so the doctor's unconscious is able, from the derivatives of the unconscious which are communicated to him, to reconstruct that unconscious, which has determined the patient's free associations. (1912b, 115–16)

The analyst should be in a position "to use his own unconscious in this way as an instrument in the analysis" (115), since "everyone possesses in his own unconscious an instrument with which he can interpret the utterances of other people" (1913b, 320).

Freud captures in these images the dynamic interplay between transference and countertransference. This unique form of communication is the instrument that opens the way to interpretation. "On the other hand," Ferenczi writes, "the doctor must subject the material submitted by himself and the patient to a logical scrutiny, and in his dealings and communications may only let himself be guided exclusively by the results of this mental effort" (1919, 189). The analyst then no longer resonates with, but rather deliberately pulls back from, the patient. Ferenczi formulates this step in interpretation still more clearly ten years later in "The Elasticity of Psycho-Analytic Technique": "Before the physician decides to tell the patient something, he must temporarily withdraw his libido from the latter, and weigh the situation coolly; he must in no circumstances allow himself to be guided by his feelings alone" (1928, 90). Ferenczi here reiterates the same set of ideas and conveys the rhythm of analytic work:

One gradually becomes aware how immensely complicated the mental work demanded from the analyst is. He has to let the patient's free associations play upon him; simultaneously he lets his own fantasy go to work with the association material; from time to time he compares the new connexions that arise with earlier results of the analysis; and not for one moment must he relax the vigilance and criticism made necessary by his own subjective trends.

One might say that his mind swings continuously between empathy, self-observation, and making judgements. The latter emerge spontaneously from time to time as mental signals, which at first, of course, have to be assessed only as such; only after the accumulation of further evidence is one entitled to make an interpretation. (95–96)

Thus, Ferenczi again distinguishes between the blind spot, the analyst's interfering "subjective trends," and his enabling "fantasy," the countertransference in a contemporary sense.

Empathy

In contemplating the most favorable moment for offering an interpretation, Freud had from the outset drawn attention to the requirement that the analyst be able to listen empathically. Freud cautioned the analyst not to proceed "until a transference has been established in the patient, a proper *rapport* with him. It remains the first aim of the treatment to attach him to it and to the person of the doctor. . . . It is certainly possible to forfeit this first success if from the start one takes up any standpoint other than one of sympathetic understanding" (1913a, 139–40).

Ferenczi further elucidates the importance of this empathic resonance: "In general it is advantageous to consider for a time *every one*, even the most improbable, of the communications as in some way possible, even to accept an apparently obvious delusion. . . . Thus, by leaving on one side the 'reality' question, one can feel one's way more completely into the patient's mental life" (1931, 235).

In a letter to Freud of January 15, 1928, which comments on "The Elasticity of Psycho-Analytic Technique," however, Ferenczi sharply delineated the boundaries of empathy: "I . . . mean that one must at first put oneself in, 'empathize' with, the patient's situation. . . . The analyst's empathy dare not take place in his unconscious, but in his preconscious" (quoted in Grubrich-Simitis 1980, 272). It is a kind of identification, as Ferenczi notes in his effort to proffer a metapsychology of the psychic processes in the analyst during analysis: "His cathexes oscillate between identification (analytic object-love) on the one hand and self-control or intellectual activity on the other" (1928, 98). R. Horacio Etchegoyen (1991, 270–74) has attempted to understand the concept of empathy not in the manner of social science, but, following Ferenczi, psychoanalytically. As Etchegoyen makes clear, empathy is a matter of concordant countertransference. The analyst experiences every feeling that the patient has experienced and identifies himself with the patient, or rather with the affected part of the patient's psychic apparatus (see Racker 1948, 124–25; 1953, 134–36).

The Counter-Question Rule

A number of Ferenczi's later reflections on technique have passed into the received wisdom of standard technique without necessarily having been credited to their originator. For example, Ferenczi is the forgotten creator of the counter-question rule (Thomä and Kächele 1985, 252–57). He writes:

I made it a rule, whenever a patient asks me a question or requests some information, to respond with a counter interrogation of how he came to hit on that
question. If I simply answered him, then the impulse from which the question
sprang would be satisfied by the reply; by the method indicated, however, the
patient's interest is directed to the sources of his curiosity, and when his questions
are treated analytically he almost always forgets to repeat the original enquiries,
thus showing that as a matter of fact they were unimportant and only significant as
a means for the unconscious. (1919, 183)

Silence

Ferenczi also concerns himself with the meaning of silence:

In such cases it is better to encounter the patient's silence with silence. It may
happen that the greater part of the hour passes without the doctor or the patient
having said a single word. The patient finds it very difficult to endure the doctor's
silence; he gets the impression that the doctor is annoyed with him, that is, he
projects his own bad conscience on the doctor, and this finally decides him to give
in and renounce his negativism. . . . The fact that the doctor at many interviews
pays little heed to the patient's associations and only pricks up his ears at certain
statements also belongs to the chapter "on counter-transference"; dozing may
happen in these circumstances. (1919, 179–80)

Racker's attitude to the foregoing is interesting, especially since he places
only a limited value on Ferenczi's contribution to the understanding of
countertransference:

He [the analyst] listens most of the time, or wishes to listen, but is not invariably
doing so. Ferenczi (1919) refers to this fact and expresses the opinion that the
analyst's distractibility is of little importance, for the patient at such moments must
certainly be in resistance. . . . At any rate, Ferenczi here refers to a countertransference response and deduces from it the analysand's psychological situation. He says
"that we were reacting unconsciously to the emptiness and worthlessness of the
associations just presented by the withdrawal of conscious excitation" (1919, 180).
The situation might be described as one of mutual withdrawal. The analyst's
withdrawal is a response to the analysand's withdrawal, which, however, is a
response to an imagined or real psychological position of the analyst. If we have
withdrawn—if we are not listening but are thinking of something else—we may
utilize this event in the service of the analysis like any other information we
acquire. (1953, 138–39)

Ferenczi continues to laud the silence of the analyst in the later phases of
his development, and, it should be noted, not simply at the time of his

active technique of renunciation but in the final period of his relaxation technique. In his posthumously published *Notes and Fragments,* he writes: "The disadvantages of 'going on talking.' Obstacles to 'relaxation.' Communication makes things 'clear conscious' and speculative. Associations remain on the surface (or go round in circles; *piétiner sur place*). Relation to analyst remains conscious" (1932c, 258). Ferenczi then has recourse to clinical practice and offers two cases. In one, "The patient felt disturbed and irritated by the often repeated 'signs of agreement' ('Hm' — 'yes' — 'of course,' etc.) on the part of the analyst; had the feeling that something was being interrupted by them" (1932b, 259). It is, he observes elsewhere, up to the tact or concordant countertransference — in other words, the capacity for empathy — of the analyst to know "when one should keep silent and await further associations and at what point the further maintenance of silence would result only in causing the patient useless suffering" (1928, 89). In Ferenczi's first case, "Interpretations given prematurely were particularly disturbing. Perhaps he would have arrived at the same interpretation (explanation) on his own if only it had not been 'communicated' to him. *Now* he did not know how much of the interpretation was spontaneous, that is, acceptable, and how much 'suggestion.' The greatest possible economy of interpretation is an important rule" (1932b, 259). Ferenczi had already recommended earlier: "Above all, one must be sparing with interpretations, for one of the most important rules of analysis is to do no unnecessary talking; over-keenness in making interpretations is one of the infantile diseases of the analyst" (1928, 96). The need for caution in the handling of interpretations has been widely recognized and seconded through the years. Ferenczi mentions a second case in his late fragment: "Analysis of B.: she literally shouted at me: 'Do not talk so much, do not interrupt me; now everything has been spoiled again.' Frequently interrupted free associations tend to remain more on the surface. Any communication or talk brings the patient back into the present situation (analysis) and may hinder him from sinking deeper" (1932b, 259).

Abuse of Free Associations

Citing the example of the case of an obsessional neurotic who associated nonsensical material, Ferenczi regards the misuse of free associations as a resistance (1919, 177–83). If the analyst draws the patient's attention to his unconscious resistance, the person suffering from obsessions tries to lead the analyst astray, to get him to abandon the fundamental rule in order to be able to arrange his communications systematically, or even demands that he be interrogated or hypnotized by the analyst. If the patient remains silent too long, he is concealing something. In some instances the patient, when asked the reasons for his silence, replies that he has no clear ideas. That only confirms he is engaged in resistance, since he thereby proves that he has scrutinized his associations and then suppressed them. Among Ferenczi's various examples one is particularly noteworthy, namely, that associations beginning with the phrase, "I think that," have already been subjected to a critical examination (1919, 180).

Activity as a Parameter

Last but not least, I should like to recall what Ferenczi wrote about the application of the active technique:

The main thing about this technical auxiliary is, and remains, the utmost economy of its employment; it is only makeshift, a pedagogic supplement, to the real analysis whose place it must never pretend to take. On another occasion I have compared such measures to obstetric forceps that also should be used only in extreme need and whose unnecessary employment is rightly condemned by medical art. (1921, 208).[4]

Seen in this light, Ferenczi's experiments in each one of his phases constitutes the search of an experienced analyst for those supplementary measures or parameters that can extend the indications for psychoanalysis, insofar as they consciously modify the standard technique, of which Ferenczi himself was the cocreator and masterly practitioner. In a letter of January 4, 1928, to Ferenczi, Freud expressed his approbation of "The Elasticity of Psycho-Analytic Technique": "Your article . . . testifies to the preeminent maturity you have acquired in the past years and in which you have no peers" (quoted in Grubrich-Simitis 1980, 271).

Conclusion

If thoughts are provisional actions, then entries in a diary are a kind of provisional thought, in which ideas flow with relative freedom from inhibition and are carried to their ultimate conclusions. In the *Clinical Diary* Ferenczi describes his practice of mutual analysis as well as the impossibility of such an undertaking. Nonetheless, Michael Bálint reports that Freud, when faced with the planned publication of the *Diary*, "did not object to any part of the text proposed by us; on the contrary, he expressed his admiration for Ferenczi's ideas, until then unknown to him" (Ferenczi 1985, 219).

Ferenczi's final entry in the *Clinical Diary* was recorded on October 2, 1932. Among the posthumous *Notes and Fragments*, an entry dated October 29, 1932, "The Analyst's Attitude to His Patient," bears witness to his continuing reflections on the analytic attitude. Ferenczi writes:

> Dilemma: *strictness* provokes repression and fear
> kindness provokes repression and consideration
> G.[5:] OBJECTIVITY (neither strict nor kind) is the best attitude.
> In any case: a sympathetic, friendly objectivity.
> Is this not Freud's technique? (1932a, 262)

Ferenczi then continues with a sudden shift, a radical change in direction, which attests to his struggle. "In some respects it is, but *forcing one's own theory* is not objective—a kind of tyranny. Also the whole attitude is somewhat *unfriendly*" (262). In a dense entry to the *Clinical Diary*, dated July 6, 1932, "Advantages and disadvantages, that is, optimal limits of countertransference," after offering a series of clinical examples, Ferenczi concludes: "All in all still no universally applicable rules" (1985, 157).

It is time to document and historicize the entire spectrum of Ferenczi's contributions to psychoanalysis, his breakthroughs and dead ends, in order to be able to do justice to the complexity of his work.

NOTES

1. "Are not both these principles inherent in the method of free association? On the one hand, the patient is compelled to confess disagreeable truths, but, on the other, he is permitted a freedom of speech and expression of his feelings such as is hardly possible in any other department of life" (Ferenczi 1930, 115).

2. See Axel Hoffer's nuanced exposition of this theme in his contribution to this volume.

3. For a critical discussion of the definition of concordant and complementary countertransference, see Etchegoyen (1991, 269–70).

4. Ferenczi's caveats can be compared to Kurt Eissler's (1953) conditions for the adaptation of analytic parameters and his contrast between parameters and pseudoparameters.

5. This initial is Ferenczi's abbreviation and disguise for a patient whose case history appears also in the *Clinical Diary.*

REFERENCES

Bálint, A. 1936. Handhabung der Übertragung auf Grund der Ferenczischen Versuche. *Int. Z. Psychoanal.,* 22:47–58.

Brabant, E., E. Falzeder, and P. Giampieri-Deutsch, eds. 1992. *The Correspondence of Sigmund Freud and Sándor Ferenczi.* Supervised by A. Haynal. Trans. P. T. Hoffer. Cambridge, Mass.: Harvard University Press, 1993.

Cremerius, J. 1983. "Die Sprache der Zärtlichkeit und der Leidenschaft." Reflexionen zu Sándor Ferenczis Wiesbadener Vortrag von 1932. *Psyche,* 37:988–1015.

Deutsch, H. 1926. Okkulte Vorgänge während der Psychoanalyse. *Imago,* 12:418–33.

Eissler, K. R. 1953. The Effect of Structure of the Ego on Psychoanalytic Technique. *J. Am. Psychoanal. Assn.,* 1:104–43.

Etchegoyen, R. H. 1991. *The Fundamentals of Psychoanalytic Technique.* Trans. P. Pitchon. London: Karnac.

Ferenczi, S. 1909. Introjection and Transference. In *Sex in Psycho-Analysis,* pp. 30–79. Trans. E. Jones. New York: Dover.

————. 1912. On the Definition of Introjection. In Ferenczi 1955, pp. 316–18.

————. 1919. On the Technique of Psycho-Analysis. In Ferenczi 1950, pp. 177–89.

————. 1921. The Further Development of an Active Therapy in Psycho-Analysis. In Ferenczi 1950, pp. 198–217.

————. 1925. Contra-Indications to the 'Active' Psycho-Analytic Technique. In Ferenczi 1950, pp. 217–30.

————. 1928. The Elasticity of Psycho-Analytic Technique. In Ferenczi 1955, pp. 87–101.

————. 1930. The Principle of Relaxation and Neocatharsis. In Ferenczi 1955, pp. 108–25.

————. 1931. Child Analysis in the Analyses of Adults. In Ferenczi 1955, pp. 126–42.

————. 1932a. The Analyst's Attitude to His Patient. In Ferenczi 1955, pp. 261–62.

————. 1932b. Once Again on the Technique of Silence. In Ferenczi 1955, pp. 258–60.

————. 1932c. The Technique of Silence. In Ferenczi 1955, p. 258.

————. 1933. Confusion of Tongues between Adults and the Child. In Ferenczi 1955, pp. 156–57.

————. 1950. *Further Contributions to the Theory and Technique of Psycho-Analysis.* 2d ed. Ed. J. Rickman. Trans. J. I. Suttie et al. New York: Brunner/Mazel, 1980.

————. 1955. *Final Contributions to the Problems and Methods of Psycho-Analysis.* Ed. M. Bálint. Trans. E. Mosbacher et al. New York: Brunner/Mazel, 1980.

————. 1985. *The Clinical Diary of Sándor Ferenczi.* Ed. J. Dupont. Trans. M. Bálint and N. Z. Jackson. Cambridge, Mass.: Harvard University Press, 1988.

Ferenczi, S., and O. Rank. 1923. *The Development of Psycho-Analysis.* Trans. C. Newton. New York: Dover, 1956.

Fliess, R. 1953. Counter-transference and Counter-identification. *J. Am. Psychoanal. Assn.,* 1:268–84.

Fogel, G. I. 1993. A Transitional Phase in Our Understanding of the Psychoanalytic Process: A New Look at Ferenczi and Rank. *J. Am. Psychoanal. Assn.,* 41:585–602.

Freud, S. 1912a. The Dynamics of Transference. In *The Standard Edition of the Complete Psychological Works.* Ed. and trans. J. Strachey et al. 24 vols. 12:99–108. London: Hogarth Press, 1953–74.

————. 1912b. Recommendations to Physicians Practicing Psycho-Analysis. *S.E.,* 12:111–20.

————. 1913a. On Beginning the Treatment. *S.E.,* 12:123–44.

————. 1913b. The Disposition to Obsessional Neurosis. *S.E.,* 12:317–26.

————. 1915. Observations on Transference-Love. *S.E.,* 12:159–71.

————. 1919. Lines of Advance in Psycho-Analytic Therapy. In *S.E.,* 17:159–68.

————. 1933. Sándor Ferenczi. *S.E.,* 22:227–29.

Freud, S., and K. Abraham. 1965. *A Psycho-Analytic Dialogue: The Letters of Sigmund Freud and Karl Abraham 1907–1926.* Trans. H. C. Abraham and E. Freud. London: Hogarth Press.

Greenson, R. R. 1967. *The Technique and Practice of Psychoanalysis.* Vol. 1. New York: Aronson.

Grinberg, L. 1979. Projective Counteridentification and Countertransference. In L. Epstein and A. H. Feiner, eds., *Countertransference,* pp. 169–91. New York: Aronson.

Grubrich-Simitis, I. 1980. Six Letters of Sigmund Freud and Sándor Ferenczi on the Interrelationship of Psychoanalytic Theory and Technique. Trans. V. Mächtingler. *Int. Rev. Psychoanal.,* 13:259–77.

Haynal, A. 1987. *The Technique at Issue: Controversies in Psychoanalytic Method from Freud and Ferenczi to Michael Bálint.* Trans. E. Holder. London: Karnac, 1988.

Heimann, P. 1950. On Countertransference. *Int. J. Psychoanal.,* 31:81–84.

Jones, E. 1957. *The Life and Work of Sigmund Freud.* Vol. 3. London: Hogarth Press.

Lacan, J. 1951. Intervention sur le transfert. In *Écrits,* pp. 215–26. Paris: Seuil, 1966.

Racker, H. 1948. The Countertransference Neurosis. In Racker 1968, pp. 105–26.

————. 1953. The Meaning and Uses of Countertransference. In Racker 1968, pp. 127–73.

————. 1958. Classical and Present Technique in Psycho-Analysis. In Racker 1968, pp. 23–70.

————. 1968. *Transference and Countertransference.* Ed. J. D. Sutherland. London: Hogarth Press.

Thomä, H., and H. Kächele. 1985. *Lehrbuch der psychoanalytischen Therapie.* Berlin: Springer, 1989.

Fourteen

A New World Symphony: Ferenczi and the Integration of Nonpsychoanalytic Techniques into Psychoanalytic Practice

■

R E B E C C A   C U R T I S

One night last winter, after having purchased a guidebook that day to eastern Europe, I was planning my trip to Prague and the Ferenczi conference in Budapest. Having seen the movie, *The Music Box,* with many scenes of Budapest about a year before, images from the film came to mind as I perused the travel guide. The images from the film were the only pictures of Budapest I had ever seen. The movie starred Jessica Lange. Not surprisingly, Jessica Lange was in a dream of mine that night. (I won't discuss what dissociated and/or wished-for aspect of myself she might represent.) There was also music playing that I didn't quite recognize. A musician friend happened to call me the next morning, and I hummed the tune to her. "Dvorak's *New World Symphony,*" she said. The music in *The New World Symphony,* a beautiful blend of classical themes with Native American and African spirituals, seems an appropriate metaphor for psychotherapy integration—a blend of Freud's now "classical" technique with some of Ferenczi's innovations and strands from non-European traditions.

At the conclusion of *The Development of Psycho-Analysis* Ferenczi and Rank declare:

This chapter was presented at the Fourth International Conference of the Sándor Ferenczi Society, Budapest, July 1993.

248

If we have attempted in the foregoing pages, venturing from the present direct facts, to forecast the prospects of psychoanalysis, this seems to us more than an idle play of phantasy. . . . The most important advance in psychoanalysis consists finally in a great increase of consciousness, or expressed according to our metapsychology, in raising the instinctive unconscious mental content to the level of pre-conscious thinking. This, however, from our point of view, means such an important step in the development of mankind, that it may actually be regarded as a biologic advance, and indeed as one which for the first time takes place under a kind of self-control. Under the influence of this increase in consciousness the physician, who has developed from the medicine man, sorcerer, charlatan, and magic healer, and who at his best often remains somewhat an artist, will develop increasing knowledge of mental mechanisms, and in this sense, prove the saying that medicine is the oldest art and the youngest science. (1923, 67–68)

Psychoanalysis and psychotherapy are at the interface between art and science. Although psychoanalysis in this century has until recently been largely removed from the developments in scientific psychology and psychiatry, the return of scientific psychology to the study of conscious and unconscious processes after prolonged neglect has rejuvenated the integration of psychoanalysis with other forms of psychotherapy, some of which, such as behavior therapy, are based on research findings in psychology.

When should clinicians engage in techniques that are not traditionally psychoanalytic? This question, grappled with by Ferenczi in his spirit of experimentation, is increasingly coming to the fore for psychoanalysts today. And what differentiates contemporary psychoanalysis from other forms of psychotherapy?

With academic psychology having at last fully embraced nonconscious processes after they were effectively banned by William James a century ago, the features that make psychoanalytic therapy and psychoanalysis distinct from other forms of therapy are becoming blurred. Cognitive-behavioral therapists now tell patients to lie down and report whatever comes into their stream of consciousness; they also examine what is going on in the relationship between the patient and the therapist. Many psychoanalysts, on the other hand, no longer believe in the centrality of the Oedipus complex and work with patients who are for a very long time too anxious to discuss the relationship with the analyst. For those of us who were trained as clinical psychologists before seeking analytic training and who felt we gained a lot from the encounter groups and T-groups of the 1960s and early '70s, the question often comes to mind, "Should I try such and such a technique?" especially when we are not seeing a patient in a formal psychoanalysis.

In this chapter I propose to raise some questions regarding the integration of three types of techniques introduced by Ferenczi into psychoanalysis and psychoanalytic therapy: (1) relaxation; (2) the active techniques of suggestion and advice-giving; and (3) what I shall call active fantasy or suggested fantasy, derived from Ferenczi's idea of forced fantasy and from the imaging techniques in cognitive, experiential, Gestalt, and encounter therapies. I shall raise these questions in the tradition of Ferenczi himself, who always kept in mind the importance of unconscious and transferential processes and strove to overcome inhibitions blocking conscious awareness.

Some case examples will clarify the issues surrounding the decision whether or not to use a guided relaxation technique with a patient. Sue came to consult me initially seeking short-term therapy. She was an administrative assistant in an office and had been recommended to me as a "good patient." I found out from her that she had been hospitalized once for a suicide attempt, although she refused to discuss the matter further. She was suffering from panic attacks on the subway that were so bad that she had to get off several times on the way to work; they also prevented her from going to sleep. I agreed to work with her on a short-term basis. I taught her breathing and imaging techniques so that she could stay on the subway. With some success in allaying this anxiety, she then began to discuss her very serious problems at work and in a relationship.

Two other patients with job and relationship problems also mentioned that they had panic attacks at night. One was in analysis; the other was not, though she had therapy lying down on the couch and eventually began analysis. I addressed their panic only with intellectual inquiry. The panic attacks subsided, apparently as a result of the patients' diminished fear of the experiences and the safety of the analytic situation.

When should therapists use such direct relaxation techniques? A discussion of the history of active techniques in psychoanalysis provides a useful background to the consideration of specific uses of relaxation, suggestion, and suggested fantasy.

Psychoanalysts have traditionally been opposed to any sort of active techniques. Kenneth Frank (1992) has articulated at least five major types of arguments against them: (1) analysis should focus on the therapeutic relationship as the central agency of change; (2) active techniques violate the requirement of analytic neutrality or abstinence; (3) an awareness of the mutative impact of interpretations has made analysts wary of techniques involving suggestion and manipulation; (4) all activity is associated with resistance in psychoanalysis—denial, acting out, and other defenses opposing introspection, verbalization, and insight; and (5) the theoretical formulations about personality on which these techniques are based are too limited and fail to recognize deep structure, conflict, and unconscious motivational forces.

Recently Frank (1993) has described the disparate views held by analysts regarding the goal of psychoanalysis. For those who see the goal as understanding, active techniques may seem inappropriate. Few analysts, however, would limit the goal to understanding. Most also consider the working through and resolving of inhibitions a desideratum, and many, like Ferenczi, strive for the reduction of anxiety and the freeing of creative possibilities for problem-solving. By employing behavioral and cognitive therapies designed to reduce anxiety, the possibilities for integrating techniques drawn from these therapies are enhanced.

What has been the experience of integrating such techniques into analysis since Ferenczi? Freud, of course, frowned on Ferenczi's use of relaxation techniques, and the psychoanalytic community as a whole strongly opposed Franz Alexander and Thomas French's proposal that the therapist "at the right moment, should encourage the patient (or even require him) to do those things which he avoided in the past, to experiment in that activity in which he had failed before" (1946, 41).

Harry Stack Sullivan distinguished a "prescription of action" from ordinary advice-giving. Although he believed it to be harmful to give advice except in unusual situations, he did recommend that an interviewer indicate "a course of events in which the interviewee might engage and which, in the interviewer's opinion, in view of the data accumulated, would improve his chance of success and satisfaction in life" (1954, 212). For Sullivan, advice would simply reflect the therapist's personal values or hunches. To indicate to the patient, on the other hand, the fairly *predictable* consequences of courses of action was not only acceptable, but the therapist's responsibility (Wachtel 1977, 68).

Paul Wachtel has been the leading advocate of the integration of nonpsychoanalytic—and specifically behavioral—techniques into psychoanalysis. With Marvin Goldfried, a cognitive-behaviorist, and others, he organized the Society for the Exploration of Psychotherapy Integration, which has been growing internationally. Wachtel has argued explicitly that patients must be encouraged to approach anxiety-provoking situations after psychoanalytic exploration has determined what they are.

Frank has written recently about integrating nonpsychoanalytic techniques into psychoanalysis and psychoanalytic therapy. He has described a case in which he introduced cognitive-behavioral anger-control techniques and diary-keeping into the treatment of an abusive mother (1992) and explored the use of relaxation techniques with a patient experiencing panic attacks (1993). Frank has argued that the movement from a one-person blank screen model of psychoanalysis to a two-person interactional perspective makes active techniques more palatable and comprehensible theoretically.

Wachtel (1993), in a commentary on Frank, points out that the patient's view of the analyst's behavior—whether that be silence, interpretation, or an active technique—must be explored and analyzed. Silence and interpretations are behaviors as much as is the direct proposal of a means of coping.

Frank (1991, 742) has formulated seven guidelines to aid in integrating active techniques into psychoanalytic treatment: (1) they must be used in a way that advances psychoanalytic inquiry; (2) their use must avoid enactments and be based on thoughtful consideration of each patient's overall therapeutic needs; (3) the analyst's possible countertransferential motivations must be continually monitored; (4) the advantages and disadvantages of choosing one approach over another always need to be weighed; (5) the analyst must seek to avoid taking away initiative and control from the patient; (6) the analyst must not become overly invested in behavioral change; and (7) active techniques may need to be modified for use in psychoanalytic therapy and administered in small doses to investigate thoroughly the patient's reactions.

My own formulation as to when to use active techniques is somewhat different. Having been trained as a clinical psychologist and having taught theories and techniques of therapy (including nonanalytic ones) before seeking training in a psychoanalytic institute, I feel free to use whatever techniques seem most appropriate, whether or not I am doing analysis. As I think back over the patients with whom I have used active techniques, they are those with the most severe deficits and who functioned most poorly, such as patients who had been hospitalized before I worked with them. Upon examining the two cases Frank has recently discussed, I note that the patient to whom I taught anger-control techniques had an apparently borderline mother who was sometimes physically abusive, and a submissive, ineffectual father. The cognitive-behavioral techniques were employed in the fourth year of treatment. The patient with the panic attacks was someone with a history of hurting herself by striking her face with a hairbrush until she caused abrasions and bleeding. Both patients not only experienced severe anxiety, but at times acted in physically destructive ways.

In psychoanalysis or psychoanalytic therapy, I am unlikely to use techniques beyond relaxation, implicit suggestion, and suggested fantasy. This is because my psychoanalytic patients are already functioning without the sorts of deficits that might warrant more active techniques. I would like to turn now to a further discussion of the innovative techniques I have found useful in analytic work.

Relaxation

"Analysis begins with relaxation," Ferenczi wrote in his *Clinical Diary* (1985, 49). I would go further and say that analysis begins, continues, and ends with relaxation. But relaxation is not an end in itself. Through the relaxation of mental blocks, exciting new connections are made. Although some analysts (perhaps a small group) do not believe it is important whether a patient is on the couch or not, and some believe it is demeaning to the patient, I am a proponent of the use of the couch for all patients who will be more relaxed lying down. Recent research has shown that brain waves are different when patients in psychoanalysis are sitting up and lying down, with supine patients emitting more theta waves. Along with Ferenczi, I see the goal of psychoanalysis to be the freeing of inhibitions to conscious awareness, and this freeing occurs more readily when people are lying down. Robert Stigold, a neurobiologist who works in Hobson's dream laboratory, points out that the brain is physiologically able to make more connections when people are relaxed.[1]

In recent papers (Curtis 1992, 1993) I have presented a model of conscious and unconscious processes somewhat akin to Freud's topographical model and argued that dynamic and nondynamic nonconscious experiences are selectively attended to and recalled by the same processes. This model incorporates the data of contemporary cognitive scientific research and philosophical views of the mind. I cannot elaborate that model here, but suffice it to say that I agree with Ferenczi that "the unpleasure that arises when certain connections are made is avoided by the giving up of these connections" (1985, 38). "Relaxation . . . requires unifying the personality completely and allowing all perceptions to register on the self in an unfragmented way: that is, actually a kind of re-experiencing" (54). Psychoanalysis is a process by which connections can be made not only with conscious awareness but among other representations of which one may not be fully aware, such as nonconscious representations of self and others. (Meditation is another process by which one attempts to allow all experiences into awareness.)

Relaxation is central to all psychotherapy. The patient must trust the therapist and feel reasonably safe for therapy to occur. Just as behavioral treatments frequently involve desensitization to feared stimuli, psychoanalysis operates in a similar fashion, with the patient discussing increasingly anxiety-provoking processes in a safe place in the presence of a trusted analyst. Ferenczi introduced his relaxation technique after finding in several cases that his exaggerated frustration technique was not helping, especially when patients came to him after previous failed analyses. Although Ferenczi initially equated relaxation with indulgence, from reading his *Clinical Diary* and other papers as well as reports of others about him, I have gained a sense of the deep trust and sense of safety patients must have felt with him, which seems to have come more from his personal way of being than from his technique per se. For patients to have entered a trance state without any specific instructions, there must have been enormous trust. Ferenczi, in his use of relaxation, did not rely solely on the safety created in the analytic situation. He instructed his patients in the relaxation of the posture of their muscles (1930, 115).

Behavioral therapists use relaxation techniques as a way of applying learning theory to the treatment of anxiety. Patients are taught breathing techniques to reduce states of panic and to remain calm in desensitization procedures as they are exposed to increasingly anxiety-provoking stimuli. I maintain (1992) that behavioral psychologists have been concerned with *explicit* or self-reported anxiety whereas psychoanalysts have been concerned largely with *implicit* or unconscious anxiety. Effective treatments for both implicit and explicit anxiety give patients ways of relaxing and approaching feared experiences.

Sullivan's (1954, 104) idea that as therapists we should strive for an optimal level of anxiety makes sense only if we can be sure that patients are feeling secure that the relationship will not be terminated and that they will not be hurt by undergoing increasingly anxiety-provoking experiences. As therapists we can do this best when our patients feel safe and relaxed.

Suggestion

When I was cleaning up my library as I started to write this chapter—cleaning is something I rarely feel like doing except when I'm anxious about doing something else—I came across an article by Irwin Hoffman (1993) describing a scene from a TV show called "Sessions" starring an analyst or therapist played by Elliot Gould. The patient was thirty-five to forty years old and quite estranged from his father, who was likely scared due to his wife's illness and his own feelings of helplessness. The therapist said to the patient regarding the father, "Maybe he needs someone to talk to." The patient asked, "You mean a shrink-type person like you?" The therapist responded, "Actually, I was thinking of a son-type person like you." The patient then spoke to his father and they were reconciled. Hoffman argues in favor of this use of suggestion, in light of the long-term consequences for the patient if the father had died without the reconciliation.

Ferenczi, of course, used suggestion. Even routine questions such as, "What keeps you from doing such and such?" implicitly contain suggestions. Most analysts also offer explicit advice under certain circumstances— for example, when the situation is life- or treatment-threatening, perhaps after traditional analytic exploration has taken place. The situation described by Hoffman is an intriguing one. Even if the question were phrased, "What keeps you from talking to your Dad?" the possibility of a behavior has been suggested to the patient. It seems to be a matter of a commonsense weighing of costs and benefits. The cost of making a suggestion does not seem to be as great as the cost of a parent dying without an experience of a renewed relationship. In group psychotherapy lasting fifteen sessions, I have watched members successfully suggest on many occasions that another member reinitiate contact with a family member or friend; there is often profound joy and gratitude for the encouragement. I have watched group members alter phobias of driving cars that have existed for many years. Although reliance on the analyst for suggestions is something we certainly don't want, nor would we want suggestion to usurp analysis, there are occasions when the consequences are so enormous that it seems irresponsible not at least to inquire why the patient would not consider a particular action.

Ferenczi defines his active technique as "requesting the patient upon occasion, in addition to free association, to act or behave in a certain way in the hope of gaining thereby . . . mental material that lay buried in the unconscious" (1926, 37). He tells us that "experience later taught me that one should never order or forbid any changes of behavior, but at most advise them, and that one should always be ready to withdraw one's advice if it turned out to be obstructive to the analysis or provocative of resistance" (1928, 96). Freud (1918, 166) had maintained that phobic patients must eventually be induced to approach the anxiety-provoking experience, so an exhortation to engage in an action was not a deviation from Freud's technique.

Ferenczi eventually concluded that, if we can wait long enough, "the patient will himself sooner or later come up with the question whether he should risk some effort, for example to defy a phobic avoidance" (1928, 97). Of course, we may not have time to be so patient. Active techniques, for Ferenczi and Rank (1923), were designed to aid in the overcoming of resistance. But Ferenczi also wrote later that "analysis is preparation for suggestion" (1932, 270).

Freud, as is well known, held that "the pure gold of analysis might be freely alloyed with the copper of direct suggestion" and that the hypnotic means of influence "might find a place in [analysis] again" (1918, 168). The initial distrust of suggestion in psychoanalysis stemmed from the belief that its benefits were only temporary and that the symptoms would recur if the analyst did not help the patient to overcome the dissociations that had prevented him or her from arriving at such results independently (Ferenczi 1928).

Experiential, Gestalt, and Encounter Techniques

I shall now discuss Ferenczi's use of "forced fantasy" and the integration of some techniques from the experiential, Gestalt, and encounter traditions with psychoanalysis.

Ferenczi reports that when he attempted "actually to transport [himself] with the patient into that period of the past," Freud reproached him for it (1985, 24). He adds that, absent such an experience, the analysis will remain on an intellectual level. He points out that the analyst too must be able to relax, but not so far as to enter an actual trance state. Given the importance of fantasy and play to psychoanalytic theory, it is surprising that relaxation should not be used more often. Clearly, the theoretical hostility to acting out a fantasy in the treatment situation by role-playing derives from the view that it is more beneficial to talk about an experience than to repeat it. It is unclear, however, why this premise would extend to an inhibition regarding acting out in fantasy the scenarios of dreams, memories, and desired or feared events. If one of the goals of psychoanalysis is to free people from inhibitions regarding their thoughts and feelings, moreover, it would seem to be commendable for analysts to free themselves.

Let me describe briefly the technique used by Alvin Mahrer, a leading experiential psychotherapist. In each session, both the patient and the therapist close their eyes, and the patient is requested to report on a feeling she or he is experiencing. The patient is urged to experience this feeling more intensely, then is asked about a time recently when she or he felt this way, and then about an analogous time in the past; the session concludes with the patient being asked to imagine some ways that current situations might be handled differently. Mahrer and the patient do precisely what Freud reproached Ferenczi for doing, i.e., they transport themselves into a given period of the past. When a patient is describing the past in an intellectual fashion, happy though I am at times to get the history, I find myself saying, "Be there now."

Ferenczi advocated a technique he called "dream interpretation during relaxation" (1985, 67). With it he attempted to take the patient back into a dream during the analytic session, with the aid of conscious associative material. To do this, he tells us, a certain state of drowsiness and relaxation is necessary. One requests the patients to "penetrate deeper into the feeling, seeing, and experiencing of each detail, whereupon they produce small details and data about the dream-fragment, which by all appearances are derived from reality. This kind of submergence into a dream leads, in most cases, to a cathartic exacerbation of the symptoms, which then provide us with an opportunity to get closer to reality" (67).

A perhaps similar technique taken from Gestalt therapy that I have frequently found useful is to tell the patient to "become" each of the different people and objects in a dream or fantasy. For example, if a patient tells me that she "has her wall up," I tell her to "become" the wall and say "I am the wall," and to report what she does and feels. Having gotten thirty-five undergraduate students per semester to engage in this activity in front of their classmates (with the assurance that not participating would *not* affect their grade), I know that it can be done without much resistance. If patients are hesitant, their fears of even imagining something can, of course, be explored.

The technique of calmly imagining a hierarchy of anxiety-provoking stimuli was developed by behaviorists and is used frequently now by cognitive therapists. A different technique advocated by Ben Feather and John Rhoads (1972) is to ask the patient to imagine his or her worst fears. For example, one patient who had a driving phobia for ten years and feared he would hit pedestrians was told to imagine *deliberately* running over someone. After he imagined such scenes with increasing enjoyment, his anxiety diminished and in two weeks he was able to drive across the state. Similarly, another patient experienced a writing phobia that was related to revealing secret information. After the patient was asked to imagine *deliberately* disclosing all the secrets of his company by emptying all the file cabinets into the street, the phobia dissolved. This patient had spent years in psychoanalysis without improvement and may even have become worse. I don't see that the suggestion to imagine events and feelings is inconsistent with psychoanalytic principles.

In using the techniques of imagining feared experiences, Gordon Paul (1966), like Ferenczi, believes that it is important for patients to imagine the situation as though they were in it, meaning that they should not see themselves in the picture, for then they are viewing it as outside themselves. Instead they are encouraged to see the things around them as if they were there. If patients are reluctant to imagine an experience in fantasy, the therapist may need to point out the difference between reality and fantasy. It is crucial to try to distinguish between the consequences of wishes and of overt behaviors. Implicit in this technique is the assumption that it is beneficial for patients to be able to experience all of their potential feelings and impulses so that they do not need to keep any experiences out of awareness.

I shall now give a case example in which I went beyond the use of imagined wishes or fears to a technique I would label "suggested fantasy." The patient was a twenty-nine-year-old aspiring artist who had been seen previously for five years (usually twice a week) by another therapist, sometimes individually and sometimes in a group. The patient viewed this therapy as helping her to be able to get involved in a relationship with an available, nice man. She saw me twice a week and chiefly discussed the frustrations in her career. Occasionally she mentioned her plans to get married to the man, with whom she was living, and her fears that she might end up like her mother, who had not had sex with her stepfather for the past ten years. She had experienced sexual difficulties with her fiancé for the past year and rarely had sex, which she attributed to their busy schedules and problems with her back, although during the first six months of their relationship she had experienced no particular problems. She described her fascination with fairy tales beginning in childhood and her desire to have a prince save her and to live happily ever after. I wondered whether she might be getting married to have someone support her.

The patient had been sexually abused when she was thirteen by her stepfather's touching her vagina while telling her that he just wanted to examine her. The patient reported that she had been reading many "trashy" novels at that age and was having fantasies about sex with older men. The previous year she had told her mother that she was a twenty-four-year-old in a twelve-year-old body. She did not and had never masturbated. She described her stepfather as quite good-looking and a man to whom many women seemed attracted. She could remember nothing about her feelings regarding the incident, however, except that she felt angry, but that her stepfather must know best. When she told her mother, she responded by saying that the stepfather must have been just having fun and she was sure he hadn't meant anything.

While seeing the patient twice a week for eight months, I usually felt like another appointment during her week of physical therapy, art, and exercise classes. She could spend two whole sessions discussing a mole on her face or crying profusely because her wedding dress was not pretty enough. I felt frustrated by her plans to get married in spite of her sexual difficulties and her fears that she would end up like her mother. But these were apparently outweighed by her fears of being left unprotected in life by a man. Although the patient had no memory of her early childhood and had not learned that her stepfather was not her natural father until she found photographs in the attic, it emerged that her biological father had died when she was three years old, and that her mother's mother had died several weeks before, thus leaving the mother of two young girls very depressed.

Since she was determined to get married, I was relieved when she again decided to discuss her sexual difficulties. She felt extremely uncomfortable with any type of foreplay. When I asked about her feelings toward her stepfather, we got no further than before, so I invited her to imagine the event as if she were there now and to describe all the details. She imagined the scene, but said nothing she hadn't said before. I then encouraged her to imagine finding some pleasure in the event. Although she insisted that it was not at all pleasurable and that imagining it in that way would hurt her mother, she was able to do so. The following session she came in excitedly and told me that she had experienced pleasure in sexual foreplay with her fiancé, and so far she has not reported further difficulties.

Arnold Rachman (1988, 1991) has taken the use of suggested fantasies and psychodrama one step further in his mode of humanistic analysis. He leads patients through three phases: (1) an empathic phase; (2) an analytic phase; and (3) an action phase. Like many of us who believe strongly in the value of group therapy, Rachman thinks that patients benefit from moving from an intense individual experience with the analyst to a setting that elicits personality change with significant others in the "group family." In group work Rachman uses many active techniques associated with the encounter group movement, such as trust exercises and psychodrama. In his description of his work with the patient he has called "Oedipus from Brooklyn" (1988), Rachman reports that he had him not only enact scenes that might prove catalytic, but even wear costumes and masks and set the stage with candles, incense, etc. Rachman also employs what he calls hypnotic regression by inducing a relaxed state through the use of music, a dark room, and a glowing light.

Ferenczi wrote not only about countertransference, but also about counterresistance. As analysts, we are frequently the ones who are resistant to change. Even when a strategy repeatedly fails to work, we remain wedded to it, afraid to stray from the conventions that have been passed down through our own analyses and sanctioned by the analytic community. Ferenczi, in the spirit of experimentation, tried out many techniques and later described how they failed. We also know of the positive benefits to be derived from his successful techniques. If our patients sense that we are unwilling to engage in new behaviors, how can we expect them to make even bigger changes? If creative living is a goal of psychoanalysis, our techniques must involve an interplay between freedom and discipline.

It was a powerful experience in my own analysis when my analyst asked to enter my fantasy world. After telling him of a preanalytic dream about a ferris wheel in Vienna, he asked, "How would it be if I came on the ferris wheel with you?" In response I wrote:

What a technique-y thing to say.
Something he learned at the psychoanalytic institute
Or from Harold Searles, I bet.
"How would it be if I were to ride on the ferris wheel with you?" he said.
That ferris wheel in Vienna I dreamed about years ago
From which you can see out for miles around
That cycle of creation and destruction
That wheel of life
Attached in the center to a mountain
No place to get on or off—
I don't know how you end up there.
"Pleasant, scary, exciting,"
I thought at first—
Then I didn't want him getting that close to me and disappearing
After the ride I paid for was over.
And how would I not touch him
On a ferris wheel ride?
But then, it would be exhilarating
No one had ever asked to enter my inner world before—
My world of dreams—
So, I said, "Maybe, in September."
I can't tell exactly where reality ends and fantasy begins.
But I think someone is coming along with me.

Guidelines for Using Active Techniques

We would never insist that our children do something they are not capable of doing without first showing them how. Analogously, many of our patients have severe developmental deficits, and to expect them to work analytically all the time would be unrealistic and set them up to fail. John Gedo (1988) and Michael Basch (1988) have recently argued for the introduction of educative techniques into analysis. My guidelines for employing active techniques are the following:

1. Nonpsychoanalytically derived techniques can help to reduce severe symptoms in many patients. If they are tactfully employed, without further probing of the meanings of experiences, patients frequently find therapy useful and are then eager to present other problems. In time, they may become amenable to a psychoanalytic approach. When these techniques

are not successful, therapists, regardless of orientation, must explore more fully the meaning of events.

2. Nonpsychoanalytically derived techniques are useful in attempts to induce patients to recollect, reexperience, and emotionally understand events in their lives and the meanings they give them, and in freeing their inhibitions to awareness.

3. Nonpsychoanalytic techniques should be used when the long-term benefits for the patient outweigh the costs of not using them.

4. The therapist's comfort in using nontraditional psychoanalytic techniques will depend upon the value he or she places on simply pointing out a repetition of a pattern in the transference as opposed to freeing inhibitions against trying out new experiences.

Conclusions

The "increase in consciousness" that takes place in psychoanalysis is, as Ferenczi and Rank argue, "more than an idle play of phantasy" (1923, 67). Psychoanalysis is conducted in the interstices between actual events and the meanings people make of them, in the playground of the mind between reality and fantasy. It presupposes relaxation and may include encouragement that the patient shed his or her inhibitions to awareness, indulge in fantasies, and decide which ones he or she will attempt to make come true. When both patients and analysts are open to as many connections as our minds are capable of making, to all of our possibilities and potentialities, the psyche passes through that mysterious portal of the human spirit from passion to being that we call creation. Thus, strands from both old and new traditions can come into awareness and compose in both our professional and personal relationships our own psychoanalytic symphonies for a new world.

NOTES

1. Stigold made this comment during the discussion of papers in a symposium on "Conscious and Unconscious Processes" at the convention of the American Psychological Association, Washington, D.C., August 1992.

REFERENCES

Alexander, F., and T. M. French. 1946. *Psychoanalytic Therapy: Principles and Application.* New York: Ronald Press.

Basch, M. F. 1988. *Understanding Psychotherapy: The Science Behind the Art.* New York: Basic Books.

Curtis, R. 1992. Self-Organizing Processes, Anxiety and Change. *J. Psychother. Integration,* 2:295–319.

———. 1993. Psychoanalysis at the Edge: The Emerging Model of Motivation and Mental Processes. Unpublished paper.

Feather, B. W., and J. M. Rhoads. 1972. Psychodynamic Behavior Therapy II: Clinical Aspects. *Archives Gen. Psychiat.,* 26:503–11.

Ferenczi, S. 1926. Present-Day Problems in Psycho-Analysis. In Ferenczi 1955, pp. 29–40.

———. 1928. The Elasticity of Psychoanalytic Technique. In Ferenczi 1955, pp. 87–101.

———. 1930. The Principle of Relaxation and Neocatharsis. In Ferenczi 1955, pp. 108–25.

———. 1932. Notes and Fragments. In Ferenczi 1955, pp. 216–79.

———. 1955. *Final Contributions to the Problems and Methods of Psycho-Analysis.* Ed. M. Bálint. Trans. E. Mosbacher et al. New York: Brunner/Mazel, 1980.

———. 1985. *The Clinical Diary of Sándor Ferenczi.* Ed. J. Dupont. Trans. M. Bálint and N. Z. Jackson. Cambridge, Mass.: Harvard University Press, 1988.

Ferenczi, S., and O. Rank. 1923. *The Development of Psycho-Analysis.* Trans. C. Newton. New York: Dover, 1956.

Frank, K. 1991. Action Techniques in Psychoanalysis. *Contemp. Psychoanal.,* 26:732–56.

———. 1992. Combining Action Techniques with Psychoanalytic Therapy. *Int. Rev. Psycho-Anal.,* 19:57–79.

———. 1993. Action, Insight, and Working Through: Outline of an Integrative Approach. *Psychoanal. Dial.,* 3:535–78.

Freud, S. 1918. Lines of Advance in Psycho-Analytic Therapy. In *The Standard Edition of the Complete Psychological Works.* Ed. and trans. J. Strachey et al. 24 vols. 17:159–68. London: Hogarth Press, 1953–74.

Gedo, J. 1988. *The Mind in Disorder.* Hillsdale, N.J.: Analytic Press.

Hoffman, I. Z. 1993. The Intimate Authority of the Psychoanalyst's Presence. *Psychol./Psychoanal.,* 13:15–23.

Paul, G. L. 1966. *Insight vs. Desensitization in Psychotherapy: An Experiment in Anxiety Reduction.* Stanford, Calif.: Stanford University Press.

Rachman, A. 1988. Liberating the Creative Self through Active Combined Psychotherapy. In N. Slavenka-Holy, ed. *Borderline and Narcissistic Patients in Therapy,* pp. 309–40. Madison, Conn.: International Universities Press.

———. 1991. An Oedipally Conflicted Patient. In A. Wolf and I. Kutash, eds.,

Psychotherapy of the Submerged Personality, pp. 217–38. Northvale, N.J.: Jason Aronson.

Sullivan, H. S. 1954. *The Psychiatric Interview.* New York: Norton.

Wachtel, P. L. 1977. *Psychoanalysis and Behavior Therapy.* New York: Basic Books.

———. 1993. Active Intervention, Psychic Structure, and the Analysis of Transference. *Psychoanal. Dial.,* 3:589–604.

Fifteen

The "Wise Baby" Grows Up: The Contemporary Relevance of Sándor Ferenczi

■

JUDITH E. VIDA

Introduction to Ferenczi

Despite the certainty with which its theory is frequently presented, psychoanalysis is not a fixed body of knowledge; it is rather many theories, some compatible with what Freud wrote, some not, and with many hiccups and inconsistencies, particularly as infant research and neurobiology have been incorporated into the analyst's working vocabulary. Nor is it a single established technical practice; it is, again, many techniques, despite persistent efforts to "uphold standards" and to distinguish the "pure gold" of psychoanalysis from the serviceable but cheapened "alloy" of psychotherapy. Psychoanalysis now comprises over a hundred years of accumulating, hard-won (and painfully lost) clinical and personal experience. Some of what has been accumulated can be taught to new generations of psychoanalysts and psychotherapists, but because the analyst is his or her own instrument (and each one of us, like it or not, is different), a certain amount of reinventing the wheel is not only unavoidable but also desirable if psychoanalysis is to remain a fresh, viable, and inventive discipline.

Versions of this chapter have been presented to "Activity and Passivity Revisited," the annual symposium of Chestnut Lodge Hospital, Rockville, Maryland, October 1993; the Association of the Advancement for Psychoanalysis of the Karen Horney Psychoanalytic Institute, May 1995; and the Psychoanalytic Center of California Symposium on Primitive Mental States, Los Angeles, June 1995.

Until quite recently, Sándor Ferenczi (1873–1933), who in 1908 joined the small group of Freud's early adherents, was counted among the lost pioneers of psychoanalysis. In his biography of Freud, Ernest Jones described Ferenczi as "the most brilliant . . . the one who stood closest to Freud" (1955, 157). Also until recently, the majority of his contributions have been thought to belong to the classical tradition of psychoanalysis. John Gedo (1976) has deemed Ferenczi's work prior to 1930 as second in importance only to Freud's. The proper measure of Ferenczi's relationship with Freud is their voluminous correspondence, which consists of over a thousand letters exchanged uninterruptedly over twenty-five years until Ferenczi's death, despite growing tensions between the two men after 1927. The publication of Ferenczi's *Clinical Diary* (1985), moreover, has provided an impetus to reevaluate his contributions after 1930 and to reconsider his role in the development of psychoanalysis.

From empirical beginnings, Freud laid down a theoretical system for describing the contents and structures of the mind in both its conscious and unconscious aspects. During his lifetime, the notion of psychoanalysis began to shift from being principally a tool for psychological investigation to having treatment as its ultimate aim, so that the purpose of theoretical innovation was to improve the therapeutic result. Michael Bálint wrote that "although the technique of psychoanalytic treatment was perhaps Ferenczi's favorite topic and occupied his creative mind most of the time during his analytical career, it was always the treatment itself that mattered to him and never the working out of a tidy system" (1967, 147). At the outbreak of World War I, when analysts found themselves without patients, Ferenczi had three brief periods of what he came to regard as a "training analysis" with Freud in order to supplement his own self-analysis. Although to the end of his life he remained painfully aware that this analysis had been incomplete, Ferenczi greatly valued it, particularly for the profound effect of his firsthand exposure to the experience of transference. When he resumed his own clinical practice after the war, it was with a heightened sensitivity to how transference *felt* to the patient.

In the aftermath of his analysis with Freud, Ferenczi began thinking about countertransference, noting its presence in the development of psychoanalytic theory and practice as well as in the immediate subjective experience of the analyst. Henceforth he questioned Freud's negative notion of it purely as a hindrance to be suppressed and sought to recognize it as a major factor in all analyses, which needed to be dealt with without hypocrisy. Ferenczi's experiments with therapeutic uses of the countertransference contributed to his escalating tensions with Freud after 1927.

The controversies surrounding Ferenczi since his death have likewise in the main concerned his technical experiments—above all, mutual analysis—for which we now have the indispensable primary source in the *Clinical Diary.* So trenchant are the observations recorded in the *Diary* that it is easy to forget that Ferenczi did not intend it for publication. Ferenczi devised the experiment of mutual analysis "as a last resort to keep alive the analyses of a few patients who had been severely traumatized as children" (Vida 1991, 272). The seven major papers Ferenczi wrote after 1927 all grew out of his work with these patients; in them he began to move beyond the *cul de sac* in the conceptualization of treatment implicit in Freud's one-person psychology. Ferenczi's ideas about countertransference were far ahead of the theory, practice, and discourse of his own time, and they sounded crazy to his contemporaries. His rethinking of the pathogenesis of trauma, initiated in "The Unwelcome Child and His Death Instinct" (1929) and "Child Analysis in the Analyses of Adults" (1931), reached its culmination in "The Confusion of Tongues between Adults and the Child" (1933), the paper that Freud asked Ferenczi not to present at the Wiesbaden Congress (Rachman 1989). After Ferenczi's death, Jones quietly kept "Confusion of Tongues" from being published in the *International Journal of Psycho-Analysis,* and it did not appear in English until 1949. The paper describes the child's biphasic traumatization by the (primarily sexual) transgressions of adults, the second and more insidious phase of which involves the disavowal by adults that any harm has occurred. The child, left alone and uncomprehending, undergoes an internal splitting: a traumatized part is abandoned, another part takes on the adult's disavowed guilt, and yet another part identifies with the adult as a kind of self-protection.

The Wise Baby

A concept developed by Ferenczi with which he has often been identified is that of the "Wise Baby." Apart from being applied to Ferenczi himself, however, little clinical use has been made of this concept. Such autobiographical readings as it has been given, moreover, have often been used to "diagnose" Ferenczi's "pathology" and served not just to explain but to *explain away* the prescience of his insights regarding treatment. Jones, for example, speaks of Ferenczi's "childlike nature" and "insatiable need to be loved," which, however, were inseparable from his "lack of critical judgment" (1955, 157). Even Bálint, Ferenczi's staunchest supporter, invoked the Wise Baby metaphor to interpret Ferenczi's estranged position in the memorial essay he wrote to accompany the first English translation of "Confusion of Tongues" in 1948.

To allow a more complete understanding of this concept of the Wise Baby, it is worth quoting in its entirety the brief communication in which Ferenczi first coined the term. It appeared in German in 1923 in the *Internationale Zeitschrift;* the English translation that follows is by Olive Edmonds and was published in 1926 in a volume compiled by John Rickman for which the principal translator was Jane Isabel Suttie. The title is "The Dream of the 'Clever Baby' ":

Not too seldom patients narrate to one dreams in which the newly born, quite young children, or babies in the cradle appear, who are able to talk or write fluently, treat one to deep sayings, carry on intelligent conversations, deliver harangues, give learned explanations, and so on. I imagine that behind such dream-contents something typical is hidden. The superficial layer of dream-interpretation in many cases points to an ironical view of psychoanalysis, which, as is well known, attributes far more psychical value and permanent effect to the experiences of early childhood than people in general care to admit. The ironic exaggeration of the intelligence of children, therefore, expresses a doubt as to analytical communications on this subject. But as similar appearances in fairy tales, myths, and traditional literary history very often occur, and in the painter's art are also effectively represented (see the Debate of the young Mary with the Scribes), I believe that here the irony serves only as a medium for deeper and graver memories of their own childhood. Therefore the wish to become learned and to excel over "the great" in wisdom and knowledge is only a reversal of the contrary situation of the child. One part of the dreams of this content observed by me is illustrated by the pithy observation of the ne'er-do-well, when he said, "If I had only understood how to make better use of the position of the baby." Lastly, we should not forget that the young child is familiar with much knowledge, as a matter of fact, that later becomes buried by the force of repression. (1923, 349–50)

Ferenczi modestly adds in a footnote: "I do not believe that this communication has in any way exhausted the interpretation of this type of dream."

Ferenczi continued to develop the concept of the Wise Baby in the decade before his death. In "Child Analysis in the Analyses of Adults" he described how "the split-off intelligence of the unhappy child . . . behaved like a separate person whose duty it was to bring help with all speed to a child almost mortally wounded." He went on to comment: "It really seems as though, under the stress of imminent danger, part of the self splits off and becomes a psychic instance self-observing and desiring to help the self, and that possibly this happens in early—even the very earliest—childhood. . . . It is of course not every such child who gets so far in mastering his own pain" (1931, 136). Ferenczi here is saying that although all traumatized children may experience a splitting of intellect and feeling, they do not all have the capacity to become "Wise Babies," in the fullest sense of the concept.

Among the *Notes and Fragments,* which are isolated jottings in a telegraphic style published in English in 1955 and often pertain to matters in the *Diary,* there is an entry from April 9, 1931, entitled "The Birth of The Intellect." I shall give extended extracts:

Aphoristically expressed: intellect is born exclusively of suffering. (Commonplace: one is made wise by bad experiences; reference to development of memory from the mental scar-tissue created by bad experiences. *Freud.*)

Paradoxical contrast; intellect is born not simply of common, but only of traumatic, suffering. It develops as a consequence of, or as an attempt at, compensation for complete mental paralysis (complete cessation of every conscious motor innervation, of every thought process, amounting even to an interruption of the perception processes, associated with an accumulation of sensory excitations without possibility of discharge). What is thereby created deserves the name of unconscious feeling. (1932, 244)

Ferenczi continues:

Here we are faced with intellectual super-performances, which are inconceivable psychologically and which demand metaphysical explanations. At the moment of transition from the state of life into that of death there arrives an assessment of the present forces of life and the hostile powers, which assessment ends in partial or total defeat, in resignation, that is to say, in giving oneself up. This may be the moment in which one is "half dead," i.e., one part of the personality possesses insensitive energy, bereft of any egoism, that is, an unperturbed intelligence which is not restricted by any chronological or spatial resistances in its relation to the environment; the other part, however, still strives to maintain and defend the ego-boundary. This is what has been called in other instances narcissistic self-splitting. In the absence of any external help one part of this split-off, dead, energy, which possesses all the advantages of the insensibility of lifeless matter, is put at the service of preservation of life. . . .

Pure Intelligence is thus a product of dying, or at least of becoming mentally insensitive, and is therefore *in principle madness, the symptoms of which can be made use of for practical purposes.* (245–46)

In entries of the *Clinical Diary* between January and August 1932, Ferenczi employs clinical material to elaborate his notion that precocious intelligence originates in a traumatic rupture between feeling and thinking, a rupture which similarly may give rise to obedience and adaptation. These reflections chart Ferenczi's awareness of his own "intellectual superperformances," as well as those of his patients. A counterpoint is provided by an entry for June 16, 1932, in which Ferenczi posits that healthy narcissism— "that is to say the recognition and assertion of one's own self as a genuinely existing, a valuable entity of a given size, shape, and significance—is attainable only when the positive interest of the environment . . . guarantees the stability of that form of personality by means of external pressure, so to speak. Without such a counterpressure, let us say counterlove, the individual tends to explode, to dissolve itself in the universe, perhaps to die" (1985, 128–29).

In "Confusion of Tongues," Ferenczi analogously writes: "The fear of the uninhibited, almost mad adult changes the child, so to speak, into a psychiatrist, and in order to become one and to defend himself against dangers coming from people without self-control, he must know how to identify himself completely with them. Indeed it is unbelievable how much we can learn from our wise children, the neurotics" (1933, 165). Finally, among the *Notes and Fragments* there is an aphorism recorded in November 1932: "The idea of a wise baby could only be discovered by a wise baby" (1932, 274).

In the following section I shall introduce some material concerning a patient of mine whom I have come to recognize as a "Wise Baby." Although Ferenczi's work informed the theoretical background of the treatment, the treatment itself suggested some additional dimensions, which were absent in Ferenczi's original construct, with both historical and clinical consequences. Is it sufficient to say that wisdom results *purely* from traumatic experience? Indeed, I suspect that Ferenczi's characterization of precocious intelligence as a pathological by-product served a self-deprecating function that may have made it easier for others to undervalue his work and, unwittingly and regrettably, contributed to a now widespread notion that it is a sign of pathology for children to have extraordinary intelligence.

Clinical Material

Dr. J de A, a married computer scientist in his mid-thirties, sits in my consulting room for the first time, mildly anxious, definitely wary, and speaking of his troubled introspection in subdued, carefully poetic language. Before seeing me he has consulted a younger analyst who, upon hearing the principal concerns and an abbreviated history, seems too quickly to leap to the judgment that psychoanalysis is indicated, at an initial frequency of four times a week. Dr. de A balks at such swift certainty and declines the recommendation, whereupon my name is given to him as someone else he might interview for treatment. Now sitting opposite me, Dr. de A's primary concerns, of painful moodiness and uncertainty about himself in both work and family relationships, seem eclipsed by the impact on him of the analyst's recommendation. Such presumption in his view begs the question of whether help might be possible at all. I am supportive of his requirement to test out the working relationship, rather than to make a commitment without knowing the person with whom he is dealing. Dr. de A has a question that crystallizes his concerns: "Are you smart enough to work this out with me?" I do not hear this as a challenge; what I hear is urgency tinged with despair. His is a legitimate question. I reply: "At this point, there's no way for either of us to know. That's something we'll have to find out." I realize I am quite stimulated by this exchange. I imagine I can see why my colleague was so eager to take this man into intensive treatment, yet it is clear to me that each step will need to be explored and validated as we go. Am I smart enough? I see already that this man is prodigiously gifted. The question is a little scary.

Dr. de A has a high-level position in a large corporation at the cutting edge of technology. He has sophisticated management responsibilities in addition to being the driving force behind several controversial long-term research projects. It is highly unusual for a single individual to have this combination of duties, but Dr. de A has not just survived in this position. During the ten years since joining the company, freshly armed with a prestigious doctorate, he has risen steadily and dramatically through the ranks to have now surpassed some of those who hired him. Dr. de A observes that he sees things in quite a different way from his colleagues and superiors, and is perturbed by the darkly pessimistic, self-critical conclusions he draws. His career trajectory is at once self-evident and mystifying to him.

Dr. de A is his parents' third child; his sister and brother are twelve and ten years older, respectively. He grew up in the Pacific Northwest, where his father was a narrow-gauge railway engineer who suffered unfathomable depressions until his death some ten years ago. Locked into a monotonous job, Dr. de A's father struggled all his life with feeling unwanted and out of place. The father had been born a twin, but his brother died when they were two. The father's mother, Dr. de A's paternal grandmother, driven cold with grief and rage, proclaimed loudly that the wrong twin had died and never again addressed her surviving son by his preferred name. What eventually gave some focus to the father's life was the dogged pursuit of amateur scholarship. He studied the Civil War, the history of Native Americans during the settlement of the West, and the Holocaust. Each provided a rich avenue for developing and refining his identifications with the unwanted. Dr. de A said, "My father, weak and crippled as he was, I respected a great deal, but he had been beaten down over life with no hope of coming out. My father felt deeply, but converted it into a personal sense of loss and failure by comparing himself with others."

Dr. de A's mother was a housewife. Her dismay at finding herself pregnant again, with him, had far-reaching consequences. The paternal grandmother, with whom Dr. de A's father eventually severed all ties, tried to persuade her daughter-in-law that this inconvenient pregnancy would produce an extraordinary child. Instead of becoming emotionally reconciled to the pregnancy, Dr. de A's mother concretely incorporated her mother-in-law's notion by evolving a pattern of communication in which Dr. de A's accomplishments are the only topic on which he himself is permitted to engage her. A current example: Dr. de A calls to ask if she can babysit his children on a particular evening; she is busy, or she cannot possibly do it for unspecified reasons. If she hears, however, then or later, that the reason for the request is to allow Dr. de A and his wife to dine with an important corporate executive from the East Coast, or for Dr. de A to receive recognition from one of his many professional societies, she reverses her previous decision without a blink and proceeds to pump him for details.

His mother was both contemptuous and long-suffering about his father's depressions and made the youthful Dr. de A her substitute companion. Dr. de A eventually observed: "There was something in my mother that was as dangerous as can be imagined, and it was deftly hidden beneath an outward facade of having a completely oppressed way of behaving. She was never the source of any of the conflict, which was even more menacing because it was not clear." At the end of one of our earliest sessions, Dr. de A said: "I think the problem with my mother has to do with 'penetration.'" Perplexed, I said: "Well, we've got plenty of time to take that up eventually." In fact, we did not take this theme up until four years later, when Dr. de A resumed treatment after an interruption lasting nearly a year.

Dr. de A's siblings are so much older than he that initially he had little sense of their roles in his life as a child, and even now in adulthood he feels little warmth or connection with them. He has a besetting sense of strangeness about his family and feels that there were many experiences that didn't make sense.

Within a few months of beginning our work, a pair of events came to light that are probably linked, since both date from the same time.

Regarding the first: Dr. de A's earliest memories are of feeling strange and bewildered, and of puzzling over it. One day, when he was four, he had an idea that made great sense to him. Filled with pride and accomplishment, he burst into the kitchen where his mother had climbed up to get something from a high cupboard, and announced happily, "I've finally figured it out. I'm unwanted!" His mother's response was at first blank and silent; presently, however, she began to talk about something else altogether. Remembering and retelling this evoked humiliation and further bewilderment. I myself felt shocked speechless.

Regarding the second: Dr. de A fell ill as a four-year-old. (We came to suspect that this happened after the kitchen scene.) There were many visits to the doctor and many medicines, to no avail. Nobody knew what was wrong. Dr. de A became weak, listless, lethargic, and eventually did not get out of bed at all. His mother set up a bed near the kitchen so he could watch her. Dr. de A remembers a blank calm in his mind; he could see no end to this state. Dr. de A believes this continued for a protracted period, certainly for weeks, and possibly months. One day there was a surprise visitor; his mother said, "Santa Claus is here to see you!" Instantly, Dr. de A knew that this was a trick. It was summer; this could not be Santa Claus. Santa Claus gave him a pep talk. "What's a big strong boy like you doing in bed? Don't you want to be up and running around? Having fun? There are so many things to look forward to. I'll be bringing you a lot of great presents at Christmas," etc. Dr. de A knew his mother had somehow set this up, that Santa Claus was lying to him, and that Santa Claus *was* a lie. At the same time, he could look down the path of his own private thoughts and see nothing but a dead end. So he decided to accept this as a way out, at least a way out of bed. He recalls being extremely clear-headed about his decision. The way out of bed was to accept that life is a lie; to stick to his own truth meant no life at all. And thus, with no joy, he did leave his bed.

It is beyond the scope of this chapter to fill in the many trenchant details of subsequent events in Dr. de A's life and how he came to understand them; some, however, are highly relevant. It would not be correct to say that Dr. de A became "emotionless" after Santa Claus's visit, but a dramatic reordering of his sense of the world did take place. Nothing and nobody were to be counted on, but not in a paranoid sense; rather, the concepts of depending on and expecting understanding ceased to have any meaning. Not long after entering school, he asked what was the hardest thing for grown-ups to do. Upon being told it was computers, he determined to study them, although he had to make do with ordinary arithmetic and science classes for a long time, and his intuitive, highly creative efforts at problem-solving repeatedly ran afoul of teachers with limited understanding and conventional expectations for student performance. By the time he graduated from high school he had developed a huge capacity for persistence and making things happen, which would fuel his adult life in college, in graduate school, and now in his work. But this came at a great emotional cost, observable to none but him. His singlemindedness was less useful in his personal life. A youthful first marriage to a vain, self-involved woman, whose affairs were common knowledge to everyone but Dr. de A, ended painfully after a few years, leaving him feeling even more bewildered and out of place. In the aftermath, an attempt at therapy proved no less unfortunate when the therapist, an older woman, pressed Dr. de A to become more and more personally involved with her. When he definitively rejected her sexual advances, she became enraged and he fled. Now a second marriage, to a calm but lively and intuitive woman, is proceeding successfully and they have a much-loved and extremely bright child, although Dr. de A remains worried that his black moods and internal self-doubts, in which he questions every one of his perceptions until it seems that nothing remains, will exceed the tolerance of his new family and destroy it.

This treatment began some years ago. Shortly after the initial sessions, a frequency of twice a week was established and Dr. de A chose to use the couch after I explained that the recumbent position could be helpful in focusing awareness of internal processes. For about a year we were able to add a third session, but financial difficulties necessitated a return to twice a week. Because of his job, Dr. de A was required to travel frequently and without a lot of warning. However, he did have some flexibility. What we worked out was a system of make-up sessions that was quite successful, if not entirely predictable: some weeks he had one or two sessions (rarely none); in others three or four. It often happened that during periods when circumstances enabled a greater number of weekly sessions, we entered into much deeper, more archaic material. When there were interruptions in the ordinary flow, Dr. de A would return having worked hard in a sector of his mind while he was away. We would pick up not where we had left off, but at the new place he had come to.

To go on discussing Dr. de A's treatment in this fashion, by focusing exclusively on him, would assuredly be fascinating, but it would reproduce metaphorically his traumatically induced split and perpetuate what he hated about a traditional psychoanalytic approach. This way of working, we also discovered, created for him a virtually exact replica of the scene in the kitchen with his mother. What became quickly apparent as we began to proceed together was that purely intellectual understanding from me was of no use to Dr. de A, but neither was a situational empathic murmuring. To make an impact, I had to offer both support and insight with a content that Dr. de A had not previously thought of. Dr. de A's besetting need was to be taken in emotionally, to feel understood over and over again as the essential step in accumulating evidence that he existed, that he was real. As he expressed it to me repeatedly, "Understanding can only be demonstrated by taking it one step further." I never knew ahead of time or while it was happening whether I would be able to meet this challenge. When I failed, it never sufficed for Dr. de A simply to wait. I would need him to get agitated, to cry out, as it were, in pain, and somehow something would begin to shake loose inside me and I would be able to say something that *I* hadn't thought of before—words or an idea would suddenly shape them- selves around a vague or not so vague somatic feeling.

In fact, anticipating a session with Dr. de A was a complex experience. On the one hand, I looked forward avidly to the richness and the stimula- tion; at the same time, and increasingly so as we got into a phase of reliving the experience of his illness at the age of four, I had a visceral feeling of dread. What we learned together was that while the choice presented to him by Santa Claus could be intellectually understood as being superficially between the hopeless depression of his father, who saw the truth, and the dangerously mindless self-deception of his mother, at bottom it was really a choice between life and death. As a four-year-old, he had entered what was probably a marasmic state, and it was horrific for him to relive it and for me to be with him. He would sit up on the couch at the end of a session, and I could see him pack up his anguish and carry it out the door. It was extremely painful to witness.

I had been reading Ferenczi, including the *Clinical Diary,* newly trans- lated into English, when I began work with Dr. de A. That discovery, combined with personal experiences with "severely gifted" children who have had their giftedness treated as pathological or unreal by well-meaning parents and teachers, informed my conscious and preconscious thoughts. I began with the premise that room needed to be made for the assimilation of the exquisitely painful consequences of what his intellect knew. Con- firmation of the usefulness of this approach came early. In the fourth month of treatment, Dr. de A said, "It was so helpful for you to say that it's not going to work to try to fix things by adjusting my thinking to what everyone else sees. It's liberating because I've struggled for so long to try to see things the way others do. To imagine that there's something legitimate about my way of seeing things is remarkable." With this declaration, we launched into the first layer of reentering his experience as a four-year-old, and the phrase "the wise child" crept into my notes and interpretations. What began to be conceptualized was his terrible dilemma as a four-year-old, which he had seen with uncanny clarity (although the full meaning of it was just now being grasped), that he could not go on as a whole person; some vital part of him would have to be jettisoned. In simplistic terms, it could be said that he faced a choice between Thinking and Feeling; but if he chose Feeling, there did not appear to be enough in his environment to sustain that part of himself and he might literally die. It felt as though he had "chosen" Thinking, and now in his analysis he very badly needed enough safety to consider that he might, after all, have made a mistake. (Suicidal games that he played as a ten- and eleven-year-old were not remembered until well into the second phase of treatment, some four years later.)

After a dream of himself as a compartmentless sphere containing the skeleton of a child, some signs of life began to show. We came to understand a menacing dream of an eel surfacing from the depths of a pool as a picture of his constant awareness of being able to say something that would destroy his father or mother. Turning to me, he asked urgently, "Do you understand how dangerous I can be?" The aftermath of this exploration was his beginning to feel freer and *less* dangerous. Although he said, "It's hard to put myself into the situation of feeling something instead of witnessing it," he experienced more "black states," which he came to grasp as the essence of what it feels like to be unwanted.

He began to characterize it as being in a Dark Room. The Dark Room, he said, "has exits and entrances and objects which I bump up against and use but there is no sense of what else is there. I'm reacting; I only know myself through what I do. There are lamps, but I'm carrying them around and not turning them on—it's a potential I can't use but the existence of the potential is extremely important—the potential of my worth." I asked if the lamps were connected to his mother, but he said, "No, they are not representative of something from someone else. One of the most frequent experiences I have is asking the question, am I intellectually capable? Is my mind functional? Over the last year in treatment, talking about my father, mother, sister, brother—I'm having a sense that there's a reason the lights are off . . . I don't think the lights are going to come on. I think that opportunity was lost." At the next session, he expressed relief: "That's the first time I've tried to communicate what it felt like, and tried to get myself to become more conscious of it, and it's the first time I've succeeded in doing both." Then he wanted me to enter the Dark Room with him. As I came to understand what he was asking, I realized that it would require my completely abandoning any vestiges of an analytic stance of thinking, observing, or objectifying. It would be surrendering to "pure countertransference," and it was scary because I, too, would have no signposts. Eventually a phrase from Stolorow, Brandchaft, and Atwood (1987)—"the shifting sands of intersubjectivity"—floated into my mind. Indeed, it felt as though there were no ground under my feet. For comfort, I carried in with me the evidence that others, too, had been there.

It is difficult to say more about the experience of the Dark Room, because leaving the analytic stance behind meant that I deliberately set aside the language it would take to frame things in a form that might convey a *clinical* understanding. It could probably be said that I voluntarily underwent a *countertransference regression*. Reflecting on the experience long afterward, I realized that it was, in fact, one of pure mutuality at quite a deep—one might say, primitive—level that involved undefended trust on both our parts. It has occurred to me that an experience such as this could very well have been what Ferenczi and his patient, R.N., had been straining to accomplish in their remarkable experiment of "mutual analysis," as chronicled in the *Clinical Diary*. What persuaded Ferenczi to participate was his response to R.N.'s fear and unconfirmed suspicions of *his* consciously withheld countertransference fear of her. In the mutual analysis, Ferenczi's openness about these responses and their past and present origins succeeded in enabling R.N. better to trust her own perceptions and, equally important, allowed her to experience Ferenczi as *more real*. Ferenczi was drawn into confronting the extremity of R.N.'s mistrust of him, and I, in turn, could feel with no protective buffering how terrifying it was for Dr. de A to risk trust. Ferenczi has been assiduously criticized after his death for his supposed exploitation of analytic relationships for personal emotional gain, but such criticism avoids considering the impact on both the analytic and the *relational* process of reaching such a state of mutual trust.

Following the experience of being together in the Dark Room over a number of sessions, something was transformed that allowed Dr. de A to become aware through dreams and reflection of the desperate persistence with which he tried to interest his mother, even after he was four, and how consistently he failed. When an interchange between us left me befuddled, and I observed that he was way ahead of me, he became panicky and angry and commanded, "You can't fall behind!" This episode put him back in the Dark Room, while I struggled to understand. When I finally said that I thought he had insisted that I not fall behind so I would be with him when he needed me, he was struck by how true that felt and commented, "A shroud has lifted."

During slightly more than three years of treatment, there was a great deal of significant change. Repeated explorations of interactions at work that were internally difficult for Dr. de A revealed that far below the surface he was reliving the scene in the kitchen with his mother. Of course, no amount of reassurance or success in the present could rewrite the scene as it actually occurred. As Dr. de A became increasingly able to distinguish past from present, he eased up on himself internally and began to appreciate the very real limitations in others' capabilities, which, interestingly, made him less fearful of them. Along with his own coming back to life as a "wise child," thus recapturing his own sense of wholeness, Dr. de A was able to embrace his wife's wish for another child.

His wondering about how it would be possible to stop treatment led us to a plan to terminate in four months, shortly after the birth of the second child. Neither of us had any notion that the work was "finished," but there was likewise no doubt about the usefulness of his taking the opportunity to see how things would go. Furthermore, we agreed that resumption would be possible if or when he wished. We had been through some unusual experiences in the sessions, and I had the idea that I would one day want to write about them. I didn't say anything about this right away, but he caught me thinking something I was unwilling to say. So I told him what was on my mind and added that I would need his permission to write about the case. Both his immediate and subsequent responses were striking. He sat up on the couch and reported that my words had had a powerful effect, a validation that made both me and him feel quite distinctly *real*. Regardless of what or when I might write, he said, the fact that I wanted to meant that he was real to *me*.

In the first eight or nine months after stopping treatment he came in once to discuss some work-related issues. A year later he asked to return to tackle the next level of his emotional-perceptual concerns, but he laid down some conditions: first, that we would meet face-to-face and at a frequency of once a week, with no suggestion from me that more often would be better; also, that I would accept his need to make the interaction real, as real as *sex,* though he didn't know how we would accomplish this. What gave him hope that we could continue was remembering my comment about writing. Next, he felt that it was necessary for him to be free to get as angry with me as he did with others. What made that a difficult prospect was his fear of humiliation, that I would lose respect for him. This condition implied a significant deepening of our working relationship. (At the beginning of treatment he had felt freer to talk to me than to his wife for fear of losing her respect; that relationship was feeling significantly more real as well.) He concluded by suggesting that somehow in the previous phase of treatment we had helped him free up the part of himself that had been identified with his father; now we had to tackle his mother, a much more dangerous business.

Discussion

Ferenczi's idea of traumatically acquired intelligence owes a great deal to the Freudian conception of development as a *forced struggle*. Since each stage of development means the renunciation of more primitive pleasures, environmental impingement is essential if progression is to occur, and this impingement is then immortalized internally in the form of unconscious conflicts at successive stages of development. This could be characterized as a theory of *development as trauma*. In recent decades, Winnicott, Bowlby and his successors in attachment theory, and a veritable army of researchers have done much to establish and characterize the inborn developmental strivings and the highly variable inborn temperaments and talents of the human infant, and thus to challenge the authority of such a view.

In *Thalassa* (1924) Ferenczi argued that genitality incorporates a fundamental human longing to regress and dedifferentiate into a state of perpetual pleasure in the womb. But it is not fanciful to think that he would have eagerly taken up contemporary ideas about the role of innate, genetically mediated strivings in human development. For in the last year of his life, Ferenczi began to propose radical changes in his theories and to contemplate rethinking the whole basis of the traditional notions of masculinity and femininity. This is documented in the *Clinical Diary* and the *Notes and Fragments,* where in entries of September, October, and November 1932 Ferenczi considers that the anxiety and/or collapse that can follow a stretch of traumatically driven excessive achievement can be usefully treated with opportunities for saturation with play and "waiting for the *spontaneous* tendency of 'growth' " (1932, 265). There is real resonance here with Winnicott's ideas of "spoiling" as a management technique to allow healing and spontaneous resumption of development. In a most intriguing entry, Ferenczi asks, "Is it possible to make friends with the ucs.?" (251).

I have noted that by 1931 Ferenczi did not think that all traumatized children had sufficient intellect to master their own pain; now this needs to be extended to an acknowledgment that not all traumatized children become Wise Babies. My view is that Dr. de A's intellect was not traumatically acquired, but traumatically *distorted* by the necessity of its use for survival, in the absence of minimal conditions of emotional safety. These distortions seem to me to have been activated by his traumatic perception that what he knew was dangerous, when he appeared in the kitchen to share with his mother the extraordinary, unanswerable insight of his having been unwanted. This perception was the product of the already long-standing operation of a remarkable intelligence. Ideally, this mother might have found a capacity to respond to her child in a complex fashion that would have allowed the recognition of his insight along with a new emotional contact that energized them both to deal with their common problem. Only thus might Dr. de A's development have been transformed. As it was, he remained stranded, and he had to rely on his intelligence for defense and protection. His desire to learn "the hardest thing" was born of his awareness that there was no real help available to him; he had better equip himself to deal with life alone.

So I take issue with some of Ferenczi's notions about the Wise Baby. Just as not all traumatized children become Wise Babies, so perhaps neither are all children with precocious intelligence Wise Babies either. The concept is no less significant for having been incomplete. Alice Miller gives dramatic form to a version of the Wise Baby in *Prisoners of Childhood* (1981). Her principal idea concerns the vulnerability of gifted children by virtue of their unusual sensitivity to being exploited, principally as caretakers, by the pathologically narcissistic strivings of parents. (Miller's omission of any mention of Ferenczi seems less deliberate than suggestive of the obscurity into which his contributions had fallen.)

I too think that the gift of extraordinary innate intelligence is associated with a certain kind of vulnerability, which I identify as an experience of penetration by suffering that is significantly greater than that of a more ordinary child when, for whatever reason, there is an insufficiently responsive human environment. It is the intelligence that allows for the expanded perception of suffering. When this suffering becomes so great and unrelieved that the emotional register must be split off because the pain of preserving it as an experiencing organ is unendurable, what is left of the Wise Baby is a diminished organism. He is likely to "pass" as sufficient if the remaining conscious or accessible parts are capable of constructing a workable system. Dr. de A's system went like this: "I ask a question: Doesn't anything matter? Then I think: I can make things matter. Then I respond: Then I will try to make that happen; I will choose something I can believe in and work to create a world I can believe in. What am I trying to do and what is motivating me? The distinction between past and present is very blurred."

The split-off parts of Dr. de A passed into that realm of "unconscious feeling," which Ferenczi thought was created by the experience of mental paralysis in the face of trauma. As Dr. de A and I have continued to capture those elements in analysis, he is able (1) to feel more whole; (2) to make a sharper distinction between past and present; and (3) to use his intellect more playfully, with less strain, and more for his own purposes. This work is accomplished in the analysis through a process of reliving and reenactment. There are now countless episodes, major and minor, in which the kitchen scene has been reenacted, repeated, and relived in the therapeutic context. In fact, for a very long time, each new development began with a confrontation and continued with my failure, but Dr. de A at least did not need to leave the scene and take to his bed. We would hammer at it till something came through. There continued to be some shared anxiety and uncertainty around these encounters, but neither of us was as frightened as we used to be.

Ferenczi's idea of *counterpressure* holds that the stability of the personality as a genuinely existing, valuable entity is sustained by the positive interest of the environment. I think that this is a most useful conceptualization of how Dr. de A has been struggling to get to an experience of both himself and me as real by using metaphors of sex and penetration. Because he never did "get through" to his mother, he had only vague notions of what these words might represent. But he has become clearer. His wife and children feel more real to him, and I have progressed successively from being perhaps harmful to being neutral to being safe but undifferentiated to being possibly (or occasionally) real. Once, during a weekend, Dr. de A experienced a contentless flash of anger at me, which was shortly followed by a suffusion of contentment and attachment to his wife; in that instant he had known that *he* was real, as he had a sense of me as someone with whom he could become angry, because I could receive, hold, and acknowledge his anger.

The combination of extraordinary innate intelligence with its concomitant expansion of vulnerability to suffering means that the Wise Baby, perhaps even more than the "ordinary" child, requires an experience of counterpressure to prevent the overstretching of his capacity to contain his suffering and thus be able to use his intellectual gifts to express his personality and interests. In other words, they must form part of his experience of himself. With the provision of adequate counterpressure, the Wise Baby need not be seen as a pathological distortion of normal development, but as a variant of the developmental process that has a distinct and unconventional pattern of its own.

Ferenczi, I surmise, felt that he had missed a specific experience of counterpressure in his own life. He sought it in his relationship with Freud, with mixed results, and also in his practice, with important consequences for the development of psychoanalysis that are just beginning to be appreciated. For Ferenczi to have been a Wise Baby in my terms, he, too, had to have had extraordinary innate intelligence, an assumption about him that has not, to my knowledge, been widely entertained. Ferenczi is typically acknowledged to have been gifted in the realm of "intuition," which has always been devalued, particularly by comparison with Freud's "genius." Perhaps we should begin to recognize that Ferenczi's concerns anticipated and indeed framed the issues of psychological therapy that have only begun to be assimilated more than fifty years after his death. Indeed, Ferenczi has been discredited in large measure because what he saw and foresaw in psychoanalytic practice—both his own and that of others—greatly disturbed the answers, systems, and clarity that his contemporaries, including Freud, were straining to achieve. But a Wise Baby, whether Ferenczi or Dr. de A, has a unique perspective and something valuable to give, and it tends to be painful to know.

Because psychoanalysis will never be a fixed body of knowledge, Ferenczi's abiding relevance is to have provided the model of an analyst who was able, for a variety of reasons, to experience himself as an open system. Stimulated by that openness, he formulated questions that others could not anticipate; he waited for responses; he allowed himself to be penetrated; and he permitted something new to be created between himself and the analysand. I see this as the process by which a Wise Baby is able to continue his unconventional development. Although Ferenczi's quest for a supportive counterpressure was ultimately thwarted, it did lead him, early on, to recognize the primacy of the human need for relatedness, which he long struggled to accommodate within Freud's system. Unfortunately, he died just at the point when he was beginning to find more room for his own insights. To have access to Ferenczi as a valued, trustworthy companion on our own arduous, exhilarating clinical journeys, we do not have to idealize him, but we do need to listen.

REFERENCES

Bálint, M. 1948. Sándor Ferenczi, Obit 1933. In *Problems of Human Pleasure and Behavior*, pp. 243–50. New York: Liveright, 1957.

———. 1967. Sándor Ferenczi's Technical Experiments. In B. B. Wolman, ed. *Psychoanalytic Techniques*, pp. 147–67. New York: Basic Books.

Ferenczi, S. 1919. On the Technique of Psycho-Analysis. In Ferenczi 1926, pp. 177–89.

———. 1923. The Dream of the "Clever Baby." In Ferenczi 1926, pp. 349–50.

———. 1926. *Further Contributions to the Theory and Technique of Psycho-Analysis.* Ed. J. Rickman. Trans. I. Suttie et al. New York: Brunner/Mazel, 1980.

———. 1929. The Unwelcome Child and His Death Instinct. In Ferenczi 1955, pp. 102–7.

———. 1931. Child Analysis in the Analyses of Adults. In Ferenczi 1955, pp. 126–42.

———. 1932. Notes and Fragments. In Ferenczi 1955, pp. 216–79.

———. 1933. Confusion of Tongues between Adults and the Child: The Language of Tenderness and Passion. In Ferenczi 1955, pp. 156–67.

———. 1955. *Final Contributions to the Problems and Methods of Psycho-Analysis.* Ed. M. Bálint. Trans. E. Mosbacher et al. New York: Brunner/Mazel, 1980.

———. 1985. *The Clinical Diary of Sándor Ferenczi.* Ed. J. Dupont. Trans. M. Bálint and N. Z. Jackson. Cambridge, Mass.: Harvard University Press, 1988.

Gedo, J. E. 1976. The "Wise Baby" Reconsidered. In J. E. Gedo and G. Pollock, eds., *Freud: The Fusion of Science and Humanism*, pp. 357–78. New York: International Universities Press.

Jones, E. 1955. *The Life and Work of Sigmund Freud.* Vol. 2. New York: Basic Books.

Miller, A. 1981. *Prisoners of Childhood.* New York: Basic Books.

Rachman, A. 1989. Confusion of Tongues: The Ferenczian Metaphor for Childhood Seduction and Trauma. *J. Am. Acad. Psychoanal.*, 17:181–206.

Stolorow, R. D., Brandchaft, B., and Atwood, G. 1987. *Psychoanalytic Treatment: An Intersubjective Approach.* Hillsdale, N.J.: Analytic Press.

Vida, J. E. 1991. Sándor Ferenczi on Female Sexuality. *J. Amer. Acad. Psychoanal.*, 19:271–81.

INDEX